900

Managing Your Reputation

How to plan and run communications programmes that win friends and build success

Roger Haywood

LEEDS METROPOLITAN UNIVERSITY
FOR REFERENCE USE IN THE
LIBRARY ONLY

D0279283

McGRAW-HILL BOOK COMPANY

London · New York · St Louis · San Francisco · Auckland · Bogotá
Caracas · Lisbon · Madrid · Mexico · Milan · Montreal · New Delhi
Panama · Paris · San Juan · São Paulo · Singapore · Sydney
Tokyo · Toronto

Published by
McGRAW-HILL Book Company Europe
Shoppenhangers Road, Maidenhead, Berkshire, SL6 2QL, England
Telephone 0628 23432
Fax 0628 770224

British Library Cataloguing in Publication Data
Haywood, Roger
  Managing Your Reputation: How to Plan and
  Run Communications Programmes That Win
  Friends and Build Success
  I. Title
  658.45

  ISBN 0-07-707740-7

Library of Congress Cataloging-in-Publication Data
Haywood, Roger
  Managing your reputation: how to plan and run communications
  programmes that win friends and build success / Roger Haywood.
      p. cm.
  Includes index.
  ISBN 0-07-707740-7
  1. Public relations.   I. Title.
  HD59.H32   1994
  659.2–dc20   94-19178
                                                                  CIP

LEEDS METROPOLITAN
UNIVERSITY LIBRARY

1701053800
B35B
157073 8.11.94
26 1 95

Copyright © 1994 Roger Haywood. All rights reserved. No part of this publication
may be reproduced, stored in a retrieval system, or transmitted, in any form or by any
means, electronic, mechanical, photocopying, recording, or otherwise, without the
prior permission of Roger Haywood.

12345 BL 987654

Typeset by BookEns Ltd, Baldock, Herts.
and printed and bound in Great Britain by Biddles Ltd, Guildford, Surrey

Contents

Foreword

A public relations executive, with whom I was once associated, had a practised way of rejecting constructive contributions from colleagues.

'They all think they're public relations experts!', was his dismissive cry.

Of course they did—and quite rightly so. The enhancement and protection of a company's public reputation is a fundamental, corporate responsibility which every good manager will instinctively understand and grasp.

'Public relations', in its broadest sense, is a collective noun for all those philosophies and activities that become transmitted externally, in one way or another, to determine the popular perception of an organization's character and demeanour—in other words, that overworked phrase, 'the image'.

The generally accepted definition of the practice of public relations is really its narrowest. That is, the employment of specialist communicators, usually journalists, to refine news, views and general information for an anticipated favourable reception by selected media and, thereby, a targeted audience.

One very real danger with public relations is that misused, or misunderstood, it can create its own costly, self-perpetuating industry. This, at best, makes no real contribution to the company or, at worst, runs at odds to it.

Public relations must, therefore, be an integrated discipline in all areas, at all levels. It must reflect the genuine attributes of a company, not become an isolated activity, allowed by default to contrive artificial substitutes for them.

Nobody should be in business to achieve great public relations. The objective of enterprise is to build a great company, with all the implications that has for customers, shareholders and employees. In *Managing Your Reputation*, Roger Haywood demonstrates just how the careful, responsible development of great public relations can play a vital role in attaining recognition as a great company.

Sir Colin Marshall
Chairman
British Airways

Acknowledgements

I would like to express my appreciation to the many colleagues who either offered helpful observations on the contents of this book or who kindly provided useful examples and allowed me to quote their experience.

Thanks to the countless contributors and those stalwarts who patiently checked copy and made suggestions, particularly Mike Beard, John Dresser, Warren Newman, Douglas Smith, Ilsa Vermuch and Bob Worcester.

Particular appreciation to Louisa Rydon who put so much of this together with such good humour and patience, Michelle Powell for her commitment and unassailable belief in what this business is really all about and my researcher, Sharon Garfinkle, whose energy and confidence knew no limit.

I am also indebted to those who generously allowed me to be less than kind about their public relations efforts—often examples of when it went wrong. I hope their tolerance lasts and that the next time I see them it will not be in court. Should they feel I am being superior, may I say that I have made more mistakes in this daft business than I care to remember. But that's another book for another time ...

Introduction

Why should a book need an introduction? Surely everything necessary to be said should be said in the body of the book? Perhaps. So why this? Some things I want to say may be too subjective and personal to risk irritating the less-worldly reader. Therefore ...

> *Mental health warning*: The following contains views that might damage your well-being, undermine your equilibrium and threaten your blood pressure. Those of a sensitive disposition are invited to move straight to Chapter 1.

'No organization can succeed without effective public relations', said a pretentious young man half a lifetime ago.* He probably meant 'few organizations'. Conveniently, he ignored operations like banks, the church, the army, the police and the totalitarian governments that then controlled some two-thirds of the world. None of these cared what people thought, nor did they need goodwill to pursue their ambitions successfully.

He also left out of his sweeping statement the health service, steel, gas and electricity industries plus the many other state-owned monopolies that could rely upon an endless flow of public money with few measures of performance. He also omitted the BBC and the Royal Family which, in the UK, were such national institutions that they could take popular support (then!) for granted.

Everyone needs goodwill to succeed
Times have changed, yet have made that all-embracing assertion truer today than it was in the 1960s and 1970s.

Today, it is not just companies in the private sector that must care about attitudes. Now, governments, public services, utilities, local authorities, charities, trade unions and countless other institutions and non-profit bodies are as dependent upon goodwill for success as those in the commercial

*The author, talking at a conference of The Institute of Public Relations, Brighton, 1968.

sector. Factors that have created this include: privatization of public businesses—and the resulting accountability to stakeholders; the increasingly hostile stance of the media towards organizations, as a result of intensified competition for readers, listeners and viewers; the evaporation of automatic reverence for institution and authority; the growing public demand for information and the right to know.

Such developments in society have forced that awkward juvenile craft of public relations to grow into something approaching a mature discipline. Indeed, some of the finest commercial public relations policies and techniques were developed in the UK—particularly in the period immediately following the Second World War, as countless military information specialists were demobilized and sought to apply their talents in the more liberal environments of public and business life. Despite this, the practice of these skills was the exception rather than the rule, until very recently.

When I started my career in public relations, few managers cared about good relations with their various publics and even fewer appreciated how such relationships could be managed. All that has changed in less than the span of one career.

My generation grew up in post-war euphoria. The war to end wars was behind us. The future looked bright. Britain had an empire—well, a commonwealth—and world influence. Nuclear energy was to save us. London was the centre of the universe. Dan Dare led the world in space exploration.

We know what's best for you ...

But, remember the other side. Life was grey and predestined for most people. Those great liberators, the telephone and the car, were owned by only a few. Power, money and control belonged to a tiny minority. Opportunity and choice were limited. Universities were for the wealthy or the élite—who were usually the same people. There was no choice in radio and television—one television channel and three radio channels, all controlled by the same *ministry of broadcasting*. Newspapers tended to be deferential and polite to politicians and hardly reported business or financial matters at all.

Most commodities were nationalized and state-controlled. Electricity and coal each came from a source that was owned by the government—though you had a choice: you could take it or leave it.

The health 'service' (the health *force* would have been more appropriate) could keep many waiting for half a day for an appointment to make an appointment. If, in the course of an operation, they happened to cut off the wrong piece, it would have been optimistic to even expect a letter of apology.

Have mental malfunction, will teach

Public employees were generally secure for life, facing little te
competence and unsackable. As a child, my generation was taught b
who knew they were virtually immune from criticism and the risk
their jobs. Most teachers were following a vocation … but not all.
authorities, their nominal 'bosses', it may have been difficult to tell which was
which—but not so for their pupils.

At my state school, most of my class-mates were regularly attacked by a
'teacher' with a knotted rubber tube; every few weeks he went berserk and
rampaged around the classroom hitting whoever earned his displeasure. A
horrendous wartime experience slaving on the Burma railway gave him an
excuse that we understood. We never complained. (Or at least, only once
when, in his haste, he grabbed a tube and swung out with the bunsen burner
still attached.)

On the other hand, one gym master regularly identified some training need
among those he favoured; and would oblige them to stay behind. Some
favour!

These professionals (along with the finer representatives of their craft)
were managed by a headmaster who would probably have been certified if
examined. Oh, happy school days!

Later, my own children were taught by a generation more conscientious,
but still no more accountable; when I failed to have an intelligent interview at
a parents' evening with one master, I knew that complaining to the
headmaster that he was drunk could in no way end his responsibilities for the
young people under his care.

All for one and … well, perhaps not

Lest this sounds too political, may I add that I was a trade unionist (that
lunatic fringe, the NUJ) and labour voter in those innocent days.

Managers in industry were no more accountable. Most were secure for life,
with the toughest decisions they faced being what to have for lunch. Total job
security was not just the preserve of the professional middle classes. Trade
union leaders thrived on power. They had an iron grip on industry and public
services; they were unbeatable and unsackable, until the bold expulsion of
Red Robbo from British Leyland.

Such union excesses probably resulted from a true feeling of exploitation
over previous generations, for this social order of the *haves* and *have-nots* had
been built on a structure of a compliant, obedient workforce, generally
without the education or the economic mobility to change their way of life.

In my lifetime, universal higher education and vocational training, the car, the telephone, radio, television and an explosion in information opened new opportunities for the younger generation. In effect, this post-industrial *information revolution* also spelled the end of the working classes—if you accept the definition of these as that group of low-skilled workers with no options over where they worked or in what occupation.

As a young adult, I experienced the joys of not being able to travel to work because of strikes, and ran a company that could only turn on the electricity for three days a week because of an impasse between a weak government and arrogant unions. I saw my country lurching inexorably towards third world status. Those in positions of power, privilege and wealth continued to divide the responsibilities among themselves, while the put-upon workers, often used as pawns by their unions, took more and more for less and less.

But, forgive my nostalgia for the good old days.

Customers 'own' the organization

Today, the world is a different place. National and international economic growth brought competition. This led to a customer orientation in business, stimulated by the philosophies of marketing. Consumer power grew. Market forces were seen to apply across *all* areas of supply and demand.

State industries across the world were shifted back into the private sector. Competition was opened up and survival (let alone success) became dependent upon meeting market needs. The buying decisions of customers with wider choices became ever more influenced by the perceptions they held.

The public demand for information accelerated. The views of wider audiences also became critical—shareholders, employees, neighbours, trade bodies, suppliers and many others. The *court of public opinion* became all-powerful. Is it any wonder that the need for public relations and the demands of the profession grew, both in size and sophistication, to attempt to satisfy these communication needs?

However, now, fewer and fewer organizations have an open mandate on how they behave. Increasingly, the requirement is to perform with consensus support of the people. Churchill put it better when he said to me once, 'If you ain't got the punters with you, mate, you can forget it.'*

Public opinion can close a company, or remove a government ... stop a war, or build an international brand.

Public relations is everywhere. Public relations is life. Organizations need to create awareness of their activities and their ambitions. They need to create

*Fred Churchill, proprietor of the Fix'em Fast Motor Centre, Wandsworth.

understanding. They need to convert this understanding into goodwill. They need to nurture this goodwill to become the positive support which stimulates positive action. Customers buy. Shareholders invest. Employees work. Neighbours support. Unions cooperate. Governments legislate.

That is the role of public relations: evaluating public perceptions; developing the policies that will win approval; projecting these to win the reputation the organization deserves; and generating the support that it needs, among all key audiences.

For ease, much of the comment in this book is in the context of companies. However, as all who work in the coyly-named 'non-profit' sector will confirm, these principles apply equally in all organizations, such as charities, trade and professional bodies, societies, associations, clubs, local and national authorities, public bodies, trade unions and even governments—though few would guess it about the latter on the evidence of their everyday behaviour!

This book attempts to plot a way through this vital but confusing and ill-charted area. It is not an academic treatise; it is based on practical experience, some of it painfully gained through making embarrassing and very public mistakes.

Nor is this a textbook. There are plenty of those, including the author's own, *All about Public Relations*, from the same publisher. This book is intended to be a friendly, anecdotal journey through the worlds of reputation, goodwill and public opinion—more a travelogue than a route map.

Bon voyage, mes vieux.

1

Basic principles

Understand this public relations business

*Organizations can win the reputation
they wish; whatever they do, they will get
the one they **deserve***

A study of public relations

This book explores areas of public relations, sector by sector. Some chapters
will cover familiar territory for those directors with relevant specialist
experience or responsibilities. However, it must be appreciated that many
readers may have expertise in other disciplines.

Managing Your Reputation can only be comprehensive if it covers all the
major aspects of public relations as a corporate function. For this reason,
there is a little overlap between some of the chapters so that each can stand as
a self-contained overview. Some of the copy repeats points made in *All about
Public Relations*, the basic guide, from the same author.

The criteria for *Managing Your Reputation* has been to ensure that any
director would have sufficient information to fully participate in a board
discussion on any of these aspects of the craft.

For each of us, our reputation is one of our most precious qualities. So it is
with companies and other organizations. If you manage an organization, then
you *must* manage your corporate reputation. It is your top responsibility.
Ultimately everything—particularly sales and, therefore, profit—is dependent
on how you are regarded. Your corporate reputation may well be your most
valuable asset. To paraphrase George Washington: *With a reputation you can
do anything—without one, nothing.*

If you do not give the management of this factor the highest priority, then you may be leaving to chance what reputation you will enjoy—or, more likely, not enjoy. In the absence of positive action, you are allowing circumstance or fortune to shape this vital business asset. In effect, you are saying: 'I will leave others, many of whom may not be sympathetic to our aims, to decide how we are viewed by all those upon whom we depend for success.'

Do not imagine that you have some 'right' to goodwill and support. You will only win these if you work for them ... and are seen to work for them. If a good reputation is not your priority or you feel it does not require special effort, do not be surprised if you find it is being shaped by such factors as your competitors' unchallenged assertions; a (yet another) superficial evaluation by a precocious analyst; some *no-smoke-without-fire* gossip recycled by a headline-hungry journalist; another business-bashing report from a consumer group; privileged point-scoring by politicians; the rabble-raising, distorted complaints from an unelected pressure group; or the totally reasonable fears of your confused factory neighbours.

Why complain if these audiences and their views are ill-informed, or biased, or even malicious? You have control over the information they receive and the company actions they observe which shape their attitudes.

It is a simple and infallible rule. The company that has a poor reputation suffers from poor management. Good managers build good reputations. The company that has a good reputation may deserve it, but the managers will have worked hard to ensure that they *win* proper recognition.

The principles of private relations and of good relations with the public one serves are the same, asserts Lord Forte, founder of the major international hotels, catering and leisure group, all in the service industry. 'Reputation and respect can only be built on foundations of honesty and trust. Honesty can conceivably get you into trouble but it remains the best policy. Anything less can destroy in a day what may have taken years to achieve.'

Attitude: a vital factor in most decisions

The truth is something they certainly do not teach you at Harvard (or Henley or the LSE ... and which few economists would proclaim). The attitude of someone making a decision can be more important than all logical elements. In business, there is an understandable pressure to focus only on the tangible factors that make business sense—for example, is our price competitive?; are the working conditions acceptable?; will this earn the right return for the shareholders?; might the factory neighbours accept this planning application?

We tell ourselves that if we get these right then all those decisions will be in our favour. But many of the audiences on whom we depend for our business success are not *in business* with us. They may have a very different agenda, but one we need to recognize; employees may be looking at security or career options; shareholders comparing investments for their pensions; local politicians seeking a vote-winning business/community alliance.

Often, as managers, we apply all our skill and experience to make ours the best offer—yet still find that the customers buy someone else's dearer product; that the best graduates do not always recognize the opportunities; that the share price goes down despite the company reporting good results; that the local community rejects our plans, though they need the jobs.

Sometimes, managers rely too much on logic and believe that all decisions are made on a rational basis alone. The factor they may overlook is that decisions can be influenced by opinions and attitudes. It matters significantly what people *feel* about our products, services and, indeed, our organizations.

One of the prime functions of public relations is to manage company policies and associated communications to build the regard in which the organization is held. Favourable attitudes can be critical to success, taking ages to nurture. As Sir Anthony Cleaver, chairman of IBM UK, comments: 'Public relations is a long-term exercise; a reputation built over many years can be seriously damaged in seconds.'

Goodwill can be a powerful bonus

In business communications (on which this book focuses) attitudes can spell the difference between success and failure. For example, when we choose where we work, in which companies we invest and what products we buy, our attitude to each organization plays a part ... and, sometimes, this can be the single most significant factor.

Studies show that many graduates put corporate reputation and social responsibility even ahead of salary when deciding where they will pursue employment opportunities.

When Exxon ran a tanker aground in Alaska or Gerald Ratner rubbished his own products by calling them crap, in each case, one of the first measures of the impact was a collapsing share price. Why? This was long before any real damage to the trading positions could be calculated. It was simply that people like neither pollution nor cynicism.

When British Airways explained to its staff that customers were number one—and trained them in how to make their *travellers* feel that they were number one—sales soared. Customers liked being treated as if they mattered. In many cases, this approach proved to be more important to flyers than the ticket price.

The attitudes of the key public to your organization are shaped largely by the *attitudes of the organization towards them*. It is easy to test such attitudes. Would you expect Ford to knowingly sell a dangerous vehicle, or Shell to compromise marine safety by cutting down on crew training, or ICI to put the health of employees at risk through poor environmental health policies, or Forte to deliberately mislead its shareholders? Positive or negative, your feelings indicate your appraisal of the attitudes of these companies to the audiences concerned.

Try the 'pub-test'

It is easy to test the effectiveness of any organization's public relations. Later in this book we shall look at more sophisticated techniques, but the simple, immediate pub-test takes some beating. You are introduced in the bar or club to someone you have not met before. He or she naturally asks, 'Who do you work for then?' You answer, 'ABC.' And the response to that is a crude but valid test of ABC's public relations: either 'Oh dear, ABC have been in trouble recently. Tragic that accident, straight after the strike. Got any solution to the pollution problems?'; or 'You did well to win that great export order. Saw your chairman on "Panorama" talking about Anglo-US trade ... very impressive. I even bought a few of your ABC shares myself'; or even 'Who are ABC?'

'It's not corporate 'image' but personality that counts. Public relations helps both to create the 'personality' of the organization and to project this to the audiences it depends on for success.

Some people may be able to survive in some walks of life without concerning themselves with personality. Yet, few organizations can hope to prosper without a sympathetic, favourable personality—unless they enjoy a monopoly or some other form of protection that means they can afford not to bother about making friends and influencing people.

A few fortunate people may have such a natural, positive personality that they never need to think about their behaviour. Perhaps an occasional company falls into this category.

Usually, the strongest corporate personality will be much more than the personality of one individual, though it will be shaped by the input of many managers. A company that is closely linked to one individual may have only an 'inherited' or 'reflected' personality—consider Richard Branson and Virgin; or Alan Sugar and Amstrad; even Bernard Matthews and, well, Bernard Matthews. Do such companies have their own personality separate from that of the founder and prime mover? If not, then growth, diversification and succession can become difficult.

Defining public relations

One view of public relations describes the craft as the projection of the personality of the organization. The corporate personality is what the organization is, reflects what it believes in, determines where it is heading. But, above all, the personality can be developed and controlled by the management, to become the central factor in the building of the corporate reputation. Perhaps the most satisfactory practical description of public relations is that it is *the management of corporate reputation*.

One quality of good management is that it is stable and consistent. These are also qualities in corporate personalities that are likely to bring success. Just as we can anticipate how someone with a developed and balanced personality will behave, we should be able to predict how high-profile corporations will handle themselves.

Of course, there are many other factors that are essential to success. The best public relations will not compensate for weakness in production, quality, service or personnel and many other important business areas. Indeed, it is likely that an active public relations policy will expose rather than hide such a weakness.

Possibly the most common unrealistic request that many advisers get from prospective clients is to be asked to develop a public relations plan to fix *management* problems. For example, a manufacturing company complains that the public do not appreciate the quality of its products. If that is because the quality is not up to standard, then that is a management problem. However, if the products are excellent and the message has not been conveyed (or the competition is stealing all the 'quality' kudos), then *that* may be a public relations opportunity.

MUTUAL UNDERSTANDING

The Institute of Public Relations' official definition of the grey science describes it as the planned two-way communications between the organization and the audiences critical to its success. Such organizational communications are designed to create an understanding of aims, policies and actions. This may not go far enough.

One definition of public relations only covers 'mutual understanding'. This is not satisfactory for it focuses on the *knowledge* of the publics but not necessarily on their opinions and attitudes. Clearly, information is only part of communications, as communications is only part of public relations. For what the company does is as important as what it says.

Effective public relations is much more than communications: it should be more fundamental to the organization. Public relations should begin before the decision-making stage when issues are being debated by management and policies are being formulated.

The Institute has been developing its new definition which, at the time of writing, had not been published. My own version is:

> *Public relations is the discipline responsible for creating the optimum environment within which the organization operates, through evaluating the attitudes of those upon whom it depends for success then developing both the policies and the supporting communications to earn their understanding and support.*

Clearly, any definition should stand alone but it may be helpful to add a few comments. 'Discipline' is convenient shorthand for management function or role, while implying the planned and structured approach that is necessary. The 'optimum environment' is clear in meaning but does not limit the specific factors that might apply in each case. The phrase 'policies and supporting communications' confirms that public relations is a management function and that communications is but *part* of the process.

This definition avoids goodwill but opts for 'understanding and support'. This is because public relations must not just create an atmosphere, mood, attitudes or even, important though it is, *reputation*–it must also produce some sort of action, as *support* identifies.

You do not necessarily have to feel warmth towards an organization to be able to support it. *Goodwill* is perhaps too emotive while *understanding* is neutral. For example, you might vote for the ABC political party (but reluctantly) because they have won your understanding and support, though not necessarily your goodwill. As an illustration, you might understand and support the need for nuclear power generation, security systems in shops and offices, price rises for your electricity–without needing goodwill towards them.

Public relations policy

Public relations is an essential top management responsibility–not an optional extra, nor a mechanical function that can be delegated to administrators. Policy must be decided–and supported–from the top.

International businessman, Lord Hanson, built one of the world's largest and most diversified corporations over the course of his career, starting from virtually nothing. Effective public relations was central to this; indeed, many journalists rate him as a great personal practitioner.

One of his key abilities is to be accessible. Part of this secret is the organization of his office support staff; journalists and other commentators who receive a call from the great man may never be certain from where he is calling. Ring any of his offices and an efficient personable secretary takes the message, as if he had just popped out for a moment. In fact he may return the call, sometimes in minutes, from halfway round the world.

He believes that the basis of good public relations is 'do it yourself'.

> Do not delegate the key elements. You may get a Tim Bell or a Roger Haywood to give you the advice or set up the procedures—but never let them become the spokesman for your organization. That is the job that senior executives must undertake themselves. Creative people may be able to develop great advertising for you, but this principle should not be applied to public relations. This is essentially a personal skill and a senior responsibility.
>
>   Winston Churchill said something about accountants which I think applies to all consultants and particularly those in public relations—*have them on tap but never on top*.

Businesspeople sometimes ask whether their company should have public relations. They should not ask such a question. They have public relations whether they are aware of it or not. The real question they should ask is: Do we want to plan, control and manage it ... or rely on chance and the uncoordinated activities undertaken by whoever wants to get involved?

The best public relations policies will not be developed by instinct alone, though it may play a helpful role; there is no room for the enthusiastic amateur in the sensitive and critical area of human relations.

Good public relations needs thought, planning and organization. No manager can claim to have a 'natural' public relations talent any more than a natural talent for law, personnel, finance or production. The development of a worthwhile public relations policy needs as much thought, attention and professional skill as does the financial, personnel or any other business discipline.

Public relations must be a two-way activity: listening to what the public thinks, as well as projecting the organization's messages. It follows that public relations efforts can only be effective where the aims of the organization are compatible with the aims of the public. The concept of the hidden persuader in public relations is nonsense.

Sir Denys Henderson, chairman of ICI—one of the largest chemical manufacturing companies in the world—oversaw a dramatic reorganization of its operations when the bioscience activities were successfully separated out as Zeneca; and this bold move created two distinct and buoyant companies able to concentrate on their different markets.

The manager and communications

Public relations was an essential element in smoothly and efficiently completing the complex and far-reaching changes that had an impact on all stakeholders in the company. Sir Denys believes that integrity in communications is central, as is the basic need to be honest:

The most skilful use of 'smoke and mirrors' can disguise fundamental problems for no more than a limited period. In the end, there must be substance behind the promise—truth will undoubtedly out, regardless of any camouflage efforts by the most expert 'spin' doctor. Management has to accept responsibility not only for the success or otherwise of the message but also for the facts behind it. It is for this reason that I view the professional management of communication as an essential tool for business success.

The ability to communicate key messages, with fluency and integrity, is a vital skill which managers must acquire if they are to succeed in today's complex, ever-changing business world. The audiences to be addressed may well cover employees, customers, shareholders, politicians, local communities and the general public, often, both at home and across the world. The different concerns of each group must be met sensitively. The relevant messages, whether good or bad news, must be communicated with consistency, clarity and honesty. An evasive, inarticulate introvert is unlikely to be successful!!!

As such top leaders as Henderson and Hanson state, directness and strength of character are essential for a good communicator. It is the responsibility of the chairman and chief executive (among other senior executives) to ensure that the company behaves properly; one of these must also take the role of top spokesperson.

However, the public relations professional may well act as the normal day-to-day voice of the company and plan the public presentations by his or her senior executives. A prime responsibility will be to advise management colleagues on any proposed policies that are not considered to be in the best public interest.

ENLIGHTENED POLICIES TEND TO BE PROFITABLE POLICIES

In a commercial democracy, an organization may deceive some of the public all of the time and all of the public some of the time, but never all of the public all of the time.

As experienced public relations practitioners will confirm, the company that decides that only the highest standard of corporate behaviour is acceptable will find that the best corporate behaviour is almost always the most profitable behaviour. Certainly, cut corners on corporate standards and you risk serious damage to reputation, credibility and commercial success when (rarely *if*) this behaviour is exposed.

Behaving well should be a happier, more comfortable, responsible stance. Personally, I do not always find this argument sufficient, alone, for a doubting management. Far more persuasive is the demonstrable fact that good behaviour can be measured on the bottom line. Ethics is a marketable asset!

The requirements of communications

We all communicate. It is one of the joys (and frustrations) of the public relations business that, because everyone can communicate to a greater or lesser extent, everyone can understand the importance of this ability.

The difficulties arise when managers believe that communications is no more than a natural talent. The reality is that communications is a sophisticated and complex process; in business it is a discipline and can be practised well or badly. As with any discipline, it has rules, can be tested, measured, learned and examined. Why would practitioners spend 3 or 4 years full time, or 7 or 8 years at night classes, to gain qualifications (followed by the lengthy and painful apprenticeship involved in making all the concepts work in practice) if this gives no advantage over an enthusiastic amateur with a weighty thesaurus and an interesting theory?

Of course, there are matters of judgement and a good public relations amateur may be better, sometimes, than a poor professional. But a good professional should always be worth listening to and his or her advice should not be rejected lightly or without considering the possible outcome.

A good public relations professional gains no satisfaction from being proved correct when recommendations are ignored and everything goes wrong. We all have too many horror stories of disasters. Too many of them begin with the boss or the client saying something like 'Everything's going so well that the last thing we need to worry about is good relations', or 'I think we can tackle this as we go along without wasting money or time on any fussy complex plan', or 'Believe me, I'm a natural communicator. There's no advice I need from some public relations person', or 'Let me play this off the cuff. We don't want to spoil our spontaneity with any briefing or rehearsal', etc.

Once in a while, ask a public relations professional to stop going on about past successes and talk candidly about some failures. Here is one of mine.

REDIRECTING A SKILLED WORKFORCE

Build confidence, be honest—and be sure to say what you mean to say

Mike MacIntosh (not his real name) was a tough Scot, an engineer and a no-nonsense manager. He was my boss at the time that the group board of the aerospace company for which we both worked asked us to plan the redirection of an unprofitable division. An excellent team, under his direction, looked at the problem and identified that the operation needed to change methods and move into new markets. This would require substantial investment and complete retraining for 100 of the division's technical people.

My job was to manage the internal and external communications around the reorganization. Everything in my area was carefully planned and coordinated with my personnel, production and marketing colleagues. I organized an internal briefing for the senior managers. This would be followed immediately by a briefing to the 100 key individuals. Bulletins, newsletters and briefing meetings were planned to cover other audiences such as the managers and employees of other divisions, overseas associates, the local and specialized trade media, the unions, professional bodies and so on. All clicked together smoothly into one coordinated plan.

The only problem was Mike. He knew the importance of the decisions and the need for careful communications; he had approved the plan. He accepted the discipline—on everyone else, that is, except himself. He felt he was a persuasive communicator and resisted all my efforts to get him to run through his talk to the employees, which would be the keystone of the whole operation. He reluctantly outlined to me what he intended to say and, later, accepted my draft of how he could best express it. He refused to rehearse this presentation.

The end result was a disaster. Eventually most of the staff either left or were made redundant. The division, a shadow of what it should have been, was sold to a competitor for a give-away price. The sad irony was that Mike also lost his job after he had finished the closure forced on him. What had gone wrong?

It would not be fair to blame Mike. It was my fault. I should never have allowed him to speak without that dummy run. I should not have been cowed into submission.

(Clients in later years have sometimes wondered why I am so obstinate on certain points and always insist on a run-through of any important statement or briefing or any questions and answers session. The reason is simply that I would rather risk upsetting the chief executive than have it all go wrong. That price is too much to pay for deferring to someone's vanity.)

The briefing notes were fine. The media coverage was great. The excitement and anticipation as the 100 employees took their places in the canteen—the only room in the division large enough to take them all—was exactly what was needed to build a new joint-venture between management and a dedicated, skilled workforce.

But, within seconds, the anticipation had turned to worry; the best craftsmen and women had decided to look for new employment. The weaker ones could do little but keep their heads down. The spirit of the team was irreparably broken and any hope of building a new future was out of the window.

You could not fault Mike's intention, but the effect of his impromptu first sentence was exactly the opposite of what he intended. He had smiled and gave them all a thought that, I am sure, from the excited atmosphere that day, had never occurred to anyone there:

'Now, I don't want you to worry about your jobs.'

The use of skilled professionals

There are right ways and wrong ways of doing things. There are times when a newsletter is appropriate and times when a video will be the best method. Some techniques will help win approval while others, used at the wrong time or in the wrong way, will antagonize. There are problems that demand face-to-face discussion when no other substitute will do.

If the aim of communications is to get people to do something differently (and if it is not, then what is the point?) it is critical to realize that information alone will rarely change behaviour. Information may create awareness—of your product, your organization or some key issue. If such information is accepted and believed, then it may change knowledge. This is where many communications efforts end. Too many are involved in a one-way dissemination of information. Is this not enough?

INFORMATION ALONE CANNOT CHANGE OPINION

An informal study of a couple of dozen commercial communications programmes showed that more than half were predominantly information-based. These might have been effective at developing awareness, improving knowledge of the particular issues but would be unlikely to change opinions, attitudes and, most important, behaviour.

Not a penny should be spent on any communications programme unless you have a clear understanding of what changes you expect to achieve. Different techniques are needed to change, say, awareness and opinion.

Consider this simple example. You are in a pub enjoying a debate with a business colleague. She votes for one political party and you vote for another. You ask her why she votes the way she does. She expands on some of the philosophies of the party she supports and explains that they are aligned with her own feelings.

You do the same with your perspective. You did not know about each other's party political affiliations. By now you both may have a little more knowledge and better awareness of the other party—possibly even a better understanding. However, there is not the slightest possibility that either of you would change your political affiliations.

You continue the discussion. She gives you more facts. You give her more facts. If you both believe these, then you continue to become better informed. But you still have no intention of changing your voting behaviour. Why? Because this decision—along with all others that matter—is shaped not just by knowledge but by opinion and attitude.

Your opinion may be that her party (let us call them the Bendies) discourages enterprise and encourages low standards of personal responsibility. *An opinion is a view or belief on an issue which may or may not be related to the facts.*

Your attitude may be that supporters of the Bendies are passengers in society. *An attitude is the stance or the position adopted on an issue. It could be deep-seated and may have taken some time to develop. We can imagine an 'instant' opinion but hardly an 'instant' attitude.*

Directors need to understand these fundamentals, or ensure that they employ and listen to someone who does. When the chairman thinks a television campaign will improve the share price, or the chief executive asserts that the facts will win the support of the shareholders in a takeover battle, or the production director feels that more investment and more jobs will ensure good local media coverage for the new plant or a cabinet minister berates the media for an obsession with trivia that makes managing the country almost impossible, all are demonstrating ignorance of some of the basics of communications. No one in management can afford to be in this position.

Some observations, in summary

1 All decisions are affected by attitude—and sometimes (often) that can be the most important factor. Ask yourself, would you be happy to invest in a company that boosted profits by skimping on safety regulations?
2 How the organization views the public decides how the public view the organization—we all tend to like people who like us. Is it any wonder we warm to companies that make it clear they care about us?
3 A spontaneous reaction to your company name can be a measure of public relations. There are more sophisticated tests, but few surer than the instinctive appraisal of your credibility by someone relevant but with no axe to grind.
4 Build the corporate personality to which people can relate. Integrity and character are qualities we all respect and the well-managed company can develop these just as effectively through its style and ethos.
5 Public relations should be viewed as the management of the corporate reputation. We expect the finances, production, marketing and workforce

to be managed, so why not that precious asset, the company reputation?

6 Communications is only part of public relations. We tend to think that all problems can be solved by listening and talking, but how the organization behaves is a critical factor in its stance to its public.

7 Policy must be endorsed from the top, even if it is implemented at operating levels. Indeed, public relations is one of those important top management responsibilities which must be executed properly.

8 The soundest policies are those closest to the best public interest. You win wide support through pursuing actions that are of maximum benefit to the audiences whose backing you need for your success.

9 Effective public relations needs planning, resources and commitment as the wise company does not leave such an important area to chance. It should be treated as a professional discipline with resources and responsibilities.

10 You cannot *choose* to have public relations—you *have* them and company behaviour is constantly shaping attitudes towards the corporation, perhaps in a positive coordinated way or perhaps not.

11 Management problems cannot be solved by public relations alone— particularly where communications is being called in to solve problems created by poor management decisions.

12 Communications must be a two-way process—otherwise, strictly speaking, it is not communications. Feedback is vitally important to check how well your messages are accepted by the audiences you are trying to influence.

13 All senior managers should be communicators. Therefore we must train those who are likely to advance through the corporation, as well as those who might have communications needs in their current work.

14 The best corporate behaviour is likely to be the most profitable. Behaving well usually turns out to be the best commercial option because we all prefer to deal with people of integrity.

15 Information alone will not change opinions and attitudes. It can develop awareness but where negative attitudes exist, more information can actually reinforce these unhelpful perceptions.

16 The end result must be a change in behaviour. More goodwill and better understanding may be desirable aims, but the real measure is support that will produce action among those targeted.

2

Board policy

Win a good reputation through action from the top

Determining communications responsibilities

The chairman must take the final responsibility for the effectiveness of company public relations. Every member of the board owes it to the chairman to share that responsibility—and to ensure that the necessary information is available to allow intelligent discussion of key communications issues at board meetings.

However, it has to be said that outside the most sophisticated business leaders, only a minority of companies are giving these matters the level of attention they deserve. Where the chairman or the chief executive does not get independent advice from a public relations professional, the need for board reviews becomes even more important.

The company management might reasonably ask when is it involved with public relations? As Brendan O'Neill, managing director of Guinness Brewing Worldwide, has stated, whenever you have contact with people or organizations you are, like it or not, in the public relations business. Few corporations question the need for a finance or personnel function; those who doubt the value of effective public relations are deluding themselves, he believes.

Review corporate communications at board level

Any failure of the directors to be on top of communications could be most damaging. Should the company experience difficult times, it is likely that shareholders or statutory bodies might become interested in how the public relations aspects of key issues were being considered at board level, as they unfolded.

For example, when did the board of Townsend Thoresen last review its crisis plan before the *Herald of Free Enterprise* tragedy? Did Hoover directors sign off marketing communications proposals that led to the ill-fated free tickets to the USA promotion? Did Ratner directors approve the speech that their chief executive made to the Institute of Directors that virtually collapsed the company? Were the board aware of the Guinness media relations practices that were part of the infrastructure behind its takeover violations? Did BA senior executives authorize those briefings of key journalists on the financial state of Virgin? Did directors of South West Water mislead the public for some days if they knew that aluminium sulphate had accidentally been put in the wrong tank?

These and other critical questions on public relations can and have been asked when problems arise; companies that do not review their corporate communications at board level are taking a risk. And most companies still are taking that risk, as a check of most board agendas will confirm. Indeed, very few companies have agreed public relations policies and even fewer publish these objectives.

Of course, many directors will protest that too much is being squeezed on to overcrowded agendas. But communications policy is not something that can be delegated. It can and does make headlines. It can and does close companies.

Yet with proper planning, the review of a responsibly run programme takes little time. Indeed, the fact that the board signs off policy may be one vital element in ensuring that the programme is run responsibly.

Initially and understandably, Sir Adrian Cadbury, chairman of the Committee on the Financial Aspects of Corporate Governance, was reluctant to extend the debate, during the early deliberations of his group, through the inclusion of the Institute of Public Relations. However, as I was president of that body at that time, I advanced the view to him that communications, particularly investor public relations, was an essential and integral element within proper corporate governance, as was well appreciated by the City. He agreed this point and the Institute submitted evidence.

The Code of Best Practice on the Financial Aspects of Corporate Governance specifically requires that the board should have a formal schedule of matters for decision to ensure that control of the company is firmly in its hands. This refers of course to financial matters where communications will be central. In addition, the code also says that it is the board's duty to present a balanced and understandable assessment of the company's position. Again, this is focused on financial communications.

There are, however, many other aspects of company operations that can impact on its financial position; and in each of them public relations will tend to be the main communications link between the company, represented by the board, and the audiences whose goodwill and understanding are being sought.

There is no other company discipline that can give a broader overview of company operations than public relations, yet most directors have no idea what is being done in their names, across vital areas of operation, involving all the audiences of importance to the company. It is not difficult to guess whether this lack of knowledge implies supreme confidence or dangerous ignorance.

The responsibility of directors for investor communications may be clear. These responsibilities are extending steadily to encompass all aspects of corporate communications. Few companies in the UK have written communications policies and even fewer make them public. Such policies can be an invaluable way to help define the responsibilities of the board and senior executives.

In this book, the emphasis is on commercial companies, but public relations principles apply as effectively to all organizations. Experience of many in the non-profit sector, for example, is extremely positive. Colonel Iain Ferguson is the vice-chairman and director of the group of military personnel who plan and run The Royal Tournament. They retain public relations professionals to help raise the profile and improve attendances at this event. He identifies the major achievement of this campaign as transforming the event from a purely military tattoo to a thoroughly entertaining and enjoyable family show. He points out that the needs of the three services are still being met but The Royal Tournament now attracts many young people who know little or nothing of the services.

Companies get the support they deserve

The ideal reputation for your organization will not be earned by accident. It will be won through application and direction. Therefore, there must be a commitment to ensure that the public relations implications of all company operations are considered in all appropriate policies and plans.

Ideally, the mission statement (or the corporate objectives) will include an appropriate commitment to the development of the corporate reputation. This will also need to be reflected in all business and marketing plans.

As an illustration, marketing may be all about *satisfying customer needs profitably* ... but it also has a responsibility to develop and reinforce the reputation of the organization. A suitable statement in the marketing plan about the reputation objective will help avoid the adoption of unacceptable sales techniques or promotional activities—for example, those that may be better for short-term results than they are for the longer term's perceptions among those who matter. It is a circular argument. Will you go to heaven because you are good or are you being good so that you will go to heaven?

Perhaps if Hoover had had a corporate reputation objective written into its marketing plans it would have been less likely to develop a promotional scheme that depended on misleading customers.

Sainsbury's, as an illustration, follows policies that reflect its belief in behaving properly. People relate to such decent values. Being well regarded by the public creates a good reputation. People prefer to buy from and work for those that have good reputations. Companies that people like to deal with have an advantage over those they don't. If Sainsbury's products and prices are as good as its promised services and proven values, it will have a competitive edge. Companies with a competitive edge tend to be those that prosper. Companies that prosper can afford to behave properly.

Those that believe in public relations like to think that Sainsbury's prospers because it cares. Others think it cares because that is the way to prosper.

MAKE THE POLICY SHAPE COMPANY BEHAVIOUR

Many companies are choosing to define and publish their mission. It is undeniably true that these will tend to have a certain sameness in feel with quite a high level of usage of words like *excellence, responsibility, encouragement, efficiency, productivity* and so on. However, they do make a formal commitment against which individual managers and employees can measure their own performances or, indeed, direct their staffs, peers or even their bosses when standards appear to be in conflict with some of the points in the mission statement.

One of the weaknesses of some corporate mission statements is that companies tend to write them to be broad enough to cover most eventualities, which means they do not have quite enough focus. One helpful recommendation might be to start with a general mission statement but to refine it over a period of time. Certainly, no company should be publishing the identical mission statement year after year in, for example, the annual report unless they are convinced that this is the definitive version. It can always be improved and the sharper the focus of the mission statement, theoretically, the sharper the focus of the organization.

Take an actual example. The following appeared, attractively laid out in white type face on a dark blue page immediately following the chairman's report in the annual report and accounts of a leading UK company, GEC.

> At GEC, we will do our utmost to provide value and high standards of service to customers and will encourage our suppliers to do the same.

We will play a constructive role in the communities in which our facilities are established, paying due regard to environmental considerations.

We will encourage and reward the productivity and the ingenuity of the people who work in the Company.

We will ensure our technological leadership by maintaining excellent research and development staff and providing them with the facilities they need.

We will continue to exercise the style of management which has been proven over many years.

We will achieve profitable growth from within the Company, with imaginative management of our assets.

We will encourage further growth through acquisition, partnerships, joint ventures and technical collaboration.

We will seek to maximize the value of our shareholders' investments by consistently raising earnings per share while maintaining prudent accounting standards.

(GEC Report & Accounts, 1993)

GEC is among those leaders prepared to spell out its aims for all to see and consider. The spirit of what the company is trying to achieve is very clear. Such statements of responsibility help companies decide priorities during good times and bad.

It is interesting that, in this eight-point statement by GEC, customers are set at the top. Yet in seven of the points there is no quantified element that might set standards against which the company could compare its own and competitors' performances. The exception is the eighth point which is very specific in saying 'consistently raising our earnings per share'. Of course, this is an annual report to shareholders and so it should not be a surprise that— whatever the ranking of the key audiences—the financial performance to the owners of the company is the only one that is unequivocal.

It would be churlish to be critical of a company that has had the courage to state its intentions. One would hope that these would be refined and developed over a period of years to give GEC the continuing advantage that it enjoys over its competitors in so many areas.

The company reputation is *everyone's* responsibility

Whatever his or her role in the organization, each employee has some personal responsibility for its reputation. As the old saying goes: *you can't take the money and knock 'em!*

In fact, it is reasonable for management to expect all members of the company to do more than resist criticizing their employers in public; each should be an enthusiastic ambassador for the company. If employees are not, then something is seriously wrong. It would be wise to include some suitable reference to these reputation responsibilities in contracts of employment, staff booklets and induction programmes.

Obviously, such a positive, supportive environment allows (indeed, should encourage) constructive criticism, designed to help the company improve performance—though even that should be 'in the family'.

Clearly, the responsibility on those at the top is more demanding. Managers and directors have both their personal and the corporate responsibility for reputation. They will not be able to exercise this properly unless they know and understand how the organization's communications work.

This is important for all managers; it is essential for directors. Indeed, it could be argued that a director who does not understand the processes by which the reputation of the company is developed is as ill-equipped as one who does not know where the product is sold or how it is manufactured.

A leading cabinet minister, still in office at the time of writing, said to me: 'There's something suspect about public relations. After all, if your product or your company is any good, then everyone will know.' He was not wrong; but nor was he quite right.

He was not wrong, for public relations can never be a substitute for doing the right thing. Reputation is dependent on far more than polished words and impressive visuals. What the company *does* matters as much as what it *says*. Its products and services create goodwill (or otherwise) as much as its communications. Its attitudes towards its publics also influence the attitudes those publics will have towards the company. (In fact, all of these elements should be part of the public relations mix, but that's another story.)

Nor was my cabinet friend right. *Build a better mousetrap and the world will beat a path to your door.* Many great mousetrap designers have starved as a result of believing that. Good products, good services and good companies deserve effective promotion. Your competitors will be presenting their case to the media, to your customers, to your employees and to your shareholders. If you do not vigorously project the values in which you believe and which shape your approach to these audiences, do not be surprised if they are more impressed with competitive offers.

Directors and the communications policy

Recent tightening of company laws in the UK means that all directors, effectively, are responsible for everything that the company does, or that they should reasonably have known it was doing. The introduction of codes, such as that on corporate governance discussed earlier, set standards of behaviour expected even where not statutorily compulsory. Like the Highway Code, such guidelines may not have the weight of the law behind them, but someone in trouble who has contravened the 'suggestions' may have a little explaining to do. Equally, increasing concern about business ethics, among the public at large and informed observers in particular (notably the business media), also exerts pressure for better behaviour and more openness.

A company that has no communications policy is unlikely to be able to carry out its responsibilities to all its stakeholders, for information will be one of their prime requirements. Each director should be concerned that the communications policy is sound; that it ensures that all who have a right to know are properly informed; that effective feedback systems exist; that early warning of problems can be assured; that the processes exist to deal briskly and sensitively with any crisis; and that a (very) senior director is personally responsible for public relations with proper, regular reporting procedures to the whole board.

Put your reputation on the agenda

The only satisfactory reporting method must be for public relations to be a regular and *routine* board item. Directors should not just be concerning themselves with communications when there is a problem. Winning a good company reputation is, perhaps, a little like building a good marriage—it requires constant work, through the good times and the bad. When problems strike, it may be too late to apply remedial treatment. Effective relations between the organization and its various publics require constant attention.

It may not be necessary for the board to become involved in the detail but each director must be comfortable that he or she has a good overview. Public relations strategy might be reviewed once or twice a year with brief progress reports in between. A strategy review paper presented to the board might cover the following areas:

1   *Objectives*. What is to be achieved over the coming period to support the mission statement or corporate objectives? Aims for the communications efforts may be acceptable; however, could these be quantified to identify a specific point that should be reached over an agreed period of time?
2   *Strategy*. What *tone of voice* is being adopted to achieve these objectives? Do all the elements support this and how do they combine into an overall plan? Is each activity complementary? Can any be extended to reach broader audiences and improve cost-effectiveness?
3   *Perceptions*. How is the company seen? What are the attitudes of those

whose goodwill you need for success? (Periodically these must be identified by research, but interim reviews should note the observations of public relations, marketing, sales, personnel and other professionals in contact with prime audiences.)

4 *Messages*. How do you wish the company to be seen? What gaps are there between reality and perception? Is the company communicating in the way that will win support—and *behaving* in the way that will win support? Are all the communications activities reinforcing these agreed messages?

5 *Tactics*. What communications methods are to be used? How will these relate to other corporate activities? Who is directing and implementing the programme? What company contingency plans have been proposed to deal with the unexpected?

6 *Initiatives*. Are there special events of which you should be aware, such as the preview of the new corporate video or the launch of the new sponsorship? Are these *on strategy* and, if so, how can they best be tied in to the broader company business timetable?

7 *Calendar*. What are the major activities in the corporate calendar that have public relations implications? What are the plans to support these? Is the programme scheduled realistically to coordinate such events with any new communications initiatives?

8 *Concerns*. What issues might the communications professionals wish to discuss? Are there areas of policy where the directors' views and support are essential? Will members of the board be expected to participate in functions? If not, might these be enhanced if they did?

9 *Competition*. Are there public relations activities by competitors that should be discussed? How is their public relations effectiveness, say, in the tone of media coverage, in comparison with yours? Is this competitive position improving?

10 *Appraisal*. How effective is the programme overall? What performance criteria are set so that the effectiveness can be appraised and the direction fine-tuned? What are the achievements to date, ideally measured against the objectives that were set?

11 *Management*. How is the competence of those charged with managing the function? Do directors have any commendations or concerns that should be voiced? How are consultants or other advisers performing? Are there any changes that need to be considered?

12 *Resources*. What is the total cost of the activity proposed, including staff time? Does anything require additional company resources, such as regional seminars, factory open days, wholesaler briefings? How well prepared is the communications team to handle any crisis that may arise?

Public relations is more than insurance

Some organizations spend money on public relations because they see it as insurance, to protect them should things go wrong, and some see it as a way of putting a gloss on their activities. Public relations can perform both functions, but these are negative approaches that will never create the real benefits that can come from whole-hearted commitment to communicating properly.

Good public relations *does* have an insurance value. Crisis plans are an essential part of any company's proof of its preparedness. All organizations should know, in advance, how to react to a fire, a security alert, fraud, accident or other unwanted eventuality that may befall them. The public relations aspects of these may be critical and may even affect the survival of the company. The wise company will not only have a developed plan but it will take its responsibilities to its publics seriously. It will test this plan and ensure that all employees are familiar with their role and are trained to handle it.

But do people behave well or badly because of a plan? Do they communicate effectively because of this plan? In fact, it is almost the converse; those who believe in behaving well will insist on a plan, and they will communicate effectively because they care about their responsibilities.

Public relations that just exists as insurance against a disaster is passive and calculated. It may also not be the most effective. It may not even guarantee the expected benefits ... less certain than giving to charity to secure your place in heaven!

Equally, public relations that exists only to put a gloss on the good news, but which disappears when there are problems, is not the wisest. The best policy must be to tell the bad news as boldly as the good. Prepare for the impossible, then use that resource, continuously and positively, to listen to the views of your partners in business, your staff, customers, suppliers and others; and use that resource to inform these publics. Consistent, open, honest communications builds trust and goodwill. You can never have too many of those qualities.

AVOID THE 'DOWN THE CORRIDOR' MENTALITY

The reality is that public relations is something in which you do, or do not, believe. Try to impose it through an unwilling management and the public will see the artifice. Good public relations does not come just from the professionals, it comes from the chairman, the chief executive, and the directors to whom it is part of their thinking, not an afterthought or a bolt-on extra.

The chief public relations officer is the chief executive. The professionals advise, manage and offer specialist skills. It is exactly comparable to other company disciplines, such as finance. In any company, the *chief* financial officer is, of course, the chief executive and the financial professionals advise, manage and offer specialist skills to their board colleagues.

Directors are constantly making decisions that have public relations implications. Indeed, there will be few senior decisions that do not have such implications. It is wise to have the most senior public relations professional very close at hand. Many companies such as British Gas, Dalgety, Grand Metropolitan and Taylor Woodrow have the public relations expert reporting directly to the chief executive or chairman.

The industry journal *PR Week* regularly interviews top executives and editor Stephen Farish observes a link at this level between personal relationships with the public relations professional and the effectiveness of company communications.

> It is interesting to see how companies that achieve and maintain a good reputation are so often led by chairmen or chief executives who clearly trust their public relations advisers. They enjoy a direct relationship that allows, even encourages, the public relations person—staff or consultant—to say what needs to be said. The company profits from the integrity and independence of this comment. After all, a good public relations adviser should be as concerned about how well company policies are accepted by those they affect, as by how well they are projected.

It could be argued that the chief executive with such candid but supportive advice can be confident that he or she is tuned into issues and concerns. Perhaps, though, the same confident chief executive always makes sure that some reliable person is available to provide up-to-date information! Whichever way it may be, the companies with good public reputations seem to employ the best practitioners in the business. In truth, the best is always the cheapest option. Good people make fewer mistakes.

A depressing topic of conversation among professional public relations people meeting socially is the misjudgements of those who should know better but who have not bothered to get public relations advice or, worse, have appointed some junior to do a senior's job. Mistakes in public relations can be desperately expensive. In choosing public relations professionals, the wisest solution is to choose the best you can find. Anything cheaper could prove too expensive.

Do nothing to compromise integrity

Transparency: that is the first requirement for any management policy for a company seeking a good reputation. It may be a cliché but it has to be the best way to describe the style of management that is as open and honest as possible, with no hidden agendas. Corporate life becomes much simpler when decisions are made openly and are exposed to as many people as possible, as quickly as possible. Of course, there are decisions that have to be taken in private and which may not be revealed immediately—commercial needs, alone, may dictate some.

However, conspiracy management can become quite infectious and too much confidentiality can lead to paranoia about security of information. Taking secret decisions can be exciting, but any decision that matters will become known sooner or later and it may well be better to consider making it known sooner, rather than letting it be discovered later.

Journalists tend to smile when advised of a piece of information preceded by a 'this must be treated in the strictest confidence'. Nine times out of ten it turns out to be something already widely known, often common gossip up and down the corporate grape-vine.

Transparency in the decision-making process is also much easier because it is a policy based on honesty. No one needs to remember the truth, but subterfuge requires a totally reliable memory if the pretence is to continue in any consistent way.

Consider an example. The company needs to save costs and, say, the Hartlepool factory is making losses. The commercial director outlines the facts to the board and it is discussed in detail. You decide that you have to close it at some date to be agreed.

But when do you tell those people directly involved? At the earliest moment that wisdom and judgement will allow. Such actions need much consideration and planning, but the risk of a leak increases with every hour and with every person advised. As more people become involved in the decisions, the chances increase that someone will feel a certain loyalty towards the other workers and, so, a discreet word in the ear of a journalist might be an idea.

Try to get everything 100 per cent and you may delay too long. If so, when you are finally forced to make the announcement, all will know that you made the decision much earlier. Indeed, all will know that when you should have told the truth you did not. Even worse, circumstances may have required you to be more than economical with the truth in that extended limbo period.

If you follow this logic, you should therefore operate as if everything that you are doing is (or shortly will become) public knowledge. It is a good approach for personal integrity and so it works equally well for corporate integrity.

If you do not want your action to become public knowledge, then the simple rule is: Don't do it!

BUILDING A BUSINESS OF INTEGRITY

Unite all the board behind a common, shared and uplifting philosophy

One of the world's largest chemical companies with significant operations in virtually every industrialized nation had a problem. A public relations consultant* had been called in because the company had been getting some pretty negative media coverage. His brief was to improve the media coverage. After a little investigation, it seemed clear to him that not all the negative coverage was unfair. Some of the stories were reasonable reports of what the company was doing. The *real* problem was that some of the things it was doing were not winning the approval of the community nor of the journalists reporting on community affairs.

He pointed out to the chairman that negative comment was often justified. If a company, for example, polluted local rivers, suffered from fires and site accidents, annoyed the neighbours with nasty smells and woke them up in the middle of the night with unexpected bangs, then declined to explain these occurrences, you could hardly criticize the journalist for reporting this. And the lack of balancing good news could be explained by the fact that nobody told the media about any good news—like major investments, important new products, splendid community initiatives, VIP visits.

Fortunately, the chairman laughed at this extreme exaggeration, and invited the consultant to attend the next board meeting to expose such simplistic views to the assembled colleagues. Our hero readily agreed.

On that memorable occasion, he decided not to go into detailed presentation on managing the media nor even to refer to the researches that had been undertaken. The foolhardy consultant decided to keep it very simple and said something along these lines:

'In the main, companies get the media that they deserve. We have very little to complain about in the media coverage that we have been getting. If any of us here around the table were the editor of "Panorama" or the *Financial Times* business correspondent, we might well produce similar stories. As a company, what we are doing is of great interest to their viewers and readers. We do not complain about good news, but sometimes we make mistakes. These range from irritating to potentially dangerous and we have to accept that it is the job of the journalist to report such matters.'

*The reckless public relations adviser was the author, the company was Rhone-Poulenc and the visionary chairman was Dr Keith Humphreys, later to become a distinguished president of the Chemical Industries Association.

'Outrageous,' responded one director. 'I would never write such irresponsible, trivialized stories!'

'You would, if you were a responsible, popular journalist,' the consultant replied as calmly as he could manage. 'Because the behaviour of big companies when they ignore their responsibility to the neighbours and the community is of interest to the readers of, say, the *Daily Mirror*. If you did not, your editor would replace you with someone who did understand this fundamental of journalism.'

'But the stories are so unrepresentative,' murmured the personnel director in a conciliatory tone. 'One tiny fire and a little smoke, entirely from cables and nothing to do with chemicals, does not deserve that sort of front page coverage.'

'It was only front page on the local paper and, in my view, it *did* deserve that treatment,' responded the consultant, equally gently. 'If we were unable to provide the information that it was an electrical fire, then the journalist cannot be criticized for not divining this. Equally, if you lived next door to a chemical plant and had your house engulfed in clouds of billowing black smoke from the local chemical works, your first thought might not be ... *I am sure that is only a little electrical fire and some harmless sooty smoke from cables burning*. We need to understand what is news. One fire in a chemical plant is news; 364 other days when there is not a fire is not news and nobody is interested.

'If one taxi driver sets fire to his cab, that is news even if 10 000 others do not do such a thing on that day. News is not about balance and it is not the media's job to project the routine of our activities. But I do protect their right to project the extraordinary and if we are sufficiently unprofessional to create their news then we deserve everything we get.'

'Where does this lead us?' asked the canny chairman, keen to get back on the track.

'Well, chairman,' responded our brash young adviser. 'As you know, many of the practices which they continue to discuss have long since been stopped. We are vigorously tackling safety. We have established an environmental policy and are about to publish this. I am happy to project this good news to the media. But I believe it is much more important that we are totally confident that, if we want a good reputation, we are not doing anything of which we are not proud.'

The chairman considered the point. 'I am proud of the company. We all are. We may have inherited some unhappy situations from generations of previous management working to the standards of their day, but I am convinced that we are doing it all right now and that things will be even better in the future. What are we doing, do you think, of which we cannot be proud? Why don't we go around the table and check?'

They duly did. After some vigorous and positive debate, the board confirmed comprehensive new safety procedures in all plants. It also agreed to pull out of the manufacture of a product responsible for severe pollution, even though it would lose some £50 million in sales. It also agreed to adopt an open-door policy at each of its plants—any member of the public could phone up for any information at any convenient time. And, in addition, any professional group, any environmental or community association could come into the plant at any time to take any samples or make any tests of effluent, ground water or any other materials at any time they liked. Finally, the board recommended a more proactive approach to community and media communications.

These actions were eventually translated into a policy which was published. Because it was credible and backed by the open-door policy, this was positively and extensively reviewed by the media. Every incident thereafter, as had been warned, attracted even more negative coverage. There were very, very few.

And, at the end of the first twelve months at the plant which had experienced the most media problems, how many community bodies or pressure groups had asked for access? *None.* There was no necessity for it was quite clear that the company no longer had anything to hide.

Some observations, in summary

1 The chairman is ultimately responsible for how the company communicates. Everything is effectively said in that person's name.
2 The chief public relations officer is the chief executive.
3 All board members must be happy with communications for they have a duty to support the corporate public relations policy.
4 Public relations policy must be decided at board level. Plans can be developed elsewhere but only the board can authorize the programme.
5 The board should regularly review issues that could affect future performance, usually as analysed by the public relations professional.
6 Make sure the public relations professional is close at hand, has regular access to directors, is up to date on developments and allowed to advise.
7 An experienced head of public relations can provide a useful perspective for the board, probably having the broadest view of the company.
8 Guidelines on corporate governance put a responsibility on directors to ensure that the company position is properly communicated.

9 Any mission statement should set public relations policy in terms of fair dealing with the publics on whom the organization depends for success.

10 Where possible, the mission statement should try to put levels of performance on each element and improve these, year on year.

11 All plans and proposals submitted to the board should include an analysis of the public relations implications and any effects on existing policy.

12 As everyone is responsible for the reputation of the organization, a requirement to support this should be written into contracts of employment.

13 What the company *does* is vitally important, not just what it *says*. Public relations must project positive and truthful messages.

14 The ideal starting point is a written communications policy which should be prepared by the professionals for board discussion and approval.

15 The time to concentrate on getting public relations policy right is when all is calm and going well. There will not be time when problems arise.

16 Do not try to keep information confidential for too long. Everything will soon be public, so issue the news as widely and as early as possible.

17 Those responsible for implementation should present the public relations programme and performance to the board, say, quarterly.

18 Factors to be reviewed should be objectives, strategy, perceptions, messages, tactics, new initiatives, timetable, competitive position, performance, management capabilities, and resources.

19 The quality of the company reputation will be related to the personal relationship between the chief executive and the public relations adviser.

20 If you truly would not wish some considered action—personal or corporate—to be publicly exposed, then don't do it!

3

Managing the function

Manage your communications investment

Developing the brief

Some elements must be approved at board level. The public relations needs of the organization will be clarified once the process of developing the objectives has been completed. However, what needs to be done to *achieve* these objectives will not yet be agreed. Indeed, little will be clear to those who did not take part in the discussions that led to such clarity.

The key to managing the function is to agree the brief. The chief executive needs to be certain that proper management processes are established so that he or she and the board can be fully up to date on developments. While much of the public relations activity may need no more input from the board than an occasional review, some elements cannot be delegated. Policy *must* be set by the board. Key issues must be reviewed at this level. Crisis strategy must be approved.

The level of detail in which the chief executive wishes to be involved will vary with the company and the individual concerned. These notes suggest areas that might be worth considering.

Getting the whole company heading in the same direction in public relations is vital. For example, there will be confusion, irritation and frustration if the public relations professionals are vigorously supporting sales and marketing objectives while personnel are concerned about staff turnover, production about local restrictions on night working and so on. In many cases, with a little thought and planning, such diverse aims may be compatible. Some priority or weighting of the activity needs to be decided.

Agreement on these matters is fundamental. Fiskars, the Finnish engineering group which owned the Wilkinson Sword brand in gardening and tools, brought in public relations professionals to support a major marketing drive. The advisers soon found that one director wanted all promotion to be built around this famous name, but another wanted the parent company to be more strongly featured.

The difference of view was significant and there were valid arguments both ways. The Fiskars name was not as well known as Wilkinson Sword; the ownership of this international brand name would be subject to review and renegotiation at some stage in the future. Should the short-term need take priority and the better-known name be promoted, or should public relations be used to develop the awareness and, therefore, brand value of the parent name over a period of time?

It was perfectly reasonable that there might be differing points of view on how public relations should address this issue. However, if the consultancy had only had access to one point of view, they may well have been criticized later for undertaking a programme of action that was not achieving the aims that other members of the board might have considered to be a priority.

Such matters need to be resolved and the ideal solution is for the board to prepare (or at least agree) a written brief.

The elements in any programme tend to be the same even when the aims and techniques are widely varied. The ideal brief may reflect these. I tend to use a simple *aide-mémoire* for these factors:

Who?	—	audiences (*those we are trying to reach*)
What?	—	messages (*what we want them to understand*)
Why?	—	objectives (*what we are trying to achieve*)
Where?	—	locations (*where these audiences are located*)
When?	—	timetable (*the schedule of activity*)
... and ...		
How?	—	techniques (*the methods we propose*)
+ how much?	—	resources (*budget and personnel*)
+ how effective?	—	appraisal (*how performance will be measured*)

Ideally, the senior executive responsible for public relations will be attending board meetings or, at least, part of such meetings. Even where this is not the case, it is important that he or she is given the opportunity to have an input into the discussions before a final policy on public relations is confirmed. However, before the brief is finalized and agreed, the organization should seek the views of external professionals.

Philips Business Systems decided to launch a sophisticated energy management system through advertising and with public relations support. The public relations consultant was asked to the management meeting discussing this strategy and was able to point out that once the system had been broadly advertised then it would be of limited editorial news interest. The logical approach would be to launch it via editorial first and delay the advertising until phase two when it could give a secondary boost to the product. This advice was accepted.

In practice, the public relations maintained interest at such a level that the sales targets were exceeded and advertising was not necessary until the second year. This revised approach ensured that sales budgets were met, but saved well over £400 000 in costs in the first budget year.

Develop a written plan

Misunderstandings and differences in perspectives can be eliminated by insisting on a written plan. This need not be produced by the board but it should be to the board's brief and approved at board level. Normally, it is best that this is prepared by the senior public relations professional, who should participate in board discussions on strategy issues so that the background is fully understood.

A one- or two-page summary may be sufficient for the board to give approval, though the full plan will be a more substantial document covering audiences, messages, objectives, timetable, resources, methods, appraisal and reporting back, as noted above.

The focus of the board should be on the messages to be projected and to which groups, rather than on details of the techniques to be deployed. As suggested earlier, the plan should be related to the mission statement or the company credo to ensure that it is consistent and reinforcing the broader aims of the organization.

CONFIRM RESOURCES TO BE DEPLOYED

The company will be committing a team of people and a budget to the achievement of the objectives of the public relations programme. The most important point is the confirmation of the person who has overall responsibility for the effectiveness of the work.

There may be diverse elements of public relations involved—for example, a customer-care team, internal communications staff, press office, marketing and city consultancies. One executive needs to coordinate these efforts and take responsibility for reporting to the board.

Public relations activity should be undertaken within an agreed budget. Only rare contingency activity might be outside the confirmed budget. Public relations should be operating within the same disciplines that apply to any other business function. This control not only applies to those running the activity but to senior management; all must resist the temptation to adopt their favourite activity for sponsorship or be wooed by the latest electronic technique, and adjust the budget accordingly. If the sponsorship is a cost-effective way of achieving the objectives, then it should be part of programme recommendations. If not, it should never be considered.

Too many programmes have been hijacked and too many professionals demoralized by disproportionate resources being allocated to peripheral activity at the expense of the planned, strategic events. As Peter Ward, managing director at the time of Korrugal, the Electrolux speciality aluminium division in the UK, used to ask me firmly, 'Is it on strategy?'

Equally, some companies spend *too much* through resources not being properly directed. When Peter Sanguinetti was brought into British Gas as director of corporate affairs, he found what he believed was a classic case of a failure to communicate effectively at the strategic level. He explains that he inherited a large team spending millions but there was a complete lack of focus and much of the expenditure was counter-productive. His first step was to sort out the fundamentals and get the strategy agreed at board level—targets, messages, techniques and so on.

His view is that there are two vital stages before planning any programme: first, management must agree the reputation they want to achieve against a number of criteria; second, use research to measure precisely the company's existing reputation among the target audiences. If the reputation does not match management aspirations, yet performance is good, then that sets a communications challenge; but if the research confirms low regard and this is because performance is below par, then management must improve this first. A company has only to fail to deliver the promise once for the reputation to be shattered, he comments.

ENSURE THAT DECISION MAKERS ARE CONSULTED

The managers of the public relations function will need to have access to senior management to obtain their endorsement of key initiatives—and possibly participation in some of these. The new product launch may need to be fronted by the marketing director. The analyst meetings may require the financial director and the chief executive. The AGM and final results briefings demand the chairman. The regional workforce development policies may be best presented by the personnel director, and so on.

Such senior executives can reasonably make suggestions for improving the activity but should avoid unnecessary significant changes. The time for radical suggestions is at the planning stage. The public relations people are no more likely to be prima donnas than, say, their production or financial colleagues; however, equally, they thrive best in a stable environment where they know the ground rules, and these are not changed on a whim.

I once organized a European visit for the parent board of Air Products & Chemicals Incorporated (a company for which I have great affection, as shown in other places in this book). They were booked to stay at the best national hotels in each of the capitals they were visiting on this goodwill mission. At these, they would meet business leaders and the media.

The whole schedule was prepared, approved and developed into a printed booklet form for distribution in advance. Just a few days before the event, a US senior executive changed all venues to the Hilton in each city.

Whether it was the right or the wrong decision, the many executives who had spent time planning the event were not consulted. Their view was that the board lost an opportunity to gain local knowledge, and countless numbers of confused employees, customers and community leaders had to change their arrangements. But, above all, this change gave out the unhappy message that the company was more American than European.

Listen to advice

Much public relations activity can be divided into the policy considerations and the reality of implementation. For example, the board of Cadbury-Schweppes subsidiary, Sodastream, felt that the business was too dependent on one major retailer, Boots. At one time, this retailer accounted for 35 per cent of sales. The policy was clearly established to develop other retail outlets while retaining the goodwill of Boots which, obviously, would always continue to be a key customer.

The marketing director at that time, Harry Hemens (later to become managing director), made his sales and marketing recommendations to support this strategy. Among these, his consultancy suggested that other retailers might take the company more seriously if they appreciated the proportion of the take-home soft drink market that the company represented.

The consultancy account director did the appropriate calculations which showed that Sodastream represented some 6 per cent (at that time) of the soft drink home consumption market. This made it one of the biggest brands in that sector and a plan of action, following this, resulted in very significant coverage among the appropriate food and drinks trade media. In turn, this was used by the salesforce to strengthen negotiations with major retailers and to increase sales through such outlets as Asda, J Sainsbury and Marks & Spencer. The Boots business did not decline but became a smaller percentage of an enlarged whole.

The board decided the policy and the public relations professionals came up with the solutions to meet that. Do not be tempted to reverse this by allowing the public relations professionals to define policy while the board discusses implementation details!

Your management should be tough, but fair

As with most professionals, public relations people prefer to place their efforts where they will be able to see success. Public relations effectiveness depends on getting the policies right. However, if the public relations professionals are in constant battle with management to try to persuade them to undertake policies that are in the best long-term interests of the public, it will not be a surprise that such efforts will prove exhausting and, sooner or later, lead to friction and a breakdown in the relationship. The most loyal public relations people in the world are still likely to be attracted by sympathy for their views.

Organizations that maintain a high profile in competitive markets usually have chief executives with a direct involvement in public relations strategy and the management of the function.

This hands-on approach can be even more important where the public expect stability and reliability. Chief executive of the Halifax Building Society, Mike Blackburn, explains his own involvement.

> Public relations is vital in maintaining good relations with the public. They often judge the organization—knowingly or not—by what is said about it by the media and others. Done well, public relations can represent the most effective and best value method of promoting the business, its products and services. But it demands to be treated seriously. In my view, monitoring what is happening must be the personal responsibility of the chief executive.

By all means, the chief executive can be tough with the public relations people. The rule is to expect a lot but do not expect them to jump through hoops. It is dispiriting and, ultimately, counter-productive to expect them to expend considerable energies in rectifying problems that might not have arisen if they had been involved in the decision at an earlier stage. Any decent professionals will bear with management to resolve a problem; but if managers persistently ignore their advice or, worse, do not even ask for it, then the enthusiasm will tend to fade after the second or third frustration.

When Hap Wagner came over from California to run the European operations of Air Products, many of those on his team were a little nervous. He was very young, and this was his first major management job—the first time he had ever worked outside California. Some felt they could take advantage of his lack of knowledge. Inexperienced he may have been, but naive he was not.

A typically pushy public relations person, I was through his door before he hardly got his feet under the desk, with a report on communications activity plus a presentation of the activities of my department. Politely (and patiently) he allowed me to run through my high-speed, whistle-stop tour around the company's public relations achievements and the amazing results that I claimed to be producing. When I had finished, he asked some perceptive questions and, sensing that the interview was coming to a close, I said to him, 'Well, now we've got that out of the way, I can forget that and get on with the job.'

'Not so,' said Hap, smiling. 'I expect you will be presenting your credentials, in one way or another, every day. We are all of us only as good as our achievements each day. It is true we work together as a team but we also challenge each other to achieve more and to set ever higher standards. Whatever you may have done, you will not be able to rest on your laurels.'

I think that is a reasonably accurate recall of what he said, though it was not my laurels that he suspected I might be wanting to rest on. He was right.

He and members of his management team did challenge his public relations team. We produced some of our best ever work as a result of this. However, he was always a sympathetic, positive, enthusiastic as well as a demanding boss. I never felt I was fighting against him but, rather, fighting for him.

As most chief executives appreciate, good public relations people are very rare. Good writers there are aplenty. Good journalists (in or out of journalism) there are aplenty. Polished public relations salespeople, there are aplenty. Strategic advisers who want to philosophize (and do no work) there are aplenty. But the public relations professional that can be trusted for wisdom, judgement, solid advice and, very importantly, the practical follow-through are few and far between. They should be sought out, cherished ... and challenged.

The personality mix can be important. Managing public relations sounds as if it ought to be easy, suggests Richard Carrick, marketing director of leading travel company, Airtours. 'It can backfire, for it is an art that cannot be entirely taught. Success will owe much to the personality of the public relations person.'

Whether you need your experts to work on your staff or to advise you through consultancy roles is a different question. It is probably much less important whether they are in house or not than whether they can win your confidence and deliver. Above all, they can tell you not only what you want to hear but, sometimes, what you need to hear ... and may not actually want to hear.

ENSURE THE PROXIMITY OF THE PUBLIC RELATIONS EXECUTIVE
Whatever other decisions may be taken, make sure that the senior manager of

the public relations function is close at hand. Public relations factors are involved in many company decisions and the chief executive will need regular input. This will not happen if the public relations executive has to be 'called in' from some distant office.

Where this is the case, public relations becomes a publicity activity and not a strategic one. Some time after the Hap Wagner experience, I turned down the position of public relations head of Air Products in the USA when I was head of the function in Europe. The main reason was that the public relations office in the US company was not even 'down the corridor' from the chief executive, but a half-mile drive away across the headquarters' campus in Pennsylvania. This told me more about the status and relevance of public relations, at that time, than the salary or any other factor.

Perhaps I could have taken the job and changed the attitude? Imagine a scene inside the executive suite, something like this.

'Hello Roger, what are you doing here?'
'Just hanging around in case any of you senior executives want to make a decision that has public relations implications.'
'I wouldn't waste your time. Don't worry, we'll give you a call when we need you—when we decide we need your input.'

Buy the best person you can afford

Once an organization has established that it has a public relations need, there may be a number of options on how this can be covered. The three main methods are:

- the nomination and training of an existing executive
- the appointment of professional public relations staff
- the appointment of a consultancy.

Sometimes the ideal solution may involve a combination of more than one of these three options.

One of the major functions in deciding which route to pursue will be the level of commitment to public relations that the organization will adopt. A company operating in a competitive market, under public scrutiny, possibly operating in a sensitive area, will find public relations absolutely fundamental to trading success. Therefore, it is likely to have to use skilled, professional executives—whether staff or consultancy or a mixture of both.

APPOINT A PROVEN PROFESSIONAL
Where the decision has been taken to put a professional public relations

person on to the staff, the best option must be to appoint someone with proven capabilities—and in public relations, not in marketing, advertising or media. To the uninformed, these may seem closely related but are actually distinct disciplines.

Sad mistakes in the public relations arena are regularly made by companies that choose to put a non-public relations person into the public relations slot.

Imagine another not-a-million-miles-from-reality scenario. Bob has been a marvellous company servant for years. He knows the company inside out. He ran sales, later managed the national contracts office, set up the Australian subsidiary, won his seat on the board. The problem is, he has run out of steam and he can't go any higher.

'I know what,' cries the chairman. 'Bob can add up a bit. We'll make him financial director!'

Unlikely? I hope so. Why, then, are so many key company public relations jobs filled by people who do not have the skills and qualifications? Can public relations be left to enthusiastic amateurs, any more than finance or marketing? It is daft ... and dangerous. Bob is unlikely to become finance director, but there is a much better chance that he will be offered public relations—where his undoubted but irrelevant talents and hurt pride become a recipe for disaster.

In some of these companies Bob will have a professional reporting to him— nearly always because Bob has been imposed on this unhappy individual and seldom because he or she was recruited to work for Bob.

Surely that professional can give him the right input?

But when the chairman is discussing plant relocations, acquisitions, analyst briefings with the head of public relations (Bob), where is the professional? Will Bob resist giving instant advice or making his comment?

'Sorry, chairman, I need to talk to the professional before I give you an authoritative view.'

Not likely. So he gives the advice and the professional is saddled with sorting out a situation that is already disastrously heading in the wrong direction.

'My view, chairman, is that if we keep quiet, there is little chance that anyone important will ever find out about that leak we had.'

Soon the professional looks for a better job. And once he or she has gone, there is no one to understudy Bob discreetly, so he can go on making bigger and more damaging mistakes. And if you do not believe me ask the chairmen of xxxxxxxxxxxx or xxxxxxxxxxxxx—or, I should say, the ex-chairmen.

Another less than intelligent option that some companies favour is to appoint a credible figure from within the media to the public relations position. That seems to make sense. That person will know the ladies and gentlemen of the media, and how they work. But will he or she know public relations? And might not some former media contacts resent that person for changing sides? In any case, what are a journalist's capabilities in strategic advice, or marketing? How proficient will he or she be at planning, budgeting, managing, controlling resources, the consultancy and the research company?

These are not skills that are normally required by many journalists. So the newcomer may be credible in the media but unless and until someone offers training in the essential skills (also assuming he or she has the right aptitudes), then that person will not be credible in public relations. Who is going to do the training? Where is that individual to turn if, because of a prior media profile, he or she has been appointed to the top job and cannot afford to appear not to know what to do? Success in the media is no guarantee of competence in public relations.

Shaun Woodward is an intelligent and professional journalist. But from his position as an editor on 'That's Life' he was recruited into the top job at the Conservative Central Office. He worked hard and effectively—but the fact that top television journalists considered him too young and not senior enough, while newspaper journalists resented anyone from television briefing them, made his position impossible.

Why take the risk? Appoint a professional; appoint the best man or woman you can find and can afford. Someone shifting from the media should go into a subordinate role for a significant period—both to acquire the special skills and to avoid being a primary adviser before gaining the necessary experience.

Some organizations (such as companies with a monopoly situation, statutory bodies, professional associations and some government authorities) may feel that they can relegate public relations to a purely information role.

(Equally a restructured role for public relations also tends to be shown in those organizations where the function is defined by giving the executives such titles as press officer or, even more restricting, information officer. Clearly, a press officer is responsible for only part of a broad public relations function: press relations, however efficiently operated, can only be part of public relations.)

Of course, many organizations have to rely on part-time or untrained assistance in public relations, because of the limits on their budget. This may well be the case with voluntary groups, churches, small charities, local arts societies and so on. However, even in such cases, there is usually a public relations professional within the group or community who has an interest in the particular cause and who can be persuaded to lend his or her expertise in a voluntary capacity. Similarly, many consultancies will accept a 'good cause' client, often on a cost-only basis.

SELECT THE BEST RESOURCE AVAILABLE

The least satisfactory option for handling public relations is to allocate the responsibility to a non-specialist executive. A limited budget is not always a legitimate reason for not tackling public relations properly. Often, the reason why the budget is not available is that decision makers do not rate the public relations function highly enough.

If the management does not need a significant public relations resource, then this may be acceptable. Sometimes, the contention that it cannot afford a proper resource is very questionable. Effective public relations, ultimately, costs no more than ineffective public relations; the returns from an investment in public relations are usually so significant that a company has to be spending a very substantial amount before it reaches the point of diminishing returns.

IDENTIFY THE BEST CANDIDATE FOR THE JOB

If a non-specialist executive has to be used to handle the public relations function, make sure that the candidates have the right temperament, the right brief, the right commitment and the right training.

- *Temperament*   The candidate must be articulate, responsive, energetic and have plenty of initiative. Courage is one of the essential qualities; the practitioner will frequently have to make decisions and must be able to stand by them.
- *Commitment*   The nominated executive should be someone who is open, direct, a believer in good communications, and must also support the aims of the organization.
- *Brief*   The writing of objectives is, perhaps, even more important where the public relations is being handled by non-professionals. The candidate must report in at the highest possible level and should not have to combine public relations with other responsibilities.
- *Training*   Level of skill may not be the most important factor. The candidate must have the right attitudes and motivation plus normal writing and language skills. He or she will need training either in-house or through specialist external courses.

BUY CONSULTANCY TO MEET THE NEEDS YOU IDENTIFY

Consultancies can offer a range of expertise. The company can choose the consultancy to suit the identified needs. The best way to handle the public relations activity may not be staff personnel or a consultancy; it may be a combination of these resources.

Whether you decide to undertake the selection process yourself or rely on a trusted senior colleague, it is helpful to follow a consistent procedure. The appointment needs to be right for much will depend on it. Ideally, both sides will need to invest heavily and will be looking for a long-term relationship.

Above all, following a procedure reduces the likelihood of being influenced by attractive but irrelevant aspects that can affect the best of judgements.

A speciality products subsidiary of the Swedish giant Electrolux once asked me to select a market research company to conduct the programme of evaluation across Europe that I had recommended. We all agreed that this research should be run from the UK and I undertook the preliminary evaluations to a procedure very similar to the one noted below.

The managing director, Ulf Ahman, and his marketing director joined me for the final presentations by the three shortlisted companies. All were excellent, but it was clear to me which was the best and most appropriate to the client's needs.

The Swedes have their own special way of handling situations and they informed me that they were not too certain which company was most suitable. As I began to offer advice, Ulf started to discuss the terrible quality of coffee we seemed to accept in the UK. They agreed that the company that had served the best coffee was the one they wanted to work with—which, fortunately, happened to be the best agency in my view. I sometimes wonder if I would have been able to persuade them to make the right choice (regardless of the coffee quality) if their 'selection' had been different! This was an unexpected selection method and, though it worked, it is not one to be recommended.

Public relations consultancies range from one-person outfits to international organizations. The first decision is to determine the resources required; for example:

1 Do you need special experience of your industry?
2 Do you require national or international representation?
3 Do you need specialization, e.g. in parliamentary, industrial, environmental areas, or general public relations?
4 Do you want advice or advice and implementation, with or without an internal public relations operation?

The selection process

Produce a list of public relations consultancies which appear to be able to offer the services required. To produce a shortlist you may:

- talk to companies whose public relations work you admire;
- ask key journalists which consultancies offer them an effective service;
- talk to a relevant professional communications body;
- check established directories.

Time and money will be spent by both your organization and the consultancies before the final choice is made. Therefore, it is advisable to reduce your list of possible consultancies to perhaps half a dozen before approaching them.

Look at their existing client lists. In Britain, this might be published in the *PRCA Year Book*, *Hollis* or *Advertisers' Annual*. Check on the ownership of your prospective public relations advisers. It may be to your advantage (or disadvantage) if they are members of an international group, or subsidiaries of an advertising agency. It may be important to know whether the directors have been in business for two or twenty years, or whether the consultancy has two or twenty directors. You may also be able to eliminate one or two from your shortlist at this stage.

PUT THE FIRST ENQUIRY IN WRITING

Approach the prospective consultancies. Try to adopt a consistent approach—with the first contact in writing. This preliminary introduction should invite each consultancy to reply with written details of its expertise and service.

You should ruthlessly eliminate all those whose letters are not of an acceptable business standard. (If they cannot project themselves, they will hardly be able to project your organization.) Do not eliminate those whose experience or skills do not appear to match your needs, as this may not be a fair test at this stage.

From the responses, you will have perhaps two or three consultancies you would wish to invite for further discussions. Suggest a date for a meeting and clarify your requirements, giving every consultancy the same information and the same opportunity. However, if one asks more perceptive questions, then this could be a critical factor. There is no need to provide this extra information to the others who are less enquiring.

With one prospective client, a small consultancy with special expertise spent days in research, including time on the road with the salesforce. From this, they revised the client's broad brief and produced a substantial and closer-focused document. They were astonished when the client gave copies of this to their competitors, all of whom realized they had been on the wrong track. Perhaps because of this embarrassment, the client appointed an international competitor with a name, but to whom the business was less critical—another nice name on the client list. Sadly, this consultancy was going through an unstable time and badly let them down within six months.

So, what procedure should your executive follow at the preliminary interview to be sure you are setting the correct course for the ultimate right choice? The interview should be conducted as seriously as any personal job interview. (An appraisal form where you can note responses is helpful when it comes to comparing the strength of the cases presented to you.) Avoid any lunch or drinks appointments unless you extend the same opportunity to every contender.

As the next stage, your selection team will visit the premises of the candidates—assuming that this preliminary interview will have eliminated one or two of your prospect consultancies. Give the consultancies you wish to visit a brief on what you wish to achieve—for example, meeting the team, assessing their facilities, looking at client work and so on. Advise them of those members of your organization who will be attending this meeting. Again, only accept a meeting running over lunch or dinner if this opportunity is given to each public relations company.

APPRAISE THE CONSULTANCY'S HOME ENVIRONMENT
If you have given the shortlisted consultancies a fair brief then you will be able to assess their response by direct comparison. Factors to be considered might include:

- their research into your organization
- the physical resources available
- the expertise of the team offered
- the success of other client campaigns
- their investigation of your claims
- their understanding of your aims
- their empathy/compatibility
- the relevance of their observations.

Do not expect the consultancy to present a programme to your team or field a particular account executive. It is more important to decide whether they have the skills to contribute to your organization's public relations aims than to be too concerned with details of staffing. By now your shortlist should be down to two or three. Write to the consultancies you have visited. Those you have eliminated should be informed and politely told why. You should now be

LEEDS METROPOLITAN UNIVERSITY LIBRARY

able to give the remaining consultancies a written brief expanding your aims. You should also clarify to whom they report, when and how.

ASK FOR RECOMMENDATIONS NOT PROPOSALS

Those you have selected for further discussion should be invited to write a report on how they believe they could assist your organization. It is also fair to explain to them the position of your selection: 'You are now in our last three consultancies under consideration.' Do not expect full proposals. These take considerable time to prepare and require a deeper knowledge of your organization than would be reasonable to expect at this stage.

Give each consultancy an opportunity to revisit your offices with the executives they wish to put on your account. Keep your own team constant.

Ask each consultancy to discuss their report and any recommendations they may have. Points to discuss should include creativity of their work, suitability of the executive, the back-up team, ancillary services (print, design, house journals, exhibitions, for example), calibre and reputation of existing clients, the reporting and control procedures, fee structure.

ASK FOR BUDGET RECOMMENDATIONS

Relate your company size and needs to their size. It may not be ideal for you to be either their largest or smallest client. If you are too big they may become nervous of jeopardizing the business and soft-pedal on their advice; equally, you may become wary of moving the account if they do not perform for fear of creating redundancies. Conversely, if your account is too small you may not get the level of service you wish—or feel able to assert authority when necessary.

Three main methods of fee charging are followed by most consultancies. All are based on hourly charges for executive time. The most popular method of calculating fees is on a fixed monthly retainer (representing y hours at $£x$). The other common methods are fees billed monthly according to hours (or days); and a basic fee charged for an agreed programme plus increments for additional work.

Additional projects or costs above an agreed level should normally be quoted and approved in advance of commissioning. Consultancies also tackle projects on an *ad hoc* basis where they quote for an identified activity. This tends to be expensive and the least satisfactory way to build relationships between consultancy and staff personnel. It can be helpful, however, to support staff public relations departments at times of particular need for additional personnel or special expertise.

Do not judge solely on the hourly rate; an average executive at $£x$ may be a poorer buy than a senior man at $2 \times £x$. Alternatively, you may not want $2 \times £x$ an hour charges for writing a simple appointment story.

Ask the consultancies to prepare a budget or give recommendations on the breakdown of your own suggested budget. This will cover fee, operating costs, press conferences, print, photography and any other items that will involve significant work and expenditure. Avoid an open-ended fee system and agree a level of expenditure you would allow without prior consultation. Clarify how their invoices will relate to the activity reporting procedure.

CHECK THE CONSULTANCY RELATIONS RECORD

You should talk to clients. Ask each consultancy to give you three or four senior client executives with whom you can discuss their public relations service. Talk to key journalists or members of other key audiences to check whether they have any experience of your preferred consultancies.

Should you need more detailed proposals, then agree some nominal fee with your final shortlist of two or three consultancies. This will also help to avoid problems should more than one candidate consultancy suggest similar ideas, and the fee can be negotiated to cover such an eventuality. (If they want confirmation of your budget and the names of their competitor consultancies, both are fair requests which should be answered.)

Finally, make your decision. Write to the chosen consultancy and ask them to attend a final meeting to confirm working arrangements and financial matters. At this stage, you may well agree a fee for a limited period, say three months, to enable them to prepare full recommendations. Alternatively, you could pay them to prepare full proposals and costings; or you can agree an estimate of the workload for the first year, perhaps with an option to review at six months.

Some consultancies will offer a contract rather than simply letters of agreement. Write to the unsuccessful consultancies, thanking them for their efforts and explaining the reasons for your choice.

Begin with a cooperative team spirit

Part of the skill in getting the maximum from the client/consultancy relationship is for the director responsible to manage this, as they say, firmly but fairly.

The Nationwide Building Society's head of corporate communications, Nigel Snell, thinks that objectivity is one of the key benefits. Consultancies should be expected to work to the company's agenda and the client must, in turn, try to avoid changing this. Be tough on the financial side, he advises, and agree fees and costs, where possible, in advance; also be sure that you do not pay twice—for example, through 'mark-ups' on work covered by a fee. But respect the fact that consultants have a business to run.

Some organizations talk about their consultancy as if they were in opposition—and not a vital part of their resource to help them succeed in a tough, competitive world. Equally, some consultancies talk about their clients as if the relationship was a constant battle of wits. And perhaps it very often is.

Here are a few suggestions for both consultancy staff and clients on how to get the best out of the cooperation. Both parties usually have a team, but, nonetheless, the relationship *does* depend on goodwill and understanding between individuals.

1 *Let your consultant act as a consultant.* Listen to advice; the consultant has some expertise. Always try to tell your consultant what might be happening *before* it happens. He or she will appreciate having an input into the policy-making. Also create opportunities in which the consultant's views can be presented.

2 *Play fair and keep to the rules.* It is supposed to be a partnership, so treat your consultant as a colleague and not as a disposable 'supplier'. Hold regular meetings and supply copies of all relevant reports and documents.

3 *Praise and criticize first-hand—and with equal candour.* If the consultant does a good job, have the sense to acknowledge that, preferably in writing. Such a letter gets circulated within the consultancy, pinned on notice boards and mentioned at internal meetings. All the best people in the consultancy will want to work on an account where the client is appreciative. Equally, if you have a criticism, make it plain, direct and verbal.

4 *Allow creative scope and a fair deal.* Allow your consultant the scope for creativity. You should ask him or her to solve problems and take advantage of opportunities, not simply to handle the communications activity you have decided. Otherwise you might as well do it yourself.

5 *Keep it worth while.* Make sure your account is profitable to the consultancy. Enter a long-term relationship so that both sides can develop the activity. Expect value for money but do not expect miracles for pennies.

INTEGRATING COMMUNITY AND CHARITY ACTIVITIES WITH MARKETING AND CORPORATE

Good programmes almost manage themselves*

A broad public relations programme may cover many activities, targeted at widely varied audiences. One difference between good and poor public

---

*This case study is based on an article by James Croall in British Airways' in-flight magazine, *High Life*, reproduced with thanks. The author of this book took not a tiny part in this programme of employee/community/charity relations!

relations is the coordination that can be developed across such activities. Sometimes, one big idea or activity can be tailored to cover diverse audiences. Sometimes, an activity can be developed that has relevance to more than one group. British Airways undertake charitable activities that have an impact on both community and employee relations. The end results also involve business partners and suppliers and have a positive impact on customer relations. In total, it is an attractive and well-managed programme, less familiar to the public than its high profile marketing-support effort. But, in its way, driven as it is by the enthusiasm of employees, it is just as relevant to positioning BA as the company it wants to be.

How do you fancy a 50-foot bungee jump from the end of a crane over a West London gravel pit? Or abseiling down the vertical side of a multistorey car park on the end of a rope? Or a muscle-toning 700-mile cycle ride?

The common thread of all these activities is that they're among the ways in which British Airways staff raise money for scores of good causes around the world. The company recently appointed a senior manager as Head of Community Relations to ensure that its involvement in the community is as effective as possible. The airline is a member of the Per Cent Club, a group of British companies contributing the equivalent of half of one per cent of dividends to community action. But it also encourages its staff all over the world to support their own favourite causes.

Every October, a Boeing 747 chartered from British Airways leaves London for Orlando, Florida, carrying nearly 200 children and around 160 adult helpers on a week's trip to the wonders of Walt Disney World and all the other delights for which the area is famous, including Sea World and Universal Studios. All the children are ill or disabled.

Most are from Britain, but this year's contingent included children from Zimbabwe and Hong Kong. Children are carefully selected on the advice of specialist paediatricians.

Dreamflight started in 1987 as the brainchild of two BA flying staff, Pat Pearce and Derek Pereira, and has been growing ever since. So has the cost; each annual Dreamflight now costs about a quarter of a million pounds to run. It's very far from purely a British Airways' staff charity, however. Organizers and donors all over the world help to raise the money, like the group of elderly ladies in Scotland who sell home-made cake at £1 a slice. Then there's purser Stephen Clarke, who grew so fed up with sitting in jams on the M25 that he researched and wrote *Jambusters South*, a highly successful guide to how to dodge the hold-ups on the motorways. Part of the proceeds go to Dreamflight.

There are children in Britain today who have never even seen the sea. Every year, Operation Happy Child takes 400 children, aged from 4 to 10, on holidays and days out. For around 100, there will be a stay at Bournemouth, Torquay or Jersey, while for hundreds more there will be a day out at an attraction such as Chessington in Surrey. Most of the children are nominated by local authorities. Some will be handicapped; nearly all will come from deeply underprivileged backgrounds.

Literally thousands of people, inside the airline and outside, help to raise the £30 000 a year that the charity costs to run, but most of the organizing will be done by a team of around 15 volunteers, many of whom, like chairman Doug Wood, who works in the BA engineering department, have been supporting Happy Child for anything up to 17 years.

When stewardess Pat Kerr visited a crowded Bangladeshi orphanage during a stopover in 1981, she left deeply moved by what she had seen. She persuaded scores of cabin crew colleagues to bring in urgently needed supplies when they visited Dhaka. Later, when a complete new orphanage became essential, Pat Kerr persuaded Lord King, the then chairman of the airline and now its president, to back the project. As well as making a large cash donation to match funds raised by staff and other helpers, the airline lent technical experts of all kinds to help plan, finance and build the new village. By 1987 the new children's village at Sreepur was open, and now holds about 650 children. Pat Kerr later left to work full time on the project, but many of her former colleagues continue to raise money for the village, which costs over £12 000 a month to run.

The airline's cargo staff have their own special charity, though it is supported by staff throughout the airline. The Cargo Kidney Machine Fund began a decade and a half ago as a one-off appeal to buy a kidney machine for a colleague's child. After the youngster had undergone a successful transplant, the machine was donated to a local hospital. Since then, the fund has raised well over £300 000 for hospitals and for individual patients.

The dividing line between the airline's own corporate community programme and the private generosity of its staff is often very fine, according to Gary Gray, head of community relations: 'We can offer immense resources, not least of ideas and experience, but we take great care to offer encouragement on charitable activities only if the staff concerned ask for help.'

When British Airways refurbished its supersonic fleet recently, it was left with 350 pairs of unwanted Concorde seats. It auctioned them off and gave the money to staff-supported charities. Now, it has invited its cabin staff to nominate community causes around the world that can make good use of 55 000 surplus blankets.

The BBC's annual Children in Need appeal is a natural opportunity for airline fund-raisers; passengers who check in with British Airways while the appeal is in progress will find themselves greeted by a jazz band, banners, balloons and staff in fancy dress rattling collecting tins.

Local charitable appeals are run all over the world. Finance staff in New York raised over $2000 for a children's hospital in Memphis by a traditional American Christmas Bake.

Long-distance sponsored cycle rides are popular fund-raisers; one group of five colleagues pledged themselves to raise money for charity by cycling 700 miles from Heathrow to Aberdeen. One fell off and broke his wrist *en route*, and when the saddle-sore survivors, tired but triumphant, pedalled into Aberdeen Airport to fly back to London, they found the airport shrouded in fog. But they raised the money.

Some of the ways of raising money, such as abseiling and bungee-jumping, are strictly for the bold and brave. Towing a 90-tonne Concorde against the clock in competition with other teams is a favourite way of raising cash that appeals to the physically fit. Some fund-raising efforts spring directly from people's jobs. A Manchester-based cabin crew set out to collect aluminium cans and foil from the aircraft they flew, and raised enough money to buy two guide dogs for the blind.

Not all charity ventures are team efforts. Heathrow check-in agent Ken Wheeler meets the great and the famous every day of his working life. So he invites them to sign his celebrated visitors' book in aid of Tadworth Court Children's Hospital. By auctioning the autographs of such celebrities as Elizabeth Taylor and Michael Jackson, he has raised over £100 000.

'Good works' aren't always charities; they can be civic efforts, too. When Radio Clyde launched a 'Clyde Pride' campaign to clean up Scotland's most famous river and its tributaries, British Airways Glasgow staff literally waded in to help. In five filthy hours their half-mile of river yielded, among other things, 30 supermarket trollies, ten gas cylinders, a load of motorway cones and 400 golf balls.

None of the good cause organizers would claim that British Airways staff are inherently more kind-hearted or generous than the rest of their fellow citizens. On the other hand, many of them have acquired substantial organizing skills in their day-to-day jobs. Moreover, the travel industries as a whole, says Gary Gray, have a tradition of helping good causes. 'It seems to be true that people who work in successful companies often have a particular flair for responding to others' needs. I am constantly impressed by the level of dedication that members of our staff show in raising funds for worthy causes.'

Some observations, in summary

1 The starting point for managing the function is to agree what public relations must achieve in support of corporate and commercial objectives.

2 Public relations policy may be developed by the professionals but, before the programme is commissioned, this must be endorsed by the board.

3 Involve the head of each major company division and business function in the planning process, for example, by asking for reactions to the brief.

4 Coordinate objectives across all disciplines, particularly where different communications activities need to be targeted at different audiences.

5 Use formal or informal research, appropriate to the needs, to identify clearly where the organization stands at present.

6 Ensure that the strategy and the programme are in a written form and that a summary of this is presented to the board.

7 The development of the programme is the responsibility of the professionals but it must support the corporate aims as defined by the chairman or chief executive.

8 Ensure that all agencies and consultancies with company knowledge and special expertise are involved in the development of the plan.

9 Relate the budget to the importance of the work and the value of the expected results, and not to any historical allocation.

10 Make the commitment that all future activity will be expected to be on strategy—and ensure that this requirement is binding on all, including the chairman.

11 To develop the strategy and run the programme, the public relations professional leading the team needs access to the board.

12 To gain the best from the programme, do not change the objectives in mid-stream and try to keep stable all those factors that you can control.

13 Make all information activities part of the broader public relations plan.

14 When you ask for advice, be prepared to listen and take action—and expect advice even when you have not asked for it!

15 Do not judge yourself what may have public relations implications but ensure that your adviser is aware of all decisions so that the best advice can be offered.

16 If you use staff personnel, make sure that someone has been given overall responsibility and is readily accessible—ideally in the next office.

17 Appoint the best person you can afford and avoid someone from an allied discipline unless you are sure you have the training resources necessary.

18 When selecting your top executive, be certain that your choice will be acceptable to those with whom he or she will have to deal—your colleagues, the media, etc.

19 If you decide to use a consultancy, select one according to an agreed plan.
20 Try to keep the same selection team throughout and keep all stages consistent for all candidate consultancies.
21 Remember that, inevitably, selection is an artificial, arm's length process, so choose the team you can work with … not the programme.
22 As you can change the suggested activity but not the people, it is wiser at the early stages to ask for recommendations and not a definitive proposal.
23 The least satisfactory selection criterion is price, so state your thoughts on the proposed budget and do not expect the consultancy to guess.
24 Whether in-house staff or consultancy personnel, you will get the best from them if you treat them as team members and colleagues.

4

Objectives

Plan public relations that will achieve real advances

Setting objectives

Setting objectives can help to ensure that the board is in touch. The bigger the organization, potentially, the further the directors can be from the sharp end—customers, shop-floor employees, new recruits, individual investors and so on. One of the splendid side benefits of setting and approving the corporate public relations objectives is that the communications specialists presenting their recommendations to the board must demonstrate where the company stands at present.

An objective is a point to reach, not just a direction in which to head. This cannot begin to be defined unless it is quite clear where the organization stands at present. However, it can be tempting for some at board level to wish to withdraw from the hurly-burly of relations with diverse publics upon which the organization depends; yet the truth in the most successful companies is usually the opposite. The chairman, the chief executive and their board are closest to these publics, either directly or through the quality of information on which they make decisions.

In his introduction to *The Company Chairman* by Sir Adrian Cadbury, that notable one-time chairman of ICI, Sir John Harvey-Jones, says:

> While the responsibilities of the chairman do not alter, the role varies with the changing social, economic and political environments in which we operate. Moreover, it behoves the chairman not only to be aware of the massive changes occurring in his own company and his own country but also those in many other parts of the world. There is no company that is immune to the changes which are occurring all round us.

OBJECTIVES CAN HELP DECIDE THE BUDGET

The allocation of the appropriate level of resource to public relations and, later, the calculation of the cost-effectiveness can only be certain if meaningful objectives are agreed. Some measures of the public relations programme are simple to quantify if these original objectives have been well drafted.

As detailed in Chapter 5, these objectives can help in the calculation of a realistic budget and resources. Clearly, the drafting of the objectives must be related to the methods that are proposed to measure effectiveness.

If it cannot be measured, how can you tell if it is worth doing or how much should be spent? Too few commercial public relations programmes have specific objectives. Many have some vague aims, often buried in a document long since lost in the files. Consequently, criticisms of poor performance are meaningless where that level of performance anticipated has not been spelt out.

SETTING SPECIFIC PERFORMANCE MEASURES

Subjective judgements of performance are no real measure. Differences of opinion on the effectiveness of the programme prove one of the biggest areas of complaint, research confirms, when relationships break down between consultant and client. This was quoted by 60 per cent of consultants and 70 per cent of clients questioned about areas of disappointment, according to an informal RHA study.

It is not unreasonable to imagine that the same confusion might apply where problems arise in the area of relationships between in-house professionals and chief executives within companies. Anecdotal evidence confirms many cases of senior public relations people being puzzled to find resources cut back by managements for whom they felt they were running effective programmes.

Interestingly, some 70 per cent of the consultancy programmes where such problems had arisen had no agreed measure of performance.

Disagreement over levels of performance is no problem. These can be discussed and resolved. The problems begin where assumptions are made and no such discussions take place.

The managing director of one consultancy told me he had been surprised to get notice from a company where he had handled two plant closures, one product recall and the firing of the marketing director—all with minimal negative media comment. On asking the reason for cancelling the contract, the client's chairman said he had expected to be quoted more often. 'Once a week or so in the *Financial Times* or *The Sunday Times* with some good story would have been reasonable.'

The wishes of the chairman may have been ambitious even for a company going places, but for one in crisis they were unrealistic. However, whether it was reasonable or not, they had the conversation *after* the problem, not before.

Public relations professionals (in-house or consultancy) may feel they are better off without the exposure of measurable objectives. Clients may think they are not necessary or are not prepared to pay the small budget percentage to appraise performance. Both are wrong. There are four simple steps.

- Agree what is to be achieved.
- Plan a programme to achieve this.
- Run it, with any fine tuning that may be necessary.
- Measure the effectiveness of the efforts.

The best objectives will set targets to be met relating to such factors as audiences, messages delivered, awareness developed, opinions changed, goodwill built and so on. But remember that, initially, any measure, however crude, is better than none as long as both sides agree to it. You can refine and develop the criteria in each succeeding year.

BUILD ON SPECIFIC TARGETS, NOT ASSUMPTIONS
It is easy to waste money on communications. Some organizations run major campaigns based on assumptions about the target audience feelings. If these assumptions are wrong, then such efforts can be wasteful and, sometimes, even counter-productive.

Writing objectives
The British government wasted £20 million of tax-payers' money on a campaign about Aids—not my uncharitable view, but the opinion even of some involved in the planning. This campaign was based on advertising in media that target groups did not read—media that they saw as 'establishment' and irrelevant. Also, the messages were inappropriate. The objectives were not clearly defined to ensure the right expenditure in the right areas to project the right messages to the right people and get the right feedback.

All this was happening at a time when public and editorial concerns about the illness were at their peaks. Public relations would have been a more relevant method of communications. For example, more appropriate would have been a stronger contribution to that debate, more information, published research, seminars, road shows, briefings for those personalities who could reach those audiences (actors, musicians, disc jockeys, radio presenters, student union executives and so on), plus the use of underground media to reach high-risk groups and so on.

The result of the campaign was a minimal change in understanding, let alone behaviour—but the politicians could point to some high-profile action. Companies can rarely afford such luxury.

Some years ago, GEC ran a heavy but belated press campaign to try to influence public opinion—particularly those in positions of influence—to back their sophisticated Nimrod early-warning radar aircraft which had been running into problems. The incoming GEC chairman, Lord Prior, later agreed when I suggested it had been too late. Public opinion had been formed by countless media reports of the problems, not balanced by effective 'good news' stories on that excellent British-designed and built option.

The company also faced tough and wily competition for a key government order. Boeing had built a better reputation among opinion leaders, through a planned information programme that had been run for years on its corporate activities: good public relations can be unbelievably cheap when you look at the potential returns.

A little less than the GEC budget for the last-ditch advertising, but spent on real communications over a longer period, might have better protected their £900 million investment and built the public support necessary to win a crucial billion-pound order. It may not be a coincidence that Boeing sets specific objectives for its public relations which, at that time, GEC did not.

Panic communications can irritate

Before attempting to write objectives, it is important to have a proper understanding of present perceptions. You need to know the views of the key audiences if you wish to undertake activity to move these more favourably towards the organization. This may require formal research or simpler forms of evaluation, or perhaps just asking the right question of one or two of the right people.

Remember the heady takeover days? From its palatial Mayfair head-quarters, Thomas Tilling mounted an extravagant, but doomed, campaign which was hastily produced to stave off predatory approaches from Trafalgar House. These efforts were not just unsuccessful, they actually worked against the Tilling defence. Shareholders and analysts were already concerned about company extravagance and many were irritated that they were only being asked for support when the company was in trouble. They would have explained this if asked. The planners of that campaign would have had a better understanding of perceptions on which to develop more realistic objectives if they had asked the right questions and if they had asked them earlier. In 1980, they rejected research as 'our divisions lead their fields'.

These and similar bid campaigns involving Allied Lyons, Burtons, Dalgety, Debenhams, Spillers and others, led to the Takeover Panel setting out restrictions in 1986 which, if anything, have meant that companies have had to put more sustained, consistent efforts into building their corporate reputations. Advertising has rightly taken its place as *one* of the possible communications techniques to be considered in a broader public relations programme.

Indeed, one major help that good objectives can offer is that they will often indicate the most likely communications media. Advertising can look like a powerful fast fix but it is not always appropriate, as is discussed in Chapter 9.

Understand the other point of view

Experienced managers know the dangers of basing decisions upon personal observation. We all know that we tend to see what we want to see, and hear what we want to hear. It is almost a truism, as an illustration, that every company thinks it is better known, better understood, better supported than it actually is. Keeping in touch is central to public relations and the chief executive may often have to accept that he or she is not closest to the key audiences.

As a rough rule, the higher up the company executives move, the more remote they can get from the publics upon whom the organization depends for its success. Often, managers of vision recognize this and set up procedures to ensure they get a full feedback of views. Some become sadly seduced by this isolation from the daily world of those who produce or buy their products.

Happily, this is not universally true; some successful company chairmen and chief executives make particular efforts to keep in touch with feelings that matter. All directors and senior executives of McDonald's spend time behind their counters and that includes the infamous non-executive, Sir Bernard Ingham. And why not? The fact that this simple policy receives media comment shows how rare it is. All top managers must be in touch and understand the points of view of those that their decisions will affect.

The chairman of a large quoted company—now a shadow of its former self—was asked by a press photographer to talk to a lathe operator during a board visit to its largest regional manufacturing site. Desperately searching for a topic of conversation, he remembered he was in the country and asked the bemused man: 'What's the hunting and shooting like round here?'

Fortunately, the journalists did not hear the reply above the machine-room noise—but the chairman did, and reddened. Later, in private, he commented on worker hostility and their failure to appreciate their jobs. In touch? Understanding the other's point of view? Qualified to make decisions based on subjective perspectives?

Cabinet minister, John Gummer, who travelled by chauffeur-driven government car, berated Londoners for whingeing about the collapse of the capital's services—ironically on the day that 20 000 were to spend frightening hours trapped underground in crowded, claustrophobic tube trains, crippled by maintenance failures. In touch? Understanding the other's point of view? Qualified to make decisions based on subjective perspectives?

Choose your words carefully

The most sensible objectives will include some measure of feedback from important groups. All communications must be based on a two-way flow of information or views. Effective communications needs to be built up from an understanding of all points of view. Often, a lack of knowledge of an issue among an important public has been mistakenly interpreted as resistance. As noted earlier, you cannot be certain you will change opinion or influence attitude in the way you intend unless you know what these are in the first place.

Yet, too many commercial communications make assumptions about knowledge, opinion and attitude and do without putting these assumptions to the test. At best, this will be a considerable waste of money; at worst, it may actually produce hostility in the audiences being wooed. Even the language acceptable to the audiences you wish to influence can be a factor. For example, the owner of a large nursery garden in an attractive valley, lined with a handful of quality country homes on the edges of an English county town, decided to use part of his spare land to build a small development of expensive houses. He believed this would enhance the value of all properties in the valley and wrote to his neighbours telling them of his plans. He concluded that he felt sure that he would get their support.

His assumption was wrong.

While he was wise to write to them in advance, he might have done a little homework. This could have helped him to put a more persuasive argument. To most of the readers of the letter the one word that stuck with them was 'estate'. That county town had been blighted, many felt, by 'estates' of housing and they wanted to see no more. Whatever he might have said after that, he had already lost their vote. The outcome was that the objection at planning stage was so strong that the project had to be completely abandoned.

If he had undertaken any investigation into their views, then he might have found a way of presenting his proposals that would have made an attractive scheme acceptable.

AN ILL-CHOSEN WORD CAN LOSE THE ARGUMENT
The Worldcom communications group partner in North Carolina, Epley

Associates, uses a sophisticated computer-based response system for focus group research called Continuous Attitudinal Response Technology (CART). This allows selected representatives of any audience to show instant reactions to any stimulus being presented to them. Even the reaction to individual words can be analysed.

One proposed television commercial for a new imported car was achieving very high acceptance scores with a target group of professional women—until the voice-over reached the phrase 'The ultimate driving experience'. Audience approval scoring instantly dropped drastically, never to recover.

Explains president, Michael Herman: 'Interviews with members of that audience showed that they consciously rejected that phrase as over-the-top. The ultimate driving experience for most people might be a Ferrari, a classic racing car or a vintage Rolls-Royce, not a popular sedan.' Their rejection of the remainder of the commercial followed because they felt that if the company could 'lie' about that, then perhaps all the other claims were exaggerated. Once credibility is lost, it is almost impossible to regain.

A study of awareness of the logo of a major insurance group failed to produce any intelligent result because so few could recognize the recently changed company name, including some 50 per cent of its existing clients! One banking group was shocked to find that only 6 per cent of its customers recognized a logo that had been in use for 100 years.

Gerald Ratner certainly was not thinking of his customers when he made cheap remarks about the 'crap' he sold, to win a laugh from his peers at an Institute of Directors' conference. He may have got his laugh—though I suspect it was more of a shocked gasp. He won that, but lost any goodwill among his customers. Did he really despise those who controlled the future of his company through their spending decisions? Had he really lost such touch with 'the other half' that he could joyfully disparage those who could only afford a few pounds on a gift for a loved one? If so, it was doubly tragic for he not only lost his company, he lost his humanity.

Contrast that attitude to the view expressed by Clive Thompson, chief executive of Rentokil, which summarizes the philosophy behind the vigorous growth and diversification of the company. 'Our corporate identity is red, white and quality.' Fortunately, the positive outgoing approach of a business leader like Thompson is widely appreciated and respected. Senior executives making decisions on matters relating to public relations need to be certain that they have the right independent input.

Top directors may not need constant, day-to-day contact with, say, customers; but, if this is so, then they should not be deciding the advertising, the store design or the packaging. These decisions need to be managed by professionals who can give sound, credible and confident advice. One certain rule for top executives is to be sure to choose those with the courage to say what needs to be said.

Mike Beard, a distinguished president of the Institute of Public Relations, believes that every chairman and chief executive needs one or two senior staff people who will have the courage to give frank and fearless advice at any time and in any circumstance. He feels this advice can be most important when the top executive has lost touch with the feelings of, say, shareholders or the business market in which the company operates. On occasion, there may be speculation or rumour that could be potentially threatening and needs tackling. At these times, the need is for someone inside and on side who is prepared to speak out.

Beard, through his work as director of corporate communications for Taylor Woodrow, has many years' experience in top level corporate advice. He argues that the corporate relations director is trained to take this detached view and also has probably the best internal and external grapevine of anyone in the organization. Get the personal chemistry right and that person will be uniquely equipped to handle this sensitive and critical area.

Indeed, this relationship of trust is essential if the board is to agree the correct objectives for the company public relations programme. Management pays for advice; to get value, it must create the atmosphere in which honest and detached advice can be offered.

CONSIDER THE IMPACT OF YOUR WORDS

The more senior the executive, the more important it is that he or she retains the capability of visualizing the other person's situation. The communications programme is not directed at the chairman, chief executive or other directors. This must be remembered when drafting or approving objectives.

The managing director of a company making popular home computers objected to the inclusion of local radio on an advertising schedule, presented to her as part of an overall public relations programme for a new product launch. When I asked her why, she told me that she only ever listened to Radio Four during the week and Radio Three at the weekend. Radio One was bad enough but local radio was rubbish. I resisted asking how she knew that if she never listened but went back to the objectives to remind her of the profile of prospective purchasers we had identified and agreed. Local radio would best reach these people and, when reminded of the earlier discussion and the thinking behind the decision, she agreed.

Without agreed objectives we might have lost track. Indeed, in preparing objectives, a powerful personality can push them off course if the advisers are not sufficiently confident or firm.

Encourage advice you do not want to hear

Overpowering management may occasionally bully advisers into submission. Perhaps some marketing and communications professionals consider that there is more profit in being diplomatic to the point of compliance. The failure to agree objectives for public relations can also mean that different elements within the communications mix can be working to different agendas.

When Philips was struggling through yet another of its marketing crises, I was adviser to one of its business divisions. This was being merged with two others in allied sectors. It was an eminently sensible plan, which I fully endorsed. The company was going through a difficult phase, but as it had excellent managers, fine products and a determined customer philosophy, I felt the company demanded our best possible support.

I could not, however, accept the proposed, euphoric, launch advertising; this, I felt, was naive and misleading. It suggested that all customers' electronic business problems could be solved by the new merged operation. I pointed out to the chief executive that three salesforces were still operating, not cooperating and, worse, competing. Each would exhaust the possibilities of selling their product lines, however poor the chance, before putting any business lead to another division where a more realistic sale might be likely. This problem needed tackling before such advertising could be run.

The marketing directors and advisers to the three divisions discussed this and related issues which lasted an exhausting morning. During this, one of the public relations advisers to another division said virtually nothing. After the meeting I asked him why. 'There's no bonus in risking being wrong,' he explained. 'But we are paid to advise,' I objected. 'Wait and see,' he murmured. 'Will you benefit from disturbing the client?'

He was right. Later, part of the rationalization reduced the consultancies from three to two, then, one—and the diplomat retained his role as non-adviser. It is no satisfaction to say that the manager who made that decision got the advice he deserved.

Public relations people will tell you that this is not a rare occurrence. Good advice can be right but it can be very unpopular. It takes a confident, professional and courageous management to ask for and accept advice from a confident, professional and courageous public relations professional. Weak managements sometimes fire strong consultancies rather than face these issues.

Michael Pickard, chairman of the London Docklands Development Corporation, confirms this point. Public relations is sometimes seen as a substitute for performance, he feels. Firing the PR team is rarely the solution to a company's problems. It must be a team effort, working to clear objectives. The communicators and the executive team, working well together and closely with the chairman will give you an outstanding success, he adds. One without the other will underperform.

Of course, this need to cooperate within a framework of agreed aims is not peculiar to the public relations arena. Management should appoint good advisers, with no bias, who have honesty, skill and vision. The management needs to be certain that the proffered advice is considered, independent, honest and presented with the best interests of the company at heart. That is not always the case unless extreme care is taken in selection.

The US chief executive of a group of European subsidiaries with major employee relations problems was getting his advice from a cynical and disillusioned human resources director; unknown to his boss, he was in the midst of a nasty divorce. He had not spoken to his son for two years and confessed to journalists that he hated the 'pathetic workers'.

Is this common? It may or may not be a truism that many personnel people don't like people. On the other hand, many teachers cannot stand children. Make sure you do not appoint a public relations adviser who does not like business or hates journalists; they exist!

Learn how to get true responses

Most people in senior positions underestimate the impact of their position on those with whom they work. They forget they have the power to hire and fire. They may see themselves as agreeable egalitarians yet forget that others may see them as ruthless or domineering.

When I was chairman of the Chartered Institute of Marketing and hosting a meeting of some of the most senior business leaders of many of the biggest businesses operating in the UK, Sir Alistair Grant, chairman of Argyll Group, demolished a proposal with the comment, 'With the greatest respect—which means with absolutely no respect at all—this is complete nonsense.' I was about to respond in the same vein, when the president of the institute, Sir Colin Marshall, who was sitting beside me, wisely restrained me with the quiet, good-natured comment, 'Roger, do not respond. Let him finish.'

Of course, Sir Alistair was right and his comments needed to be said. My irritation, which Sir Colin had read, was what I saw as a humiliation in the way it was said. For interest, I checked this little incident with Sir Alistair. Had he appreciated the impact of his words? He commented: 'I was irritated by what I saw as a defeatist approach to a positive opportunity. Anyone could have responded to what I said in any way they liked, but I would not have much patience for anyone arguing something that should have been dropped.'

If I had responded equally as assertively to Sir Alistair, would I have lost the support of his company for our mission? As he is a generous, open person, then probably not; but such confrontations can easily escalate, and, of course, the skill is to ensure a good balance.

TRY TO LISTEN AS OPENLY AS YOU SPEAK

If the chief executive truly wants an atmosphere in which colleagues can be outspoken, then he or she has to listen. Equally, those offering views or advice when the programme is being planned should not take advantage. All are equal, but the boss is the boss, and in that position he or she is more equal than the others!

One managing director of an engineering group regularly told his team: 'I'm a Yorkshireman. That means I'm blunt and say things as I see them.' Sadly, he did not hear things in the same way. His senior colleagues soon learned what was unacceptable. Those who cared about the company found his censorship impossible and were either fired for their 'independence' or moved on. Of course, he was soon surrounded by people in constant agreement, the company ran on the rocks, and he was eventually fired. What a tragic waste of all his talents. How sad that no one had the courage to help him build a cooperative team spirit.

Again, in Brussels I was presenting a strategy and set of objectives for a proposed programme to a commissioner with a dozen of his team in the room. Discussing the proposed aims, I pointed out an important flaw in one of his assumptions, the result of some research that we had undertaken. He listened and accepted the point and later commented, mildly, that no one on his staff had made any observation about such a curious matter in the six months that it had existed. He also failed to notice that none of his senior, experienced colleagues had made any comment of any sort during the whole of the presentation. They had learned not to debate issues with commissioners. There had only been nods and words of approval at the end, once he had made it quite clear that he was happy with the proposition.

Check observations against evidence

Good public relations is dependent on accurate intelligence. It is impossible to change attitudes effectively unless the organization has identified what attitudes already exist.

The views of senior executives may be helpful but rarely provide enough information on which to make decisions. In such cases, the only sound base should be research.

In Britain, it has been estimated that over 90 per cent of *The Times* top 1000 companies regularly use research to find out more on subjects about which (it might be supposed) they already know enough. Such research is often aimed at understanding perceptions of key publics and how these might have been developed. But what factors create such perceptions, and how do they affect our reputation? It would appear that directors use research mainly because they realize that while subjective views may be important, they do not always reflect the reality. Even where the research confirms such preliminary views, it is still valid, as decisions about the corporate reputation can be made with greater confidence. As Epictus said, 'perceptions are facts because people believe them'.

Creativity requires discipline

Public relations should be flexible, organic, responsive and creative. It should be handled effectively by some of the most talented people–the need for creativity must never be used as the excuse for a lack of discipline. It is essential that public relations is as well planned as any other activity of the organization. It must be working to agreed and understood objectives, and the best objectives will relate to a measurable change in reputation.

Though reputation is very specific, clear and tangible, it is extremely difficult to quantify. How good is a good reputation? Does the company have a good reputation in all areas–products, financial performance, environmental responsibility and so on? In reality, it is the comparative value of the reputation that matters as well as whether it is improving or deteriorating. Both formal and informal research methods can be used to establish this comparative position. For example, a study could be run to identify feelings of the organization's reputation among those publics under investigation. A representative of such publics could be interviewed to identify how they rated the organization in terms of its reputation. This might be in terms of a scale from excellent through to poor or might be classified by reputation in certain sectors from products to financial performance. For example, an analysis of the interview results will show the proportion of each of these key publics that rated the company reputation in each sector. This provides a very simple benchmark against which any changes or developments in the reputation can be measured at the end of a year or two years, or any other period that the management chooses. From this, revised objectives can be developed for future years.

Alternatively, how such publics rate the organization's reputation in comparison with other organizations can be appraised. This can be very helpful to check performance against competitors in the same sector and/or companies that are viewed as leaders in other industries.

Of course, in such studies, it is important to remember that what is being measured are perceptions, not realities. The anomalies between the perceptions and the reality give a clear focus for management attention.

The setting of the objectives should be undertaken with a clear view of how any achievement will be measured. You can realistically set an objective to make a corporate presentation to x per cent of analysts that you have identified as important. This is easy to measure, simply by counting how many on your target list attended such presentations by the end of the year. However, an objective to get y per cent of these same analysts to rate the company as well managed in, say, its sector can be pointless; it only has validity if you agree on what they would consider *well managed* and you have set up some procedure to test how many have that view, at the start, and how many have been persuaded to that view over the period of the campaign. (See Chapter 5 on appraisal of public relations performance which should be read in conjunction with these notes on setting objectives.)

Aims and objectives

IN THE DRAFT PLAN, START WITH AIMS . . .
As briefly discussed earlier, it is important to differentiate between aims and objectives. Frequently in public relations these are used interchangeably. An aim is a direction in which progress is to be made. However, an objective is a *specific* point that is to be reached. Where possible, the public relations activity should be working to quantified objectives rather than broad aims.

As an illustration, an aim for a marketing public relations programme could be to improve brand awareness; this would not be an objective, as it stands. This does not mean that it has no value. Aims may not always need to be defined as objectives, but this is likely to become necessary as the sophistication of the public relations activity develops.

A small company introducing a new product may be quite happy to have simple public relations aims. If, for example, there is no awareness of the brand in the marketplace then *any* effort that will increase the brand awareness is likely to be of *some* value. It is also going to be relatively easy to see whether an improvement has been achieved. If at the beginning of the campaign no one is aware of the brand and at the end quite a number of people in the trade are talking about it, editorial enquiries are coming through, the product is being asked for at the point of purchase, and so on, then it is reasonable to conclude that some valuable improvement has been achieved.

... AND MOVE TO OBJECTIVES

On the other hand, how do you develop from that position? How do you assess the cost-effectiveness of the activity? How will you measure how much you have recently improved in future? What budget will you allocate for what level of improvement?

In the second or subsequent years, the company is likely to find that its public relations is far more effective if it is working to objectives rather than aims. The essential factor in writing an objective is to put in a factor that can be measured. This might not be a complete measure but it must be something that would give some indication of satisfactory performance. As noted earlier, some firmly established base is necessary and this can best be set by formal or informal research.

If we continue with the brand awareness example, then it would require quantified research, before the campaign, to measure the level of brand awareness, and a similar study, at the end of the activity, to check the change. In practice, of course, this could be very expensive and could well represent a significant proportion of the total promotional budget. It could also be unnecessary: a fair indicator of the effectiveness of the public relations effort in meeting this objective can be constructed without going to the extent of a statistically validated answer.

A modest high street test may show that only 1 in 10 purchasers of a particular product could spontaneously mention your brand. The objective might be agreed to raise this to, say, 3 in 10—or whatever seems necessary for the company to achieve the commercial targets it is setting. In practice, the advice of a professional researcher in putting together an acceptable measure for these objectives is necessary. However, the principles should be understood by those planning the campaign.

Obviously, care must be taken to eliminate any biasing factors. A well-known soft drink company once developed a disappointing campaign, based upon limited research carried out in the home town where their head office was located. They had forgotten that virtually everyone they were likely to interview would have a friend or relative who worked at the company. Public awareness was substantially higher than would have been the case in a city at the other side of the country.

INVESTIGATE THE REAL PROBLEM

As well as personal interviews, this type of basic research can sometimes be undertaken through telephone interviews and post. Researchers will tell you it is important to avoid assumptions.

As an illustration, it is often invaluable for a supplier to know which companies come first to mind when a buyer is looking for a particular product—in our case, say, in the industrial or business-to-business sector. One established way to evaluate this is to place a key question in the centre of a broader questionnaire and phrase the question along the lines of: 'Name five companies that manufacture this product from which you would consider requesting a quotation.' The answer to this question will not only indicate how many people are *aware* of the company in this market sector, but also how they *rate* it in comparison with competitors.

The importance of working to quantified objectives is that they can be used as the yardstick for measure at the end of each campaign to assess the success in performance. Where public relations is a new activity with a company, it is sometimes acceptable for the initial aims to be expressed as opportunities. As mentioned earlier, these can be refined and developed into quantified objectives over a period of years.

To quote an actual example, the aims for a public relations campaign specifically designed to support the sales efforts of a manufacturer of home improvement products included:

1 to project the professionalism of the company
2 to explain the company's fair-trading policies
3 to improve product awareness at national and local levels
4 to attract high-calibre candidates for the sales team
5 to instil within the salesforce a team spirit and enthusiasm
6 to generate the maximum product sales enquiries.

INVOLVE MANAGEMENT IN THE OBJECTIVES

Any public relations professional presenting objectives to the chief executive or the board should be expected to detail how management support for these objectives will be obtained. Each aim can then be converted into an objective with some written-in measure that will give an indication of how well it is being achieved.

Take the fourth aim above, related to salesforce recruitment. This might be converted into an objective by redrafting as:

4 to raise the response to recruitment advertisements by 30 per cent over the year.

This may appear a little steep, presented so bluntly. Adding some element of strategy can make this more practical. For example:

4 to raise the response to recruitment advertisements by 30 per cent over the year, through projecting to potential applicants the rewards and opportunities enjoyed by present sales personnel.

Or consider a more complex position. It may well be a *sales* objective to increase distribution of the product from 20 per cent of retail outlets to 35 per cent. However, this would not be a fair *public relations* objective. Converting this commercial objective into public relations terms is practical, however. Depending on the industry, it might become:

1 to raise awareness of our products among trade buyers from *A* per cent to *B* per cent, or ...
2 to ensure that positive editorial coverage of our products is seen and noted by 55 per cent, or ...
3 to ensure that 45 per cent of potential stockists attend regional product presentations, or ...
4 to present the campaign video to 75 per cent of all potential retailers above a certain size, etc.

Let us suppose that, in 1 above, the awareness levels to be improved at the trade level are among key retailers. If the objective is carefully crafted then, later, it will become possible to record the increase in the number of retail outlets where the awareness had been improved to some prior agreed level. An objective for the public relations along these lines might be:

1 to raise awareness of product *X* among the managers of retail outlets, above *Y* turnover or shop size, from current 25 per cent to 35 per cent.

Before an integrated and comprehensive public relations programme can be developed, objectives have to be prepared relating to all key audiences, and not just to the sales area used in this example. These draft objectives must then be discussed across all operating divisions within the organization.

It is not sufficient for the head of personnel to approve objectives relating *only* to his or her personnel activities. If this were the case, it would be impossible to balance the proportion of the effort dedicated to personnel support with the other requirements of the programme. Therefore, it is important that the personnel chief is aware of the objectives that relate to production, finance, marketing and all the other aspects of the organization's activities—and, as regards cross-discipline understanding, vice versa.

RELATE ETHICAL AIMS TO COMMERCIAL OBJECTIVES
It is advisable that the proposed objectives should be approved at a board meeting and endorsed at the very highest level by the chief executive officer of the company. This board approval might be necessary once a year, or whenever a major change in direction of the public relations activity is necessitated.

Part of the aim of getting public relations objectives endorsed at the senior level is to make all operating division managers appreciate their own responsibilities in this area. Public relations must be seen to be closely related to the realities of commercial life–public relations can improve the calibre of recruits, help to reduce absenteeism, support the share price, see the company through a difficult phase, help to cope with consumer criticisms, influence proposed legislation affecting the organization, and establish a reputation for fair dealing (which has sometimes proved strong enough to be used as evidence in legal proceedings).

Issues analysis

Issues analysis has direct relevance to public relations planning and shows how to plan for the future. The idea is to look at all those issues that might have an impact on the organization. They will usually be external forces operating in the trading or community environment.

With the issues analysis approach, attention is focused on the external issues that may have an impact on the company and, therefore, the way the company will need to accommodate or counter these issues.

- What is the issue?
- How might it affect the organization?
- What is our stance on this?
- What are the existing external attitudes?
- Whom do we wish to influence?
- What new attitudes do we wish to develop?
- How can we achieve this?
- What are the messages we need to project?
- When will these changes be produced?
- How will they be monitored and measured?

This audit can often be run parallel to the periodic review of the crisis planning procedures. There can be some logic in this as certain issues–such as safety, industrial relations, shifts in public opinion and the actions of pressure groups–can produce crises which create special communications demands. However, it is important to consider not just the negative issues (which may create problems) but also those that offer opportunities. Issues can be positive (an increasing public awareness of an environmental matter which gives your product an advantage), neutral (new EU packaging requirements) or negative (an environmental factor where your product case is weakened).

The final objectives for the organization need to take account of the public relations needs over, say, the next three years. The current activity needs to have objectives that are specific: successive years may only require these to be drafted as broader aims. This longer look at the company can also look beyond the three-year period to try to identify trends that might prove significant to the organization. In particular, those issues that might develop over the next few years need to be discussed and evaluated, and possible action to cope with these issues needs to be discussed. Therefore, a schedule of the corporate public relations is likely to include:

1 quantified objectives for year 1 and, possibly, year 2
2 detailed aims for years 2 and 3
3 outline aims to cover those issues predicted to arise during, say, years 2 to 5
4 broad aims to cover alternative issues that might arise beyond year 5.

Although some of the examples quoted relate to commercial organizations, the same principles apply to non-profit bodies. If attitudes matter to the organizations, then activity and communications must be managed to create the most favourable attitudes possible.

Research

INFORMAL RESEARCH IS BETTER THAN NO RESEARCH
Earlier in this chapter, the relevance of research was outlined, particularly in developing objectives that will provide a real measure of effectiveness when the performance comes to be appraised. Quantified opinion research may be the ultimate, but less formal studies can still be appropriate in some circumstances.

Normally, there is considerable information that can be gathered by your public relations team through informal research. Talking to people can be invaluable. The head of public relations might be encouraged to put together a committee to represent the various operating sectors of the company, and plenty of opportunity should be allowed for colleagues to raise their own area. The chief executive may like to attend one of these meetings occasionally or, periodically, check the agenda and any debrief notes.

Make sure this panel convenes on a regular basis so that it performs a continuous monitoring operation. After a period of time, each member of this discussion group will be having discussions within the company and the group will be getting representative views from a much wider spread than could ever be achieved by one manager.

Organizations have available a large number of sources of valuable information about the attitudes of important publics. Many of these sources, which are seldom tapped, can offer information from professional advisers and trading partners who observe reactions to the organization—or from confidential discussions with such specialists as banks, accountants, solicitors, union leaders, the advertising agency, suppliers, professional bodies, financial analysts, trade editors, stockbrokers, careers officers, even government officials and civil servants. All these can put a fresh perspective on many aspects of the organization's operations.

Your public relations adviser should be getting a view of how competitors and other peer organizations are performing in comparison with your organization. Get members of that team to develop the habit of asking and listening. Make sure they carefully read reports, literature and brochures. Get them to check on complaints received by customer services and talk to personnel about the reasons people give for leaving the company. Ask them to collate all such information into an informal report, say quarterly.

The objective of this research will be to establish the gap between how the organization is seen and how it would like to be seen—the public relations credibility. This will determine the gap to be closed and indicate where a carefully written objective will help focus the effort.

START WITH EXISTING PUBLISHED INFORMATION . . .
In every sector of human activity there is a wealth of published material. This can include textbooks, publications, government statistics, journals, existing reports and so on. Many organizations maintain an information library while public or trade association libraries can be an invaluable additional source of information. Basic statistical information is available from dozens of public, industry and professional sources. For example, in the UK, it is possible (often simply through the public library!) to check on the directors of companies, the acreage of grain growing in each county, the number of radios per household, how much per head is spent on packaging, the average number of TV hours watched by women over 55, etc.

Your marketing department may coordinate this effort, if it has a research executive. Where necessary, use professionals but ask them to work in *your* offices so that members of your marketing or public relations team can develop an appreciation of the techniques involved in gathering desk research. Make sure you build up your own library of statistical industry information, company data, trends and product information, available for media and company use.

... BEFORE INITIATING NEW RESEARCH

Broadly, research breaks down into those areas that just give guidance and those that are statistically valid. The guidance information should not be used to make substantial decisions.

One widely used research method is the in-depth interview. This can give helpful guidance on awareness, perception and attitudes. Discussion groups extend this idea by giving a selected group the opportunity to explore an area under guidance from the research leader. Though they may not be representative, discussion groups can give useful indications where more substantial research might be undertaken. They can also help the researchers in drafting questionnaires to be used in any proposed subsequent survey.

Statistically valid research results are obtained where the size of the sample and the method of sampling give a response that is to within an acceptable level of accuracy of the predictable response from the whole audience. This requires the sample to be selected to represent the larger universe being investigated, in terms of age, occupation, income or other relevant factors.

Companies are recommended to turn to a professional market research organization to assist in these areas. Even in modest surveys, the professional can often produce the results at no greater cost than an in-house effort. In some cases, the professional can draft the questionnaire, advising on the method of sampling and analysing the results.

Investigation: formal and informal

Formal investigations of these matters can be undertaken professionally by many of the excellent market research companies who will not only run such studies but will offer advice on the best way to undertake the research. Good public relations professionals should also be able to guide management through the processes.

INFORMAL EVALUATIONS OF REPUTATION

However, although formal studies may be essential and certainly provide a useful benchmark every so often, informal evaluations of reputation can be very helpful in shaping management and public relations policies. For example, simple questionnaires can be circulated to management, put in salary notices, made an element in annual performance reviews, featured in the company newsletter, raised among attendants at the annual general meeting or the national sales conference, and so on.

Respondents may not be representative of the larger universe but they give a general indication of areas that might be studied more carefully. At the very least, these demonstrate that a company cares about its reputation enough to want to find out what people think and take the necessary steps to make any appropriate improvements.

Professional researchers warn against putting too much weight in such evaluations. Remember that those who are most unhappy may not respond— or may even throw the questionnaire away.

Sometimes, a most modest appraisal can be a starting point. Before commissioning a deeper study, a leading insurance broker headquartered in the City of London sent a simple single sheet questionnaire to just 25 existing clients and 25 prospectives. It proved without doubt that work needed to be undertaken on name awareness and the fuller study could then be undertaken with a tighter focus.

NOTHING BEATS ASKING GOOD QUESTIONS

The views of those you respect most can be highly valuable. I remember once being invited to fly to Allentown to interview the late Leonard Paul, the founder and chairman of the world leading industrial gas company, Air Products, for whom I worked at the time. It was a fascinating interview which confirmed in my mind why he had achieved so much in such a short lifetime. He asked almost as many questions at the interview as I did. The one I remember best was very simple: 'Tell me, Roger, what companies do you admire most and why?'

In a similar vein, earlier in my career I worked at Dexion, the international materials handling company. Some time after I had joined the company I was introduced at a meeting to the founder, Demetrius Comino, who had built an international empire on the basis of the slotted angle concept that he had invented. His first question to me was very simple but subtle and wise: 'Why did you choose to come and work with us here at Dexion?'

The boss of such a large and successful organization might have been forgiven for concentrating on what I was going to contribute to the empire. His perspective was different, more original and much more intriguing. He wanted to know what his company had done right (and what it had done wrong) that might have attracted me to want to further my career by joining them. It made me think deeply and explore views that had certainly been neither foremost in my mind nor raised at the various interviews prior to my appointment. But then, perhaps that was why he was where he was.

RESEARCH CAN IDENTIFY MANAGEMENT AND COMMUNICATIONS PROBLEMS

Focus on the correct solution for each problem

Cargill, the major international food and commodities group, takes great care to be a good neighbour. However, it had encountered difficulties within the local communities at a key UK process operation. Before deciding on a solution, the company commissioned a communications audit. This showed that many members of the community did not feel the company cared about its role as a good neighbour. Some employees were getting worn down by the continual criticism, even to the extent of being reluctant to identify where they worked when they met new people.

The reality was that the company had spent very considerable sums in improving its own operations to reduce noise, smells, traffic and other potential irritants to members of the community. This investment had used the best experience from similar plants around the world. One factor that made this situation critical was that the company had bought the plant some years before when local government allowed it to be located far closer to residential areas than would be normal practice today.

Clearly, this identification of the company and its poor reputation in the community was a public relations problem. Messages regarding investment policies and the level of care that the company took in these matters had not been effectively communicated.

However, the same study revealed that some operating procedures might need clarifying and improving. For example, open doors and windows at the plant on hot days were understandable but could aggravate noise or smell disturbance. In addition, some employees and contractors were uncertain of procedures in a variety of potential emergency situations. Both these areas were clearly problems for the management team to address.

Although there was clearly a communication element in this, no amount of communication, alone, would have solved some of the fundamental problems.

The procedural problems were most effectively tackled by publishing new guidelines, and by training and running a series of emergency drills. Some aspects of the investment programme were also brought forward to minimize production levels of odour emission.

Public relations advisers, working closely with the Cargill in-house management team, focused on explaining these moves to the community. Activities included presentations to key bodies, site visits by representatives of the local authorities, open days and improved relations with local media. The company also decided that better awareness and understanding required greater involvement in the community within which it worked. As a result, support and assistance to local voluntary groups was offered and an imaginative educational scheme was started. This provided teaching packs on industry and the specialized milling operations at this site. These were available for class study in local schools, whose pupils could also visit the plant in groups to get a better understanding of its work.

The result? A more confident workforce, improved positive news coverage, and minimal complaints—down by over 90 per cent. Also, the educational scheme was so well received that the management was asked by the local education authority to extend it to schools in a broader area.

Some observations, in summary

1 Use the presentation of public relations plans as a means of checking how in touch you are with perceptions of the company among key audiences.

2 A central responsibility for an effective chairman or chief executive is to reflect the business environment within which the company operates.

3 The public relations professional should be one of the key people inputting information and observations from inside and outside.

4 The relationship between the public relations adviser, the chief executive and the board will be important if the advice is to have any value.

5 Carefully check the integrity and commitment of your public relations adviser and, at all times, allow that person to say what he or she feels must be said.

6 A true picture of where the company stands is essential before any helpful objectives to change opinions, attitudes and responses can be planned.

7 Use research to determine current perceptions. Informal evaluations are better than nothing but use a professional researcher to guide such studies.

8 Realistic objectives will help define the plan of action, the timetable, the budget and resources that need to be allocated to the programme.

9 Objectives can only be of value if they are written with meaningful measures of performance and the methods of appraisal already agreed.

10 Aims can be developed into objectives. An aim is the direction in which you wish to move. An objective is where you want to be by an agreed time.

11 There is a rough ascending scale of achievement for objectives, from

awareness through goodwill and favourable opinion to supportive action.

12 Be certain that you include the achievement of some form of active feedback from key audiences within your draft objectives.

13 Objectives that support broad and continuous communications are likely to be more productive than those that suggest blitz action on problems.

14 Be sure that the corporate public relations objectives are applied to all communications activities and that each discipline behaves consistently.

15 Before presenting the objectives to all employees, present them first in draft form internally to line managers so that they can relate the objectives to their responsibilities.

16 If the publics you target cannot understand what you are trying to achieve they may raise unnecessary resistance. Make your aims open and clear.

17 Consider an issues audit to identify factors that could affect your business and to help develop the company stance towards each of these.

18 Issues are external elements that shape the environment within which you do business and they can be positive, neutral or negative.

19 Every crisis the organization might ever face will arise from an issue and all should be identified by the issues audit.

20 When objectives and the response to the issues audit have been agreed by the board, consider a review committee to coordinate activities across divisions and regions.

5

Appraisal

Measure the public relations effectiveness

Set some appraisal parameters

Are we agreed? If it cannot be measured, is it worth undertaking? In business, that must be the rule. Of course, we can all argue that some things are so self-evident that they do not need measuring. How can you rate courtesy, for example? The staff in our retail operations, as an obvious case, must be polite to the customers because that is the proper way to be. We must treat people the way we would like to be treated: *Do unto others as you would they do unto you.*

Ah, we add logically, being polite is good business. But is it? Always? To an unlimited extent? Does that mean the customer is always right?

In business, we set standards of behaviour towards, say, our staff or customers. They make us feel good but do they do us good? Certainly, we can measure the contribution to our commercial objectives of these policies. In much the same way, informing people may seem logical and good business. But we need to set the standards (as identified in setting the objectives in an earlier chapter), then measure the contribution these make.

Compare this with the appraisal we might make of courtesy or customer care schemes. For example, Marks & Spencer and Shell are among companies who have a *no-quibble* replacement service for their products. But no-quibble does not mean no question, otherwise you could wear your sweater or your car could wear its tyres for 12 months and you could return them for refund or replacement.

Thomas Cook has an excellent guarantee on its travellers' cheques for a refund, if lost. But if there were *no questions asked*, might not some unscrupulous customers pass their cheques to friends to forge their signature to cash them, then claim they had lost them and ask for a refund? Is that not just conceivable?

So what are the rules? Where does management draw the line? What will it invest to get a return in goodwill to justify this expenditure?

The customer, clearly, is not always right. It costs nothing to smile when talking to customers, but it can cost millions to set up and operate a customer care scheme with guarantees, refunds, replacements, repairs, and information with its attendant professional operating staff and support systems. Who would authorize such costs unless the benefits can be assured? How can they be assured unless they can be measured?

Similarly, public relations can often seem obvious, sensible, the proper thing to do and on many occasions can make you feel good. None of these factors will obviate the need for these efforts to be measured.

How can we measure the achievements of such a subjective craft? But maybe it is not so subjective to those who understand its operations. The key elements in any effective public relations programme, as noted elsewhere in this book, are: objectives, audiences, perceptions, messages, resources, tactics, timetable and performance. Each can be described and identified. The success in, say, getting a message over to an audience by a certain time at a certain cost can be relatively simple to assess. The skill is in writing the original objectives in such a way that the factors of importance can be measured.

Indeed, where a specific campaign has been planned and run using public relations as the only or primary communications technique, the measurement of performance can often be very direct. The St John Ambulance ran a campaign with very clear aims: to encourage members of the public to learn resuscitation skills and to persuade the government to subsidize courses. This campaign was so effective it won a *PR Week* award. Editor, Stephen Farish, comments,

> All good public relations—in the commercial sector or not—needs to set itself targets it should achieve. This effort not only generated invaluable, positive media coverage but encouraged members of the public to take up training opportunities—in the process winning an important government grant for this life-saving work.

In total, 1.7 million people asked St John Ambulance for information and over 180 000 were trained in the resuscitation techniques. An £80 000 grant was awarded to pilot government-sponsored courses. Not only are such achievements directly measurable, they help to set a yardstick for future programmes.

MEASURE 'CHANGE', NOT JUST OUTPUT
Such results are not often reported publicly, particularly in the commercial sector where confidentiality can inhibit openness. In consequence, some

business leaders feel that—through this inability to predict and measure results—public relations has not developed as effectively as it could as a communications discipline. They feel it is not always practical to separate its effects from other elements such as marketing, promotion and advertising.

Media relations and coverage

Too often, techniques for measuring effectiveness have really only been measuring output such as media coverage. But one of the most important aspects of measuring the effectiveness of a public relations programme is to gain intelligence to improve the activities.

A survey by Tom Watson, as part of his post-graduate studies at Southampton Institute, looked at public relations practitioners' views of evaluation. This showed that media relations and publicity efforts were the most frequently checked, followed by corporate image and identity, as well as marketing and product public relations. The weakest performer was investor/ financial relations; this seems to be more difficult to evaluate because activities can often be very closely focused. In recent years, this has been a rapidly growing sector and is likely to see a greater analysis both of methods and actions.

The majority of practitioners claimed to undertake some form of evaluation, with around 62 per cent of programmes subject to some formal review. (If these figures can be relied on, they suggest a significant improvement in the frequency of evaluation, in comparison with studies made a few years ago.) However, very little was actually spent on such appraisals, with over three-quarters of the respondents indicating that the proportion of the total budget ranged from zero to 5 per cent.

A number of companies are now offering methods for appraising public relations effectiveness. Some systems can balance a complex range of factors to give weighting to media coverage, but this still remains a measure of output and not of the true impact upon the target audience.

KEEP COMPARATIVE RECORDS OF COVERAGE AND ITS TONE

In addition, it is important to remember that media relations may only be one element of a broader public relations programme. For example, lectures, seminars, briefings, mailings, exhibitions and similar activities cannot be appraised by these methods. Even with this measure, it is important to separate out the impact of other activities, such as the effects of the salesforce or advertising.

Output measures of media coverage can be calculated relatively simply by monitoring the following factors:

- Press space or radio/television time
- The length of the stories
- The number of times company or product name is used
- The tone and news value of the headline
- The use of photograph or illustration
- The position of the item in the publication or the news programme
- The validity of the publication/programme
- Readership/viewership levels
- Total opportunities to see (OTS)
- The use of agreed campaign messages
- The positive or otherwise tone of coverage.

However, of greater value will be an understanding of:

- the percentage of the defined target audience that has been reached;
- the levels of awareness/knowledge that have been developed;
- how audience opinion/attitude may have been moved;
- above all, the change in behaviour that has been created.

Those computer-based systems which evaluate such elements and produce some comparative measure (normally given a title such as *media influence* or *audience impact*), have some limited value in comparing elements of each programme, or even the media coverage of one company with another.

Though useful, not too much weight should be put upon this; the computer is simply doing some complex calculations using a predetermined formula that might be carried out by the professional communicator. It may be more independent, but it remains mechanical. For example, could such a system truly measure the impact on journalists of the simple phrase 'I, too, am a friend of the earth', used by the then managing director of May & Baker? It was not used in the news stories but changed the attitude of reporters who had been following a company environmental issue.

GOOD PUBLIC RELATIONS SOMETIMES STOPS A NEGATIVE STORY
Even in the area of media relations, such techniques have limited relevance on those occasions when the public relations professional has prevented the appearance of a damaging story, say, through convincing the journalist that a planned approach was neither accurate nor fair.

Barratts, then Britain's leading house builder, had its reputation severely damaged and tens of millions knocked off the share price, through one damaging television programme criticizing its methods of timber frame construction. How would you measure the media relations of its competitors? Did they use superior media relations to avoid such damage or were these companies simply of less media relevance and interest?

I was once concerned about the ethics of diverting a potentially damaging review of the dangers to children's teeth of soft drinks, planned by TV programme 'Public Eye', from my client, Sodastream, to a less alert competitor.

Both examples are in media relations and yet not subject to any sort of measurement relating to quality or quantity of exposure.

Public relations is the management of reputation; therefore, the ultimate measure of the effectiveness of public relations must be the change in the company's reputation. It is reasonable to deduce that a good reputation is achieved through the planned and sustained delivery of positive messages about an organization to the publics upon whom it depends for success. These messages will have been developed as a result of the organization's study of practices acceptable to the public. A measurement of the acceptance of such messages by the publics exposed to them will complete the circle.

Public relations and management

The delivery of negative messages, or the unacceptability of the positive messages that are delivered, will both suggest that the company needs to change its policies. The chief executive should recognize this as a good indication that the company is not behaving in a way that is acceptable to these key publics. You cannot properly appraise public relations performance when it is being used to compensate for management inefficiencies.

Public relations played an important role in changing perceptions of Jaguar, the UK car maker. But only, stresses Sir John Egan who was chairman at the time, through projecting real changes in the quality of the product offered to the market. Communications cannot be an alternative to good management.

He is applying the same policy to his role as chief executive of BAA which is the entrepreneurial private sector successor to state-owned British Airports Authority. 'Truly effective communications efforts are those which are based on real achievements,' he feels. 'In my experience it is a lot easier when I can point at a business success and say, *that's how we did it.*'

Some executives fall into the trap of imagining that the veneer of a good story is a substitute for the hard slog of achieving significant improvements— and it never works. Public relations can provide some of the sizzle but you must start with a real sausage, as he tellingly puts it.

Equally, the public relations professional needs to have the confidence and authority to be able to advise management that while the delivery systems may be effective, what is being said is not meeting with approval. This is one point where public relations shifts from communications into the area of policy: not just what the company says but what it does.

The shareholders of Ferranti, as it faded away, did not want more information, they wanted more action; the customers of Ratners did not want more information, they wanted more respect; the marine staff of Townsend Thoresen did not want more information, they wanted better systems; the neighbours of Chernobyl did not want more information, they wanted better safety procedures.

APPRAISE THE ELEMENTS IN COMMUNICATIONS

Output measures of media relations coverage can only represent part of an appraisal—sometimes a minor part. There are many other factors relating to the public relations performance where measurement can be made before and after the campaign to quantify the results. These measures can also indicate the cost-effectiveness of the activity undertaken. Some of the more frequent measures include:

- *Budget.* The completion of activity within the agreed budget and timescale.
- *Awareness.* An increase in the knowledge of the organization among the defined audience.
- *Attitude.* A shift in opinion or attitude towards the organization.
- *Position.* The placing of the organization in the market among competitors.
- *Response.* The number of enquiries and/or leads generated by the campaign.
- *Share price.* The value that the investor puts upon the company.
- *Sales.* Any change in sales volumes or prices that can be related to public relations alone.

Advertising agencies and many other professional advisers are expected to quantify the effectiveness of their work. This is becoming the norm within public relations. Some consultancies are using sophisticated methods to calculate the audience exposed to favourable messages ('opportunities to see' as our advertising colleagues would describe this).

Both public relations directors and consultancies are increasingly using formal attitude research for pre- and post-campaign measurement. As chairman of *Countrywide*, Peter Hehir, says, 'Public relations professionals who complain about the low status accorded them but don't try to give their proposals a scientific platform, continue to bite the hand that starves them.'

The position identified by research will be an important part of the appraisal. Any change in awareness, or shift in opinion, needs to be related to the resources deployed to achieve it ... to appraise its effectiveness and, indeed, its cost-effectiveness.

Formal research of a substantial sample audience into such matters as perceptions of reputation, awareness, opinion and attitude, remains the best measure of the true effect of the public relations programme.

Measuring the effectiveness of public relations

CONSIDER INFORMAL REVIEWS OF COST-EFFECTIVENESS
Although a quantified measure must always be best, almost any measure is better than none.

Broadly, such practical assessments will fall into the subjective or objective categories. Certainly if the goals for the public relations performance were originally set only as aims, then there is not much point in taking the assessment beyond the subjective stage.

One well-established subjective measure is to hold a performance review towards the end of a programme of activity and before the detailed planning of the next stage. This needs to involve all the people who contributed to the original discussions and helped to prepare the aims, and might include personnel, production, marketing and international directors. Each representative invited to attend this meeting should be given ample advance warning and asked to obtain some assessment in the change of attitude in any sectors for which they are responsible.

The meeting will then look at each of the aims originally defined and will discuss whether there is any evidence to support any improvement related to the targets. As an example, the marketing director might have prepared for the meeting by talking to distributors and asking them for their views of the company's approach to the market. (He or she will find it is better not to ask directly about, say, news coverage, but rather about the influence that the coverage might have had on the targeted audience. An increase in coverage would not necessarily be recognized by the trade as better media relations.)

The marketing director should select a representative range of distributors with whom to discuss this change in awareness. This might cover, for example, larger and smaller wholesalers—northern and southern—or some appropriate balance.

The performance review has no real quantifiable validity. However, if the campaign has been working effectively, there should emerge clearly a consistency of opinion. This should be sufficient to give guidance on how to adjust the programme and perhaps, in future years, how to improve the objectives. These views might also suggest a better method of measurement, such as a more formal audit of wholesaler attitudes.

Certainly, informal reviews or small pilot studies are always a wise investment before undertaking major research. They enable you to refine the approach at an earlier stage to get the maximum from the effort.

USE FORMAL ATTITUDE RESEARCH FOR MAJOR CAMPAIGNS

Market research specialists will confirm that monitoring the effectiveness of a public relations campaign is not as difficult as many people imagine; nor need it be an extremely expensive activity.

It is essential that the measure is of the public relations effectiveness and that other changes are not inadvertently monitored; for example, other influences could include an increase in the salesforce, the effectiveness of a new sales manager, the impact of an advertising campaign, the introduction of half a dozen new products and so on. Therefore, as the original objectives should have been phrased in relation to some form of quantifiable awareness or attitude factor, it is this which needs to be measured.

In fact, attitude surveys are probably the most valuable method of assessing the effectiveness of many campaigns. On a normal annual basis, it is probably sufficient to monitor the section of the market at which the public relations is specifically aimed. However, periodically, it is valuable to look at overall public attitudes towards the organization. This is certainly useful before the start of a major campaign or, with the present pace of change, at least every year or two. If it is properly constructed, the attitude survey will be of invaluable help to the public relations advisers in their planning.

Attitude research also should provide the benchmark against which future effectiveness can be measured. Therefore, it is important that it is structured to enable it to be repeated at a later stage. This will enable the results to be compared and any advances or declines identified. It may be of less value to research attitudes among retailers then, five years later, to research attitudes among wholesalers ... and try to draw any comparisons between them. Similarly, the same research format and, ideally, the same research specialists should be used.

On some occasions, the research will reveal information about other aspects of the company's operations that have an effect on public opinion: driver behaviour, delivery methods, complexity of paperwork, telephone attitudes, salesforce structure, corporate identity and so on. A study I undertook for one engineering company showed that one of the groups that had the most influence on repeat orders were the delivery drivers. If they were helpful, punctual and reliable, the salesperson stood a better chance of obtaining the next order. Yet the drivers had not featured in any part of the marketing or public relations programme. These findings enabled the company to develop suitable policies to bring them into the planning.

RELATE THE MEASURE TO THE QUANTIFIED PROGRAMME OBJECTIVES

Some measurements of the effectiveness of the public relations programme are simply to quantify if the original objectives have been well drafted. Both these objectives and the appraisal methods to be used can help indicate the level of resources that might be allocated to the effort.

It cannot be emphasized too firmly that the drafting of the objectives must be related to the methods that are proposed to measure effectiveness. Suppose one objective has been to improve awareness of the products at retailer level, in order to help the salesforce improve distribution; it would be possible to record the increase in the number of retail outlets where the awareness had been improved to some prior agreed level. This would separate the awareness and sales objectives. In other words, sales management would be expected to take advantage of the improvement in awareness by increasing the number of stockists holding the product, say, by a comparable percentage.

An objective for the public relations along these lines might be:

- to raise awareness of product X among the managers of retail outlets, above Y turnover, from current 25 per cent to 35 per cent. Awareness to be defined as unprompted identification of X as one of the top three products in its sector.

Let us assume that public relations had developed such product awareness among retailers from this 25 per cent to 35 per cent. Then, let us suppose this additional awareness could be converted by the salesforce into actual distribution. If this potential increase in distribution were to represent sales of, say, £500 000 at ex-factory prices, then we are beginning to have a figure against which to compare the effectiveness of the public relations spend.

Alternatively, we could begin to calculate how much might be expended to achieve this goal. For example, the marketing manager might feel it reasonable to expend 10 per cent of the value of the potential ex-factory sales on the promotional effort. It might be worth spending a *bigger* proportion if it is a one-off activity; for example, this might be valid if it means that once distribution has been achieved, sales will automatically follow year-on-year. If, however, the nature of the product is such that it needs *continuous* trade support, then a lower percentage but spent regularly might be necessary.

Or, as a further example, consider the public relations activity undertaken to reduce staff turnover in a fast-growing, high-technology company. In an actual UK example, such a campaign was undertaken under a brief from the personnel director. At the end of the first complete 12 months during which this new scheme had been in operation, staff turnover had declined from 30 per cent to 18 per cent and continued its downward trend.

The direct costs that appeared to have been saved in cutting down this turnover—in terms of recruitment, training, the effect of limited performance during the induction and so on—were estimated at £120 000 per annum. The total cost of the public relations campaign (not including the time of the executives, as it was run parallel with other activities) was less than £20 000. Even if the time *had* been considered, it would still have totalled less than £30 000. This investment produced a substantial saving that would be continued year-on-year.

Use the appraisal for future planning

Whatever our limited ability to see into the future, many of us have stunning powers of seeing into the past. But hindsight can be invaluable in public relations. It can help develop alternative tactics and improve the strategy. At the end of every campaign, the analysis must identify those techniques that have worked most effectively.

Let us consider a practical example. A new public relations campaign supporting a branded packaged food included a series of presentations to housewives through tasting evenings organized across the country. These had been successful in improving awareness and directly stimulating sales. The level of sales could be positively measured in each of the towns after each of the events.

A success, you might think? Not exactly, for both the public relations consultant and the client were aware that this success had taken a very substantial investment to achieve the results—and the sales improvements were only achieved in those areas where the demonstrations had taken place. As less than 5 per cent of the market could be covered in any one year, it would take 20 years to cover the total market. To gear up the operation would create a budget out of all proportion. Yet, all were agreed that the technique had worked. A little bit of lateral thinking—plus a dash of hindsight—made the public relations advisers question whether it was necessary for the company to be carrying *all* of the costs and logistics of these demonstrations.

An investigation showed that several other manufacturers were under-taking similar exercises. One, in particular, was handling a product that was not only non-competitive but complementary to the client's brand. A little negotiation followed and the result was a modest financial contribution to the other company's costs, plus an unlimited supply of the product, supporting literature, recipe leaflets, and so on. The agreement covered how the product should be presented. .

The end result was a far broader coverage than could possibly be undertaken by a solo effort. Awareness and sales levels were monitored and found to be comparable with earlier results, but the final costs in the second year were only 25 per cent of those in the first.

Analyse competitive public relations activity

When undertaking any public relations activity, look at how other people are performing. Ensure that your press cutting service is covering competitive companies so that you can get some indication of their coverage. Try to calculate their promotional budget, by finding out what staff they have deployed on the activity, what the fees to their consultancy might be and so on. Try to establish if there are any industry norms.

This research does not need to be solely related to your industry. It might be interesting to know how much it costs to support the sales of £10 million of sports shoes every year by comparison with the sales of £10 million of gardening tools. If there are substantial differences, why? What methods are being used by these other manufacturers? Are they better than your own?

Try talking to trade associations to discover if any statistics exist on promotional activities, budgets, relevant market shares and so on. If your company is number one in a market with a dominant position, should you be spending more or less pro rata to hold this situation? Obviously, you cannot compare yourself with other companies in the same market, but find a parallel sector where there is also a dominant supplier.

Talk to the public relations professionals involved in this area. They may be as interested in your observations as you are in theirs.

CONSIDER A COMMUNICATIONS AUDIT IN TANDEM WITH
RESEARCH
One technique that can help establish clearly the present position of company communications and their effectiveness is to undertake a communications audit. This surveys the important audiences, methods of communications with them, the effectiveness of these communications channels and where they can be improved or gaps filled. A method for establishing the size of the task is to combine this communications audit with the compilation of a corporate reputation 'balance sheet'.

The aim behind this helpful procedure is to establish those factors that have an influence on the perceptions of the organization among the target audiences. For example, good products, excellent service reputation and major investment in research may be positive factors upon which you can build. An unstable management record, foreign ownership, or recent redundancies may be negative factors to be counteracted.

Remember that all activity undertaken in the public relations programme is designed to build and develop the reputation of the organization, its management and the products and services it offers—in other words, managing the corporate reputation.

Report to all involved in the programme

Whatever the results of your research and analysis, always ensure that a proper report is prepared and circulated to all executives who have contributed to the original planning.

Colleagues will wish to know if they have spent the money effectively. They will be interested to see how well the intended results have been achieved. It can be important if the results are not encouraging. The problems that will arise from pursuing the wrong course can be even worse than ignoring a difficulty that has been diagnosed at an early stage. As with all communications, remember to ask for a response to this report.

If you have been instructing other colleagues to work on this subject, be certain that you have the opportunity for a full debriefing and an appraisal of their performance related to the overall programme success. These colleagues may be members of your own team or they may be the consultancy that you are retaining. Success should be one of the factors that contributes to their motivation.

With an outside consultancy, this may form part of the renegotiation. If the consultancy has not performed to satisfactory standards, then you need to decide whether this requires a change in direction of the programme or a change in the consultancy. In either case, you will be able to base these decisions on a more substantial level of information.

Success demands as much praise as failure would demand criticism. Where the public relations work of colleagues is successful, recognize it. Praise can be the most motivating aspect of work. It does not cost a lot, but it pays dividends. The public relations adviser will gain far more satisfaction from performing to objectives. The value of his or her contribution to the development of the organization can only be assessed if it is measured. Good public relations demands effective measurement.

Some observations, in summary

1 If it cannot be measured, how can you be certain it is worth doing?
2 The most effective methods of appraisal start with the way in which the original objectives were written, making them specific and targeted.
3 True communications is two-way and will focus on the projection of acceptable messages that relate to real achievements.
4 The best appraisal will be of changes achieved and not just the *output* of the public relations programme, though that will be a start.
5 One central aim to justify any expenditure on appraisal is to gain the intelligence to improve future activity and cost-effectiveness.
6 *Output* measures include the number of stories issued, journalists briefed, media events held and level of coverage achieved.
7 Where you need to measure output, try to make this relevant to the objectives such as the use of agreed messages, the tone of coverage and the percentage of the audience reached.
8 Remember to review the control of difficult public relations situations that may have occurred in the year, including any reduction in or prevention of negative coverage
9 The real measure of performance will be the level of change achieved–for example, the shaping of opinion, development of favourable attitudes and, above all, change in behaviour.
10 Information alone may not make good communications, however thoroughly disseminated; for example, it may not be able to change poor opinions.
11 Informal reviews of effectiveness can be helpful in low-priority areas, or as the first stage in creating definitive measures.
12 Where possible, use professionals to plan the measurement of the performance either to run the studies or, at least, to plan the approaches.
13 The appraisal of the effectiveness of the communications can become a benchmark for future performance if it is properly structured.
14 Try to use the same team or company on such studies to get the best year-on-year perspective and ask them to help modify future objectives, based on this experience.
15 Use the results of the appraisal to adjust resources and activity for the coming year, putting budget where it is effective and needed.
16 Compare performance with competitors–or with companies in other industries where an exchange of information will not compromise commercial confidentiality.
17 Consider appraisal as part of a communications audit to review all public relations efforts, identifying any gaps or overlaps in reaching key audiences.

18 Make sure your public relations professionals prepare a written report on any agreed appraisal and ensure that they present this to the board.
19 Report back these findings to all who contributed to the development of the original objectives and ask for their views on next year's activity.
20 Use any relevant findings in the debrief with any external consultancies as part of the programme planning and contract renegotiation.

6

Marketing

Make public relations work closely with marketing

The board's key decision

Public relations as a marketing-support technique is well understood. Indeed, the craft has come of age over recent years. This success has sometimes overshadowed even more important areas of influence. For example, public relations is less often seen as a strategic approach to undertaking business—in effect, creating the environment within which the marketing efforts can be most successful.

Yet the growth of the Body Shop, First Direct or British Midland from nothing, or the revitalizing of BT, British Gas or Rentokil, or the decline of Dunlop, Ferranti or Goblin, or the disappearance of Townsend Thoresen, British Leyland, Ekco or Ratner, all owe something to the use, misuse or non-use of public relations—though other factors were clearly at work.

Major business successes have been built on the strength of effective public relations. Brand awareness and loyalty can be more credibly developed through communications channels. Paul Preston, chief executive officer of McDonald's in the UK, identifies public relations as central to the business strategy originally developed by the founder of the company, the late Ray Kroc.

> Some people think that the company has achieved its success by serving great food quickly, in a clean environment and at reasonable prices. It has, of course, but it was Ray's policy of making a huge commitment to local community relations, consistently, year after year, market by market that built a deep consumer trust in the business.

This philosophy has been pursued by the company. In the UK, McDonald's sponsors the British Young Athletes' league, the backbone of athletics, training over 25 000 youngsters in field and track. It now has some 300 clubs in England, Wales, Northern Ireland and Scotland. Preston feels that the ethos of McDonald's and the League have much in common, sharing goals founded in team work, dedication and the pursuit of excellence. He adds, 'From our experience, this relationship is truly a partnership at work.'

For McDonald's, public relations is not an option. As Preston comments, the payback is there for all to see.

Get the corporate projection right and your company will have the business environment in which to thrive ... with the right products, service, prices and people. Get it wrong and, whatever the quality of the rest, your company may not survive. So, where does public relations fit in ... and how does it relate to marketing?

Marketing is defined by the Chartered Institute of Marketing as the management process responsible for identifying, anticipating and satisfying customer requirements profitably. Implicit in this definition is the need to create the best business environment within which these products or services can be sold and supported. It is not unreasonable to extend this to the creation of goodwill between the organization offering the products and services and the purchasers of these.

Reputation: a central aim of marketing

Public relations is an essential element in the building of goodwill. Any marketing plan that does not consider public relations is likely to be dangerously deficit. One MORI survey confirmed that goodwill towards the company is closely linked to public perceptions of product quality—a central element in marketing. Some 70 per cent of a sample of the general public believed that reputable companies do not sell poor-quality products.

Also, shoppers are more likely to try something new from a trusted name. Such an advantage, built through marketing techniques (including relevant public relations and advertising), can be very significant in sales and market share terms.

Other studies have demonstrated the direct relationship between familiarity and high regard. All such evidence confirms the importance of the brands as well as the company behind the brands. The credibility of public relations as a communications technique which tends to be trusted by consumers can be important in the marketing mix—and certainly able to justify its own significant proportion of the spend.

However, does that mean that public relations is part of marketing? Certainly not. Is finance part of personnel or production part of sales? However closely they need to relate, each has separate responsibilities. Of course, public relations has a crucial role to play in supporting (and, sometimes, leading) marketing, but these are different disciplines with distinct responsibilities. The critical decision that management must make is where should public relations report?

Public relations versus marketing

With companies that have a major presence in consumer sectors, the most substantial expenditure on public relations may well be in marketing support. The logical decision may seem to be to make public relations report to marketing. But that can be a mistake. Public relations is involved with many company audiences that are not strictly the responsibility of marketing. These can include employees, shareholders, trade and professional bodies, educationalists, suppliers, national government, local authorities, factory neighbours and pressure groups. Make public relations report to marketing and you risk neglecting these important audiences—or creating friction when marketing management finds its resources are being deployed into areas that will not affect their success.

Some major and successful companies such as Dalgety, Grand Metropolitan, Hanson, House of Fraser and Trafalgar House have solved this by establishing a small corporate function at head office. These units—sometimes as small as one person and a secretary—advise the chairman and handle investor relations and public affairs. Marketing public relations is the responsibility of the operating divisions or companies. The corporate specialist often offers an advisory service on the recruitment of public relations professionals or the buying of appropriate consultancy services.

Some of these companies view an investment in marketing as an investment in building the capital value of their company.

Use marketing to build tangible asset value

Indeed, the goodwill of a company may well be its largest single asset. With consumer goods companies, this goodwill is often represented as the value of the brands. In recent years, there has been much debate about whether these should be shown on the balance sheet.

Sectors of the accountancy profession are concerned about intangible assets being given such a value. A football club cannot put its players onto the balance sheet; therefore, theoretically, a premier league club operating from a leased stadium, yet with a team valued at £20 million or more, may have minimal book value. The argument behind this is that players can break a leg and drop from being worth several million to virtually nothing.

Perhaps this accountancy practice is understandable with football clubs but it seems less logical with national and international consumer and business brands. Putting the value on the balance sheet strengthens the position of the company and significantly reduces the risk of unwanted takeovers.

The Accounting Standards Committee in the UK suggested that a brand value should be written off against profits over an agreed period of 20 or more years. Of course, this makes no sense as major brands like Apple, Bisto, Kit-Kat, Marmite, Rolls-Royce or Wilkinson Sword may be of vastly increased value and some of these have been around for 50 years or more. Of course, in some cases it becomes difficult to separate the brand value from the company, particularly where the same name is in use, such as Campbell's, Firestone, Hoover, IBM or Kelloggs.

The value of brand marketing

Consider the commercial value that brands can have and, therefore, the potential return on the marketing effort that can build those brands. Nestlé bought Rowntree Macintosh for a sum in excess of £2.5 billion in 1988 when the physical assets represented only 20 per cent of this price. The balance was to pay for marketing expertise, distribution capability and the range of brands. In other words, Nestlé were prepared to pay five times as much as the assets to acquire these brands and the mechanics that had been perfected for delivering the brands to the market. Similar deals carried out in the late 1980s valued companies at four or five times the asset value.

Rank Hovis McDougal had a stock market capitalization in 1988 of £1.4 billion but net assets of £265 million. At that time, it had sales of £1.7 billion and owned some 50 or so leading brands, not just in the UK but across Asia Pacific and other markets. It seemed unrealistic that the value of these brands was not recognized on the balance sheet and that RHM might be compared unfavourably with other companies in similar sectors whose brands had been valued.

The outcome was that the board decided to put a value on these commercial assets. RHM's brands were valued at £678 million, bringing the total net asset valuation of the company to a much more realistic figure of close to £1 billion.

KEEP BRAND VALUATIONS REALISTIC

Of course, one argument against this practice is that there is no certain formula for valuing brands other than, perhaps, the price on the open market; no company wants to go through a takeover situation to work out what figure it should be putting down in its books for these assets!

An over-optimistic or even unscrupulous management could protect a difficult trading position by putting an inflated valuation in the books. This was one criticism of the Maxwell Corporation which revalued a number of its newspaper titles and then borrowed against these inflated values. One sensible defence against any criticism of these valuations is to have these independently calculated.

Whether a formal evaluation of reputation (goodwill plus brand value) is put into the balance sheet or not, some estimation of this can be helpful; it will allow management to agree the budget to undertake the programme of issues management and marketing support to protect and enhance this asset.

THE VALUE OF THE 'CORPORATE' BRAND

In recent years, some companies with a strong marketing orientation have put all their public relations muscle behind their brands. These corporations face possible risk through adopting the low-profile approach—such problems can arise in the areas of public goodwill, consumer pressure, industrial and parliamentary relations. Consistently, organizations with a recognized public personality are subjected to less criticism and tend to operate with greater public support.

During the 1980s, brands were in. The top ten advertisers were all brands, yet to be overtaken by the retailers. The trend was logical. In days of yore, once the feudal system had faded, agriculture and food production became the basis of wealth.

As explorers and adventurers opened the world, trading became a route to influence and affluence. With such major world markets, cheap labour and raw materials, the industrial revolution made manufacturing the business. As those world markets became independent and developed their own manufacturing, so competition grew and, in this century, marketing became the powerful discipline. Many companies believed that brands were everything.

USING THE CORPORATE BRAND TO BUILD CONFIDENCE

As recently as the mid-1980s, the chief executive of Lever Brothers, at a conference of the Marketing Society, proclaimed that the company values were vested in the brands; it was a deliberate policy to maintain a low profile for the organization behind the products. Persil told the purchasers all they needed to know about Lever.

It was ironic that he chose Persil to illustrate his point for it was the problems over a new development of Persil, perhaps with hindsight imperfectly launched, which focused much media attention on the company behind the brands. True, it had no profile. Naturally journalists had no perception of the company, no understanding, no feeling for any reputation.

So their probing was perhaps tougher and less sympathetic than if a company with an outstanding reputation and a credible profile had made one mistake.

Compare that to the media reaction to British Midland and their one mistake when an airliner crashed on a motorway. The news reporting was probing and thorough, but nearly all focused on that flight. Any coverage of the company was reasonably positive. It had already established its credentials over the years.

Lever Brothers have since changed their policy. Of course, the company has an excellent record and much to be proud of in such areas as employee relations, safety and the environment, but had not felt this to be as important as brand promotion.

The moral of the story is make sure that the power of the promotion of your products does not overshadow the projection of the company, its values, its authority, integrity and quality of leadership.

The marketing emphasis has shifted in the last decade or so towards the retailers which, after all, are closer to the ultimate customer. Parallel with this, supportive communications have become essential as we all demand to know more and have heightened awareness of the ways of the world in which we live.

Target corporate audiences with brand marketing

The growth of consumerism has made marketing important. Brands were a natural development of the importance of customer loyalty. Inevitably, the retailers being closest to the consumers, slowly took the dominant position. Today, Comet, Dixons, Halfords, Marks & Spencer, Sainsbury, W H Smith and others are the leading brands and the leading advertisers. Most of them are also committed users of public relations both to support marketing and to project the corporate position.

This must be an obvious strategy for a major retailing public company with its important investor and corporate audiences. However, the principles can be equally effectively applied to business-to-business, technology and service companies, even of modest size.

Acorn Computers, Dowty, GKN and Smiths Industries are just as much brands as consumer product and retailing names. In these cases, the company name may be the same as the individual products—as it is in consumer sectors with names like Gillette, Hoover, Ronson or Yardley.

The strength of this is the mutual reinforcement. Indeed, such brands can have such strength that their associations create difficulties in developing into other sectors. Gillette, for example, can successfully move into male personal care products, but its association with shaving might make it difficult to move into female cosmetics. Yardley can cover male or female personal care products but might be less credible in small electrical domestic appliances, and so on.

Some companies choose to keep their corporate identity distinct from their brands, such as Unilever or Procter & Gamble. Mars trades its petcare products under the name of Thomas's Europe. The thinking is obvious; it would be odd to have your chocolate bar branded the same name as your cat food—though St Michael on underpants and pork pies may be the exception that proves the rule!

Marketing promotion versus corporate projection

Whatever your company policy, it is still important that the public relations keeps the brand statements separate from the values of the company. Ideally there should be two public relations programmes: promoting the products and projecting the corporation—separate, but coordinated.

The marketing approach to the corporation can put a fresh perspective on the management of this important asset, the company name. Sometimes companies can create an aura around an organization. *We try harder* was credible and worked hard for Avis. *The wonderful world of Woollies* was ludicrously glitzy to anyone who knew the rundown stores, as they were then. New professional management, within Kingfisher, has built a more credible stance and, as a consequence, the Woolworths brand has regained much ground—indeed, it has achieved a new slot in the market very different to that occupied some decades ago.

In the business-to-business sector, Scheering created an interesting example. The company operates in the agro-chemical world and recognized that many products were seen as damaging to the environment. Some were unsuitable, some misused and some were being blamed for environmental problems caused to outside farming. Through a skilful mix of public relations, technology, new products, customer service and marketing, the company repositioned itself under a theme, Green Science. The result was better credibility, an enhanced reputation and an award for excellence from the Chartered Institute of Marketing. Even more important it won for itself a stronger commercial competitive position.

Using brands to project corporate values

The corporate reputation is a little like your personal reputation. You know its values and what it stands for; you can anticipate how it will react. You know this not just from what it says but from your experience, from observations of how the company behaves, and from personal contact.

Would you believe reports that Sainsbury was reducing product quality without advising customers?; that BP was instructing tanker skippers to take more dangerous short routes to save shipping costs?; that Philips' electrical insulation standards were below standard?; that Vauxhall was cutting safety protection for its workers? Whatever your feelings on these, you will be making judgements on your knowledge of their reputation and the corporate personality.

Though public relations has this prime corporate role it can be used to support marketing in many areas—by improving awareness, projecting credibility, combating competition, evaluating new markets, creating direct sales leads, reinforcing the effectiveness of sales promotion and advertising, motivating the salesforce, distributors/wholesalers/retailers, introducing new products or services, building brand loyalty, dealing with consumer issues and in many other ways.

MAKE CUSTOMER RELATIONS PART OF PUBLIC RELATIONS

Good public relations cannot only build brand loyalty, it can reinforce customer relations efforts, backing both the salesforce and customer services operations.

Gardner Merchant is the market leader in contract catering. Directors and managers of the company successfully took it through a buy-out from its previous parent, Forte plc. It had always considered public relations to be an essential part of its marketing mix and this role was strengthened as the company worked to reassure clients and prospective clients of its capabilities in a highly competitive market.

Director of corporate affairs, Bob Cotton, explains that market leader status brings its own public relations problems. On the one hand, you want to promote your size as a sign of success, but many clients feel that large companies are not sensitive to their needs.

The solution the company developed was to let others sing the Gardner Merchant praise through third party endorsements in their public relations programmes. This carries a direct commercial benefit, he explains:

> Over a quarter of the company's new business comes from referrals or additional work for existing clients. Public relations is projecting a true picture of the partnership we enjoy with our clients. People like to be part of a success story, so such information is motivating for our staff and reassuring for our clients. They know a company can only talk positively about the quality of its service if it has the capability to deliver such service.

Develop public relations strengths as insurance

The best-laid marketing plans can sometimes be devastated by factors that are outside the control of marketing management. Confidence in products has been shaken by health, safety or pollution scares which often attract wide news coverage. A few angry shareholders at an AGM have been known to attract more attention than the announcement of a massive new production facility. A few neighbours have been influential in stopping planning permission for extensions to factories.

Public relations for the company, its values and aims will be important, but this will be most effective if it is consistent with the messages projected through marketing.

A historical problem with mercury pollution at one site created poor local media coverage for May & Baker (since renamed Rhone-Poulenc). Under an enlightened management, the company developed possibly some of the finest environmental policies in the industry and called in professional public relations resources to improve community relations.

These joint initiatives were so successful that, with the full cooperation of local communities, the company has since invested over £50 million on that site in new research and manufacturing facilities. Community relations was essential to enable the products to be properly marketed; a poor community reputation is equally damaging to sales.

DEMONSTRATE CORPORATE VALUES LOCALLY
A chicken production facility jointly owned by Spillers and Sainsbury had such an odour problem that local residents successfully blocked planning permissions for extensions that would have created many new jobs. The problems could not be solved by technical improvements alone. The goodwill and support of the local people had to be won through a public relations programme to show that the company listened and acted vigorously to end the nuisance and become a good neighbour.

A Cargill corn milling plant in Tilbury was threatened with closure through complaints from neighbours, also over smells. A Morton facility in a residential area of West London also faced major problems through complaints over coloured but harmless emissions. At both locations, technical improvements were successfully introduced in parallel with effective communications to win community support.

In all cases, the product marketing could not solve the problem and sales were threatened by issues remote from the normal responsibilities of the marketing function.

Leading marketing with public relations
Some marketing campaigns will be led by advertising. Everyday products of

limited news value, and which are frequently bought, may need the strength of advertising to lift them above competition, stress their special features and benefits, and remind the purchaser of their brand values. Examples might include soft drinks, coffee and most grocery products. Public relations may be used in support to reach both trade and consumer audiences. Coca-Cola has an active involvement in soccer, for example. Yet many products and services can best be supported with public relations, with this discipline taking the lead. This will be particularly relevant where the product or service has a broad interest because it is new or affects the quality of our lives, for example.

Philips used public relations to launch a sophisticated energy management system for business premises; the UK mushroom industry developed a public relations approach—make room for the mushrooms—into which the advertising was designed to fit. First Direct, the home banking service, established its position of strength almost entirely through public relations.

Your marketing professionals will be making the decisions on which discipline will play which role. However, a useful exercise is to ask the advertising, sales, promotion and public relations professionals to identify the balance and the priorities for each craft. You may be surprised how often they will agree, as they did the approach in all the examples outlined above.

Product euphoria can result from uncontrolled competition between disciplines. This needs to be watched. For example, care must be taken to ensure that all claims made are sustainable. Richard Yallop, a leading independent marketing consultant, points out the dangers of unrealistically boosting customer expectations about your offer. If these cannot be delivered, such actions will add cost (in dealing with complaints and problems) rather than customer value. This can seriously undermine the chance of achieving customer satisfaction and, therefore, weaken customer retention.

Condition the market through communications

Another area where public relations may be able to make an invaluable contribution is where the market needs to be educated to a new approach or concept. Communications targeted at the key influencers can often condition the market to allow more direct sales and marketing efforts to follow to convert interest into sales leads.

Specialist accountants, Howard Schultz Associates, found a good but limited market for their sophisticated, computer-aided accounts payable audit service. This could recover large sums for major retailers who had overpaid suppliers or not reclaimed discounts to which they were entitled. The service was too complex to explain through advertising. Direct mail was not an effective method of reaching the few dozen senior people who made the decisions, as they tended to be flooded with mail approaches. A public relations route based on editorial briefings, articles and features provided the solution.

Of course, advertising and public relations should not be viewed as competitive but should be run as complementary, reinforcing communications techniques. Therefore, liaison between advertising and public relations must be close and effective.

Get public relations and advertising together

Coordination will only be possible if marketing management brings the advertising and public relations people together and establishes mutual understanding and trust.

Both sides may resist the restrictions which the need to work together inevitably imposes. It is as important to establish areas of independence as it is to agree on the common ground between them—for example, it might be necessary to coordinate the timing of the advertising and public relations events around the launch of a new product, but it may *not* be necessary for both to work to the same creative approach.

Regular meetings between company marketing professionals and external advisers can be invaluable. Sun Valley, the leading UK food company, is among those that successfully pursue a policy of integrating marketing disciplines. All agencies meet and share ideas, therefore developing campaigns which complement each other. Marketing director, Eddie Clarke, finds this approach ensures that the company's advertising, public relations and direct marketing activities work in tandem, producing the maximum consumer awareness. He also feels that agencies should be treated as an extension to the marketing department. 'Involve them in all aspects of the company to give them a better understanding of the nature of the business and its culture,' he recommends.

Control the marketing specialists

It is essential to get all elements in the marketing mix working together. This puts a special onus on the client for there are usually quite powerful personalities at work heading up the advertising agency, public relations consultancy, marketing, research house, design company, sales promotion specialists and so on. The loudest or most powerful should not dominate the others.

However, when these disciplines work together the effect can be quite extraordinary. Quite often the advertising can be news itself. We are all familiar with the Gold Blend couple and their on/off romance over many years. However, that was an accident where a television campaign began to generate news comment, rather than being planned to be of media interest.

In contrast, the Quentin Bell Organization, the public relations consultancy, worked with ad agency HHCL to make their advertising proposition news. The agency had created a character who happened to be balding actor Jim Dunk. The proposition (hardly original but extremely originally treated in the advertising) was to try to put people off the product on the basis that there was not enough of it to go round.

The product was Molson lager, a new beer from Canada, trying to squeeze into a highly competitive marketplace. Jim Dunk protested in press and television advertisements that beer drinkers would not like it. In one memorable press advertisement, he said, 'Don't ask for a Molson as a refusal often offends.'

Editorial columns, chat shows and cartoonists took up this idea and the ensuing media coverage must have multiplied the effectiveness of the advertising by a factor of five or ten.

Advertising versus public relations personnel

The advertising and public relations elements of a campaign should each have its own distinct budget. Advertising is usually handled through external resources—though not always, as with Bernard Matthews, which is but one well-known exception. Consequently, when an agency is working alongside an in-house public relations team, budgets may get disproportionate. Effective public relations requires adequate funding and this applies as much to an in-house programme as to a consultancy programme.

Once the budgets have been agreed, there should be no competition for expenditure between advertising and public relations. The effective coordination of advertising and public relations could be assisted by following these 10 simple suggestions:

1 Involve both disciplines in the marketing planning.
2 Define complementary public relations and advertising objectives.
3 Allocate separate and firm budgets to each.
4 Agree responsibilities and planned activities.
5 Establish practical routines for coordination.
6 Have regular joint liaison sessions.
7 Get public relations/advertising to present their campaigns to each other.
8 Arrange for them to make a joint presentation to the organization's management.
9 Ensure regular exchange of all documents/information.

10   Insist that all parties work together this year, or they might not get the chance next year!

CREATING MAJOR SALES INCREASE

Integrating advertising, sales promotion, merchandising and public relations into a coordinated marketing approach

Sometimes public relations should take the lead. For example, in the mid-1980s six of the largest mushroom growers in the UK got together to see whether the industry could be developed. They were the leading members of an organization called the Mushroom Growers' Association and they ran a programme which, a year later, was adopted by the whole of the industry.

Each of the six major growers invited its own public relations and advertising advisers to look at the situation and make recommendations. Basically, at that time, mushroom consumption in the UK was only a fraction of the mushroom consumption in France or Germany. It might have been argued that these were countries that tended to go for more interesting cooking and so this might be expected. However, research also indicated that in parts of Canada the consumption was 10 times as much as in the UK.

Areas of concern were the funding for the activity and the way that the market could be stimulated without prices collapsing. Many previous campaigns had not been successful because—although they had been able to increase sales—they had simply brought down market prices. In addition, previous campaigns had been unable to distinguish the mushrooms of the advertising producers from those of other growers and importers. Such suppliers might also try to sell lower quality produce that could damage the campaign's credibility.

One consultancy was selected from those interviewed and it recommended an integrated programme of promotion. The key to the funding was the raising of a levy across all growers so that the campaign would be paid for in proportion to the turnover. Standards of quality were agreed, as it was only going to be effective if the campaign was promoting top-quality mushrooms.

The firm selected was a public relations consultancy and it recommended that a major thrust of the activity should be advertising and, therefore, identified an advertising agency which was later presented to the steering committee of the growers' group. A creative platform was built, *make room for the mushrooms*. The advantage of this was that it could run across all advertising, public relations, sales promotion, merchandising and recipe and display activities. Indeed, the programme included television, leaflets, point of sales stickers and posters, branding tags, an editor recipe service, presentations to key buyers and trade relations.

The consultancy felt that the presentation to the key buyers was the most important element within the mix. With the marketing directors of the client companies, some 88 buyers responsible for virtually 90 per cent of the UK market consumption were identified. The consultancy proposed that merchandisers should present the campaign to every single one of these *before* the campaign unrolled.

To do this, all material had to be prepared well in advance, including the television advertising. The consultancy developed a presentation package that featured all the details of the public relations programme—the stickers and posters, special promotional schemes and, of most importance, the television advertising. This was shown on a small portable video presenter and a team of merchandising specialists were selected and trained. Over a four-week period—several months in advance of the launch of the advertising—appointments were made and, eventually, each of the 88 identified key buyers was personally visited and presented with the campaign. It took six or further attempts with some to get the final appointment, but although 15 minutes was booked for the presentation, the shortest discussion was 45 minutes with many running to over an hour. All agreed that this was an impressive coordinated campaign and probably the most effective that had ever been run in this sector.

The real skill was in getting all parties to work together because the advertising had to be prepared to its finished form including a complex cartoon animation and original music—over six months in advance of it being shown on screen. The same mushroom characters had to feature on posters and displays and in an ambitious children's school competition. Eventually the school competition attracted some 35 000 entrants and the editorial coverage over the launch period, when bound, formed a pile over 10 feet tall.

But the key and central element was the television commercial and as it was shown to all the key buyers they were able to gear up in advance of the consumer interest.

It had been estimated that a 6 per cent increase in sales with prices held steady would be sufficient to justify the cost of the activity. In practice, at the end of the launch period sales had increased by 30 per cent and, by the end of the first year, they were 50 per cent up with prices being held at the same level. In other words, the returns to the growers had risen by 50 per cent over a 12-month period.

Some observations, in summary

1 Use public relations, properly planned well in advance, to make a strategic input to marketing, helping to shape the total approach to customers.
2 Consider the role of public relations in, say, market education, intelligence, countering competition and not just its publicity function.
3 The overall brief for marketing public relations is usually (and valuably) to create the favourable environment within which the business operates.
4 The goodwill towards the company is directly linked, so research confirms, to public understanding and acceptance of product quality and ...
5 ... of equal importance, research also shows that the more familiar the market is with the company, the higher will be the level of regard.
6 Public relations is essential in marketing but it is not *part* of marketing, as it has responsibilities for non-marketing audiences ...
7 ... though these two areas must be coordinated—for a pollution incident, share speculation or plant closure can all have an impact on marketing initiatives.
8 However large the function may need to be, make sure it is run by one person, reporting to the top and preferably in the next door office.
9 An investment in public relations should be considered and planned as an investment in the company capital value.
10 Make sure that separate promotional plans are prepared for each company brand, but work these consistently together.
11 Your most important brand is the corporate name so be certain that both the corporate communications and marketing reflect this.
12 Strong and well-organized public relations will help protect the company from damage when it encounters problems.
13 When planning marketing promotion, make sure the quality of company management is fully projected for they are custodians of the reputation.
14 Relate the marketing public relations to the customer-care programme so that both are working to harmonious objectives and projecting consistent messages.
15 Consider leading your marketing with public relations, say, when you are launching a newsworthy product or when the market needs educating.
16 Manage your public relations and advertising to work together, but to separate plans and budgets and with separate resources.
17 Develop advertising that has news impact, say, an intriguing storyline or characters, and use of personalities or topical approaches identified through research.

18 You, the client, must always keep control, particularly when the powerful personalities in agencies and consultancies threaten to take over.

7

Employees

Mobilize a vast volunteer army of goodwill ambassadors

Employees and public relations

The company makes more than profits through the efforts of its employees; it makes good vibrations or bad. Employees perform some important functions which most managements completely ignore. As many of these services are totally unpaid and can make a big contribution to commercial success, this seems a little short-sighted.

What are these valuable, voluntary tasks that employees undertake for free? First, whether you ask them or not, they put out messages about your operations to *all* the audiences upon whom you depend for success. Second, if you ask them, they can tell you exactly what these audiences think about your organization.

With a little imagination and management skill, all this goodwill and powerful feedback can be a bonus on top of their efforts that build your success. Peter Bateman, whose public relations work with Rentokil has made him an oft-quoted spokesperson, neatly sums up this point by saying that however many listeners, viewers or readers the communications may reach, no audience is as important as your own staff. If company personnel are not briefed and, indeed, accept ownership of the corporate stance, then external communications will be doomed as soon as this credibility gap is exposed, as surely it will be.

Why brief the analysts, inform the shareholders, woo the institutions, persuade the customers, flatter the legislators, or court the journalists if you keep in the dark those who have committed their working lives to the company? The influence of employees (for good or bad) can be very significant. Poor employee relations can bring down the company, while a well-motivated team can dramatically improve productivity.

Did British Leyland suffer appalling manufacturing problems through damaging industrial action fermented by hostile workers, or did the management antagonize workers and create horrendous industrial relations? I know who I hold responsible.

BUILD FAVOURABLE EMPLOYEE ATTITUDES

After all, Sir Iain Vallance and his team created the BT success with largely the same employees (slimmed down, true) that had made the nationalized organization an inefficient, work-to-rule, unresponsive megalith. How was Tesco changed from the *who-cares* to *the customer is king* (or queen) style? The differences lay in the management, and the business environment in which they could work.

There is, however, one factor affecting success which is equally as important as good employee relations. Those other third party publics upon whom the organization depends are likely to form opinions based upon their observations. For example, their decisions to invest in the company, write favourably about it, lend to it, work for it, listen to it or buy from it will be affected by the attitudes of those closest to the reality—the employees.

If a Dixons' salesperson was unhelpful, would it affect your attitude as, say, a shareholder if the management wanted your support to resist a hostile takeover? If the Vauxhall sales or service staff criticized their dealership bosses would you be as keen to buy from them again, regardless of the fleet deal you are offered?

The famous John Cleese training film for Video Arts *Who sold you that then?* demonstrated the damage that disaffected employees can cause. But real examples are even more telling than the fictional.

FOCUS ON WHAT EMPLOYEES FEEL AND SAY

I was once part of an advisory group planning a computer installation for the Chartered Institute of Marketing which, eventually, cost almost £1 million. An order worth having!

One company with whom I had some minor dealings approached me to see if I could get them on the tender list. As I was planning to pass their offices a few days later, I agreed to call in to discuss it. I was kept waiting in an untidy reception—not a good start, but time that proved not to be wasted. As always, I ask questions to find out as much as I possibly can, and so I launched into the standard start: 'Do you like working here?' By chance I had hit upon a disenchanted employee, and they had let her loose on reception to wreak her revenge without inhibition! With a little coaxing she told me all.

Not bad, I suppose. It pays the rent. But the way they treat you. Something chronic. They break all their promises. They told me I'd be getting a new switchboard, but they can't pay for it because they're still waiting for some big deal to be confirmed. They're just plain disorganized and unreliable. The boss is hardly ever here and, when he is, don't try talking to him after lunch because he's three parts to the wind and makes no sense to anyone.

I exaggerate a little (but not much) for effect.

In contrast, I was once picked up by the driver to Yutuka Harada, the European managing director of Japanese steel and shipbuilding company, NKK. 'What is your boss like?' I asked, slipping into the familiar routine.

Best person I have ever worked for. A true gentleman. Reliable, polite and courteous. Everyone in the office has the highest respect for him. We'd do anything he asks. You'll like him.

And I did. The chauffeur gave his comments with such genuine warmth that there was absolutely no doubt about his real feelings. He had seen the man behind the business leader and he had liked what he had seen. There could be no better PRO for that company.

Start by listening

At the top in the company, the personnel and the public relations functions need to cooperate closely to achieve the best results. In some organizations, internal communications policy is the responsibility of human resources, even if the delivery systems are operated by public relations. Coordination and consistent messages are essential to creating a well-informed and motivated workforce.

One of the best contributions that your employees can make is to act as the eyes and ears of the organization. You need to know what they see and hear when dealing with customers, competitors, factory neighbours and other groups. Everyone in the organization is a member of the public relations team. They should be listening to public comments and feeding them back as well as putting out positive messages about the company, its aims and its performance.

Feedback systems play their part and there are many excellent books on how these work—as well as organizations, such as the Industrial Society, which advise on setting up team briefings and information feedback processes. These are beyond the scope of this book, but there are some communications principles that managers should consider.

CONSIDER THE EXTERNAL IMPACT OF INTERNAL MESSAGES
One benefit of some planned internal communications system, say of the

cascade type, is that core messages will be presented consistently. These can be reinforced at briefings by notes, newsletters or other hand-out material. Local, branch and department activities can also be discussed at such meetings alongside the broader company developments.

Remember that the more open you are in briefing and providing information to employees, the closer the coordination that you will need between internal and external communications–and, indeed, this is one reason why these two aspects of public relations are better coordinated through one person.

From long experience at the top in business, Sir Edwin Nixon, deputy chairman of National Westminster, offers a word of caution.

> Spend as much time as you can on communications but, whenever you are communicating some important message internally, you must assume that what you say will be transmitted externally, sometimes to the press, sometimes in minutes, but certainly within 24 hours. Write nothing internally without considering its impact in the public domain.

LEAD FROM THE FRONT, BUT LISTEN TO THE OTHERS ...

How can the company ensure that it knows and understands what people really think so that communications are addressing the real issues and shaping the actual perceptions?

A listening philosophy starts at the top–and that means a real 'listening' style, not the artificial, advertising-imposed claims of the you-know-who bank which, incidentally, set itself up unnecessarily for countless journalistic challenges to its assertion every time one of its thousands of managers failed to listen.

Leaders must lead but it may be no sign of weakness to listen before leading. Those who consider they know best, without input, risk making mistakes; all good decisions depend upon the views of others who are better informed or closer to the action. Managers who do not listen will have to rely on others to make such decisions.

The listening chief, on the other hand, can be truly decisive; he or she can participate in all policy discussions because the views of those affected are known. The listening chief *listens*!

Listening is an infectious habit. It can spread throughout the company. Indeed, it can be made part of the business culture. True listening–not the synthetic artifice–has kept such companies as Unilever, Cadbury-Schweppes and Procter & Gamble consistently at the top. It was a key factor in making BT one of the most successful privatizations of all time.

Dr Don Spencer, then managing director of Air Products where I once headed public relations, told me: 'I don't always like what you say; but I need you to say it.' He agreed to a new company newspaper I edited without any external clearance procedures, editorial committee or supervision ('I'll tell you what I don't like when I've read it,' he said, but never did). This publication was a key factor in building superb internal relations in that company. Managers were trusted, for they listened. They expressed their thoughts and encouraged all staff to speak out. The company achieved over 20 per cent year-on-year growth throughout that decade.

The chief executive will be working with a small team who know each other so well that candour should be routine. But ensure that a dominant personality does not bully colleagues into compliance. This is likely to be far more of a problem at mid and lower level management. During and after the privatization of BT, one of the obstacles to effective internal communications that had to be tackled was the attitude of an important minority of middle managers. They acted as blocks in the communications chain for they believed that information was power and their role was strengthened if their staffs did not know as much as they did.

Make listening as much company policy as directing. Perhaps the key elements in developing the environment in which views that matter will be advanced might be:

1 *Practise listening at the top.* Ask for views *before* advancing your own. Hold listening sessions with representatives of key groups.
2 *Hold back on your judgements.* Acknowledge all views as constructive. Encourage further comment by refraining from criticizing those you do not like.
3 *Expect your managers to listen.* Encourage all members of your team to follow your example. If necessary, set up training sessions in listening. Run a stop-watch on talking and listening ratios.
4 *Ask executives to report back on views.* If none exists, set up some cascade information system or similar. Be sure that a central element is feeding back views gained from listening.
5 *Constantly monitor views.* Make an understanding of opinions a factor to be discussed constantly. Monitor these opinions in a way that allows comparison. Circulate interesting or challenging views.

Use information to enlighten not drown

Today's employees expect 'communications', as do all other audiences. But even in the most sophisticated companies too many employees are communicated 'at' rather than 'with'. Often only lip-service is paid to the concept of two-way communications.

Management needs to question seriously whether one-way information activity is productive. Effective employee communications must create understanding and support among employees to enable the company to operate more efficiently. Again, some organizations produce too much information of the wrong kind.

With some companies, communication almost becomes easier than management. This was a problem in the early stages of the spectacular growth of Sodastream, for example, before management got the balance right. At one point, decisions were delayed until everyone had been advised of what was planned, by which time opportunities had been lost.

Involvement is no substitute for leadership. It is the responsibility of management both to manage and communicate: these are inseparable. Any employee misunderstandings, confusion or lack of support must be the result of management failing to communicate effectively. This responsibility cannot be delegated or abdicated.

ANALYSE THE INFORMATION NEEDS OF YOUR EMPLOYEES

Checking the balance is simple. What would *you* want to know if you were an employee? What would you *like* to know? What would you accept that you should not know, for reasons of confidentiality, commercial sensitivity or otherwise?

Employees of an organization have information rights, needs and desires ... and these are not all the same. For example, some information rights are detailed by law—contracts of employment, rights relating to sickness, holidays, pension, safety at work and many other factors. Some companies have negotiated agreements which cover information requirements, and these soon become established as 'rights'. Across the EU and in the USA there is a growing level of legislation that is identifying and defining the information rights of all employees. We are seeing some important changes; in particular, European legislation affecting multinationals could involve companies needing to consider changing policies in countries *outside* the European community, where these have become a requirement for employees in an EU country.

Different practices in different national divisions or subsidiaries of multinational companies will increasingly become anomalous. For example, workers in the USA have the right to more information on hazardous substances than those in the UK. Some factory safety standards in Portugal are not as strict as in the Netherlands. German safe working levels with chemicals and radioactive materials are tougher than most. Building workers in parts of the Far East are not protected from asbestos risks that would not be allowed in Europe.

Where major companies operate to different standards in different markets (albeit as a result of different national requirements), the information democracy will pressure these steadily up to the highest standard. As one of the more pragmatic of the rules of public relations suggests, if you are going to have to do it sooner or later anyway, why not do it sooner and gain the brownie points for enlightened management?

However, the needs of employees in relation to information are rather different from their legal rights. At present there may be no statutory *right* for employees to know about the anticipated development of their company, but it might be a very realistic *need*; such information may ensure that they understand and support management plans. Equally, employees might want to know what new investments are likely to be made that will materially affect their jobs and so on. Where commercial factors or stock exchange regulations limit the information that can be provided, employees will appreciate this being explained.

And those who have tried will confirm how surprisingly loyal and confidential employees can be when they are trusted and brought onto the inside track. Pamela Taylor, then BBC director of corporate affairs, recalls how she encouraged the director general, John Birt, to brief the top 160 staff on confidential plans. This was at the time the BBC was going through controversial changes. These senior managers included journalists in the news business (some of whom were not totally convinced about the direction of the corporation's plans). Every single one respected the confidence and there was not the slightest leak.

Employees as corporate ambassadors

Of course, directors will need to have a clear view of the information that (a) has to be provided by statutory right, union negotiation or trade precedent; (b) should be provided in the interest of good understanding; and (c) is confidential and does not have to be freely available until the time the company decides it is appropriate.

To build a company-wide public relations force requires skill and dedication; it will not happen by accident. Even if employees are content and well-motivated, they may not see it as part of their job to be positive in their discussions. A *good old moan* is a national pastime but criticism of the company by one of its own employees can be devastatingly damaging.

There are a number of key steps to be taken to ensure that every employee is an ambassador for the company. These could be summarized as:

1 They need the knowledge of how the company stands, its strengths,

weaknesses, opportunities and threats.
2 They should understand what it wishes to achieve.
3 They should appreciate clearly their own role within these plans.
4 They must become involved and feel they can contribute in their own areas
   of skill and experience.
5 They need to support management efforts to move the operations ahead.
6 They should make a personal commitment to the ambitions of the
   organization.

Do not make the mistake of thinking that information alone is enough.
Information is often not enough to change opinions or to create the right
attitudes. It is quite possible for employees to know what the policies are but
not understand why they have been adopted, or even resent them or disagree
with the ambitions. In one study, 45 per cent of the workforce of a US high-
technology company were not familiar with the corporate mission, widely
published in literature and proudly displayed in receptions but not presented
properly to them. More seriously, even when shown this, almost 55 per cent
either did not agree or felt the company was not operating in the way it
professed.

ALWAYS BRIEF YOUR TEAM FIRST-HAND

Communications should be organized so that employees are briefed directly
and ahead of getting the information through other channels. This can
present some practical difficulties, but they must be overcome.

To be told about developments one day and to read about them the next
day in the national or local paper gives this news a special interest—and treats
the employee as a trusted confidant. Reading that same news one day and
being briefed on it the next is demeaning and can create massive resentment.
Exactly the same news can be motivating or, handled badly, can be totally
demotivating.

Stock exchange rules on insider trading may prevent a company from
briefing employees in advance. However, with a little planning, the workforce
can be briefed virtually simultaneously.

Some years ago, before its acquisition by MSI, major electrical motor
manufacturers Laurence Scott had constant industrial strife and problems
with many of the workers. The management would brief national and trade
media on information they refused to give to shop-floor employees. Some
responded by buying shares so they would receive mailings and invitations to
attend AGMs. At one infamous shareholder meeting, angry employees
picketed the AGM and voted (in vain) against every motion. This created
damaging and totally avoidable critical news reports. (This was a company

that had offered newly recruited 18-year-old clerical staff better employment terms than shop-floor personnel who may have put in 40 years' service. This is an old example from a company that has much changed in the interim. Such practices could not exist today.)

SUPPORT FIGURES WITH THE RIGHT INFORMATION

Of course, shareholders and employees may want different information. Some staff may require additional information or explanation if they are to understand fully the significance of the developments. They will certainly want to know more about how business and financial performance affects their jobs and their positions within the organization.

UK entrepreneur, Richard Branson, maintains that in running a company the priority must be employees—even ahead of customers. If employees are well informed, supportive and well motivated, he suggests that they are then more likely to provide the levels of customer service that keep clients coming back for more. And if customers are getting the levels of service they want, this is far more likely to generate the returns to meet the needs of the shareholders.

Many companies reverse this order and put little weight behind forming and motivating their employees—the people who actually generate the profits.

Some companies, such as Forte, John Lewis, Mercury and Sears, have an excellent record in this area. Whenever a major policy decision needs to be presented, their employees are treated as a priority group. They need to have the opportunity to understand and discuss such policies if they are to implement them effectively.

When Trusthouse Forte took the decision to rename itself as Forte—considered controversial by some—a complete integrated plan of communications was developed, supported by chief executive Rocco Forte and all members of his management team. The thoroughness and success of this programme won the company the coveted Institute of Public Relations Sword of Excellence for internal communications. Even more important, it won an overwhelming vote of support from employees, many of whom had great attachment to the previous name.

In this case, employees were not asked for their views. They were asked for their commitment and support, but there was no artificial suggestion of democracy in making the decision. Employees should only be asked for their views where the directors are likely to take notice of these in formulating decisions. Where a policy has been decided, it is an insult to ask people for their views when they know that these will have no influence.

Clearly, it is perfectly legitimate for a company to say: *This is our policy, this is why we have developed it, we would like to discuss this with you so that you can explore any areas of confusion or uncertainty and, when we have done that, we will be asking you to support this.*

That's enlightened leadership.

Make information believable and consistent

The organization should be at the centre of its own communications network with information radiating out to the key audiences. At the same time, as noted earlier, information should also be flowing back towards the organization. And, whether the company likes it or not, information will also be flowing between the various audiences, bypassing any official source; none of these is operating in a watertight compartment. For example, there will be communication between factory neighbours and company shareholders; customers and suppliers; prospective employees and environmental groups.

This is one reason why all information must be consistent and that the corporate personality must be reflected in all communications. If the company personality is well established, then potentially damaging information, rumour or gossip will be rejected immediately.

This up-and-down (and sideways) communications network is particularly important to employees. The well-run organization will ensure that the communications responsibilities of each manager are fully understood and implemented. Indeed, these responsibilities should be part of each manager's job description.

It is essential that *all* communications at all levels are factual, accurate and consistent. As an illustration, it is damaging to management credibility if the chairman suddenly reveals policy changes in the foreword to the annual report; this may be picked up by shop-floor shareholders but may come as news to middle managers when asked to explain. Who is managing whom? A programme relating to a substantial expansion by one consumer giant was thrown out of gear when a member of the personnel department included one short but revealing sentence in the middle of an article on employment prospects for a local newspaper survey.

The public relations adviser may recommend to management that the communications capabilities of all managers should be regularly assessed and their performance monitored (starting at the top).

Do not disseminate information from the top and allow it to filter down without checking its progress. Equally important, make sure the information coming back up to management is of the quality necessary to make proper decisions. Some people believe that information is power. Therefore, they tend to be very careful about how much of this they give away. This covetous attitude towards information can create extremely weak points in the communications network. Any information bottleneck must be identified. One manager may be reckless, while another may be miserly with information.

Some managers act as a *one-way* communications valve, constantly transmitting but never receiving; they are all mouth and no ears. Again, it is a relatively simple process to check each manager's ability to feed back information into the communications network. Special attention should be paid to any manager who is not providing any information or whose assessments are constantly adrift. Try a test: feed in information at an open level (perhaps through a story in a local paper) and see which managers react—and how they respond.

Training will help improve communications weaknesses but the most critical point is for each manager to realize that the company *requires* him or her to be an effective communicator. Include an appraisal of each manager's communications skills and motivation in annual performance reviews. Offer management communications training courses.

Internal communications
One effective way to help establish the principles of two-way communications is to work with each department in creating an internal communications programme. One of the most effective ways of communication is face-to-face, and all managers should ensure that their communications programme includes an element of this. This need not always be a one-to-one situation and can often be the manager talking to groups, but special attention needs to be paid to ensure that these do not simply develop into lectures or pep-talks.

Such face-to-face briefings by management need to be held regularly. Within a very large organization, *some* of these personal briefings may contain an element of prepared audio-visual material, such as a video interview with the chief executive. Even this must be presented by a senior manager who is able to speak authoritatively and can handle the discussion.

Such briefings must be accepted by executives as part of their responsibility for good management. All personnel giving briefings must be equipped with briefing notes covering agreed answers to all possible questions. It is the manager's responsibility to stimulate, note and take action on audience reactions. Response has to be worked at and managers have to be trained to encourage input and response.

Every company publication should arouse a reaction and a response. It may mean that the reporters on the publication need to be recruited to represent the main employee groups. The editor should be one or two steps sideways from management, should have a duty to establish strong links at all points within the organization and should report all feelings and attitudes. Perhaps the publication also needs to carry readership surveys, letters, columns and other direct response features.

USE THE TECHNIQUE MOST APPROPRIATE TO THE AUDIENCE
Perhaps the communication should not be a paper at all but a video or audio tape. Many organizations are using video to put over management or policy information. Some companies prepare a simplified version of the annual results presented by the chairman or chief executive. A number of companies have taken this one stage further and organized a video recording of a studio discussion (sometimes chaired by an independent TV or radio commentator) where selected representatives of the employees question the chief executive.

A few have gone as far as to record the discussion sessions that follow the presentation of the video: in this way, the observations and comments from employees, often at distant locations, can be fed back to the chief executive. Where this had been done, it had provided the opportunity for a second discussion on issues of concern. This creates far more acceptance of the concept of a *genuine* exchange of information and views.

Present the policy to ensure commitment
The overall communications policy should be presented to the board for approval. At the next stage the public relations practitioner should present the agreed corporate public relations programme to the heads of department to give them the opportunity to observe and react. Eventually they will need to ensure that their own employee communications activities are consistent with this corporate public relations plan.

Each divisional or departmental head should have the opportunity of agreeing on his or her priority audiences, the communications policy, the messages and methods. It is also essential to identify the potential problem situations that might arise. The company should be prepared to handle the bad news situations as well as the good. (These contingency procedures are covered in more detail in Chapter 9.)

Of all areas of public relations responsibility, there are few that have more priority than employee relations. In virtually all organizations, the major resource is the people working in the enterprise; and, above all, the people are the only *intelligent* resource ... only people can think, plan, enthuse, dream, and make things happen. The organization is as big as the ambitions of the people who make it work. David Ogilvy, the advertising guru said that if you recruit people smaller than yourself you build a team of pygmies, but if you recruit people bigger than yourself you become a team of giants. It is equally true that if you deprive people of information and treat them as insignificant, they will behave like pygmies. If you communicate properly, negotiate and treat them as important colleagues, they will behave like giants.

Train everyone in communications skills

Communications is part of life but that doesn't mean that we are all proficient, without effort. Communication skills can be learned, can be developed, and can be focused.

Although we can all communicate to some extent, you would not expect anyone to give a Reith lecture without a great deal of preparation. Similarly, we would not expect someone to handle a major sales negotiation unaided. We would not expect a novice to chair a broadcast debate with the aplomb of a Jeremy Paxman, Peter Sissons or Jonathan Dimbleby. Yet all these areas require capabilities that are only extensions of the basic communications skills that most people possess.

Therein lies the central point. Our everyday communications skills are rarely developed enough to cope with specialized business communications.

Everyone needs training in business communications if they are to be truly effective—even the most experienced. Training teaches the inexperienced the basic principles and allows them to practise new-found skills, and make mistakes, away from the attention of peers.

For the experienced, training sessions reinforce those fundamental principles we can all forget, while allowing executives to experiment, check, test, and revise approaches in a way that would be difficult, if not impossible, in a real-life situation where penalties for a mistake tend to make everyone extremely cautious.

Use your own personnel for training in communications wherever you possibly can, even if you initially employ outside expertise to help set up the systems. Your own people will understand the real issues as well as the culture and communications style of the company. This will help to ensure that such sessions are used as discussion opportunities and become of maximum value. Outside specialists can run training sessions but you need to be very careful that lecturers do not give a lecture. An effective programme of such sessions on a regular basis for all employees can also become extremely expensive.

However, you can use external specialists to design and help put together the programme of training courses and discussion sessions. This they will often do for a fixed fee plus some retainer to keep a watchful eye on progress, and they might also include an annual review of the effectiveness of the programme, giving suggestions for improvements and the maintenance of quality.

In addition, your trainers may wish to attend external courses to keep up to date with the latest thinking and to compare notes with peers from other organizations. There are many excellent courses on communications: the Public Relations Consultants Association, the Institute of Public Relations, the Institute of Directors and the Industrial Society are among those that can offer advice.

MONITOR THE COMMUNICATIONS CAPABILITIES OF PERSONNEL

Before formal training sessions, it is useful to check the communications skills of all members of the team. Such appraisals should be available for those running the individual training so that they can structure sessions that will be of most assistance to employees and will generate the maximum results from their participation.

It is also useful if the trainers keep a note of participants and their capabilities and attitudes—as illustrated during the training and later discussion sessions—so that problem areas or progress could also be monitored. Such appraisals should form part of managers' personnel records and can be part of any appraisal process.

As with all areas of communications, it is always best to lead from the front. The chairman or chief executive should demonstrate his or her belief that effective communications at the personal level is an essential skill for all managers. Sometimes senior people will need some assistance to get rid of inappropriate ideas or habits and develop their positive skills. In addition, acceptance by the top team will demonstrate to all employees the seriousness with which the topic is being addressed.

- *Explain how staff can support company aims.* Employees need their communications responsibilities detailed. Members of the company will not communicate positively as an automatic procedure. They need to be advised that this is part of their role. They need to understand the impact that they can have on important audiences. They need to appreciate that they can help shape opinion and are therefore part of the company's public relations resource.
- *Make staff part of a feedback system.* Employees of an organization mix across a very wide range of audiences and are exposed to various types of comment, many of which may be more candid than those addressed to senior executives. Training must identify the ways in which they can feed back these reactions as part of the company's systems for monitoring public opinion.

- *Brief staff on the aims of the organization.* Employees can position their jobs within the broader ambition of the organization if they understand what the organization is trying to achieve. They will also be better equipped to explain to third parties how individual elements of the organization's stance on certain issues can form part of a larger picture.
- *Give staff suitable support materials.* Employees can quote articles from newspapers, notices, news stories and so on. Key developments may be supported by briefing sheets or newsletters that can be used externally. Employees also need to be advised what is confidential and what is available for public discussion. And why there might be a difference between the two!

Formal training in communications for all employees ought to take place at least once every year and, certainly, should form part of the induction for all new employees. Between the formal training sessions, employees need to be updated. This can be part of staff briefings. Communications should be on the agenda for every such meeting, so that such sessions can discuss whether to present externally the implications of internal policy matters. Be assured that employees will be discussing these matters with friends, colleagues and family. You might as well brief them properly so that at least they are projecting something close to a consistent picture. This will be particularly true if your organization is one that is likely to be in the national or local news.

Face-to-face communications are best
The chief executive or another senior director is unlikely to select the communications methods for the internal audiences. However, it is useful to understand the main advantages and disadvantages of each. Specialist communications books will detail these but a brief overview may be helpful.

As noted, the best form of communication is one person talking as an equal to another, with question and answer, view and counterview being debated. All other communications techniques are substitutes for this ideal. It is broadly true that the further you are from this personal situation, the less effective the communications, the more the emphasis on projecting messages and the less the emphasis on feedback.

On the other hand, the broader the communications technique, the greater its efficiency in terms of the numbers of people that can be reached and the speed with which they can be reached. While the ideal situation may involve the chairman talking individually to each person with whom the company wants to communicate, it is hardly practical. Even if the chairman had the time, some messages must be transmitted to all simultaneously. Therefore, the right mix of techniques needs to be selected for each situation, and this mix will change according to the communications need. The appointment of a new managing director may require different techniques to a name change, or factory closure, or new acquisition, or environmental campaign, or product launch, or change in employment procedures, and so on.

SELECT ORGANIC COMMUNICATIONS FOR BELIEVABILITY

It is important to appreciate the principal differences between printed communications and live/audio-visual. The arrival of popular radio and, later, television were supposed to signal the death of newspapers—yet newspaper readership is still thriving, despite set-backs in some sectors.

The obvious appeal of radio is real people talking; much of the rest is imagination. We all know what Phil Archer looks like even if we have never seen the actor Norman Painting who plays him. *You sound taller on the radio, Mr Redhead* is not a joke, 'Radio Four Today' presenter, the late Brian Redhead, told me. With television you use less imagination but add colour and movement.

However, television and radio are taken at the pace and in the order decided by the editor. At a reading speed of, say, 120 words per minute, the *Daily Mirror* contains several times as much 'news-volume' as the News at Ten. A long news item on radio or television will be 300 words or less. There will be dozens of stories of that length in most newspapers. There will be up to 10 major news stories or features of 1000 words in the *Daily Mail* or *Daily Express*, even more in *The Guardian* or one of the serious dailies.

A single edition of *The Times* might contain 4 hours of editorial reading matter. The average person reads twice as quickly as he or she talks and, therefore, can absorb twice as much as when listening to a newscaster reading. The reader can choose what to study and when, read it as often as necessary and in any order, and pass the material to someone else.

SELECTING AN APPROPRIATE SYSTEM

Therefore, some communications efforts need audio-visual techniques (the launch of a new car, say) and some need print (your new pension scheme). Many need both in some complementary combination (shareholder updates, for example).

Meetings

These are very personal and organic. The spoken word properly delivered is unbeatable, even without visual aids, and is great for chemistry, particularly if small groups are involved. People relate to people, and if you can see the whites of each other's eyes and there is no intimidation—that is real communication as feedback is instant. There are, however, certain limitations: meetings are very inefficient in reaching numbers, particularly spread across different locations, and are also heavy users of management time. Nevertheless, imagine: the chairman talks once to six people in a room ... or once to a video camera in a studio ... and as many tapes as you wish can be sent around the world.

Briefings

Managers talk to their staffs in a cascade of information, down the organization. This is also organic and powerful and is, again, the real thing with great potential for feedback of information back up the chain. Limitations include the fact that briefings maintain existing pecking orders; some managers may not communicate well, some may bully, and some may retain information to strengthen their power. Some participants may not participate. Verbal messages can be misunderstood and are difficult to retain and impossible to pass on to third parties such as other colleagues, wives, husbands and families.

Seminars/conferences

As these are extensions of the meetings technique they have similar plus and minus factors. They can be very persuasive as real people are presenting. They allow the use of dramatic audio-visual support normally inappropriate at meetings. Limited feedback is possible if question and answer sessions are allowed, though this can be a little formalized. They are relatively inefficient in reaching large audiences as groups of more than 200 or 300 tend to lose the interactive dimension and become remote. They are very demanding of management time as considerable preparation of presentations, set, room design, etc. are necessary to achieve impact. Seminars and conferences have long lead times and therefore are not suitable for urgent news.

Closed circuit television (live)

This is almost as good as face-to-face communication as real people are talking in real time, live by land line or satellite. This system can reach far more people, including those in remote locations, and often several linked together. It is very practical today as any city in the world can be linked with any other. It is also efficient in the use of time. Television adds its own little spice to some occasions; however, the mechanics can get in the way and the balance is a little less even as one person will need to manage or chair the discussion. The method carries the same strengths and weaknesses of the spoken word as in meetings.

Video television (tape)

This still deals with real people but is recorded and not live. It is also persuasive, as we are all familiar with television, and can reach a very large audience through tape copies or satellite transmission. The spoken word has power but the limitations are less severe as tape can be rerun and passed on to others. However, a professional performance is required and amateurs (most of us) look and sound less than totally convincing. Feedback is very limited, indeed, non-existent at the time of the transmission. You need a note taker or a return tape to present reactions to the messages. Recipients also need a VCR or special equipment to receive satellite transmissions, or need to travel to a special location.

Audio tapes

These relate to real people and can be effective if professionally produced. They can reach a large audience reasonably quickly and far more economically than video. Playback equipment is more portable and available than for video, which can be a factor in remote markets or with busy executives such as salespeople who can listen in their cars. Because of our familiarity with radio, this method can have a high credibility factor. Rerunning, handing on and selectivity make the method an improvement on meetings, but weaknesses include no visual element and feedback is slow and ponderous. In common with video tape, there is no certainty that messages are received or accepted.

Media relations

Communications through a third party can have great authority. Stories acquire the integrity of the medium or the journalist—if 'Panorama' and the Financial Times (or Radio Essex and the Chelmsford Chronicle) say it, that carries real weight. Though the 'public' media are external, they are a credible way of talking to employees as they can reach many people simultaneously. However, there is no total control over the message as this is ultimately decided by news value (which is why media relations efforts have credibility). Reports may carry undesired messages and there is no real feedback.

House journals

The newspaper format gives (or suggests) a news urgency; and magazines give (or suggest) an authority. The messages have some useful credibility because people tend to believe material in print, and the company has to be truthful in black and white. Certainly, credibility can be higher than verbal information alone, which may not be recorded and, therefore, difficult to challenge. The messages can reach all employees simultaneously. The quality is variable as this is dependent on the professionalism and integrity of the editor, and too many have previously proved to be compliant. Sadly, sometimes the method has been viewed as too obvious a channel for the management (1984 and all that). It is better when the editor has an obvious independence.

Information lines

Some companies run employee information telephone lines, virtually all of which are recorded and most are updated daily or less frequently. They offer great confidentiality as employees can choose when to call without colleagues being aware. They are economic but reach few people and their credibility can be limited. I hesitate to show a bias, but would you phone an information service that may seem less well-informed than the tea lady or the canteen supervisor?

Noticeboards

Regretfully, this method should only be used in desperation. I have established and run dozens (hundreds?) of such well-intentioned schemes with total goodwill, but all have been defeated by fully understandable worker cynicism. The only advantage is that management has full control of information. The minuses? Well, who reads them and who is influenced by such propaganda? Feedback is likely to be abusive or worse. One day, someone will run an effective communications scheme via noticeboards and will ensure that it has credibility. Until then, we are wiser to study chicken entrails.

Advertising

Now we are into the realms of real confusion. Some managers use the safe route of advertising when they should take the riskier avenue of organic communications. Never use advertising alone when trying to win goodwill and support. Advertising reaches defined audiences with agreed messages as often as you want, wherever you want. Benefits include the fact that you can control the message and (generally) deliver it exactly where you want, in the way you want, as often as you want. Advertising can reach an enormous audience, virtually simultaneously. If it is so effective, why bother with the rest? Fundamentally, the public fully understand where advertising is coming from and who pays for it. *They would say that, wouldn't they?* This factor makes advertising good for awareness and information—but less effective for changing opinion and attitude. It also has no feedback capability. However, advertising should be considered as part of the public relations programme and controlled by the same executive.

Leaflets/brochures

As with all print, leaflets can be read at the speed of the recipient, who can also select those items of interest or re-read those that need more study. Print can also be passed on to third parties, so messages are conveyed with great accuracy and do not get distorted. However, like advertising they do suffer from the *they would say that, wouldn't they*? reservation on the part of most readers, so are not effective in shaping opinion. Feedback is also limited to coupons or other cumbersome options.

SELECTING THE BEST METHOD

Make decisions about communications media with care. The best method should be developed from a clear understanding of the communications needs. There is a real danger that the wrong technique may fail, therefore damning the validity of the communications. Equally, an inappropriate vehicle can demand a disproportionate amount of time and management effort to maintain on a regular basis.

One company I was called in to advise was concerned about the effectiveness of their very attractive series of video news magazines which did not seem to be producing the results they expected. These were eating a sizeable chunk of the communications budget. They had been introduced as a result of a survey which suggested that only 18 per cent of employees felt satisfied with company plans and activities. Yet few attended company showings of the videos and the take-up of copies for free home use was minimal and declining!

Management, it transpired, had tackled the wrong problem with the wrong technique. The briefest of surveys undertaken showed that there was resistance to company portrayals. Some perceived these as indoctrination. However, the majority wanted to question management to discuss policy and did not seek more information alone. Also, although over half the workforce had access to a video player, less than half of those felt they had the time to play a 30-minute management tape.

Quite a proportion of those with VCRs explained that it was difficult to get access to a family television set at convenient times. Even those who felt that they could find the time said that members of the family always drifted in to watch it and often caused considerable embarrassment with derogatory, ribald and generally unsympathetic comments. We interviewed 100 employees and found only 11 who believed that video was appropriate and watched any proportion of the material available.

The solution to the company communications needs was a structured series of briefing meetings supported by simple hand-out briefing sheets plus feedback questionnaires that every meeting organizer had to complete and return to the chief executive. The result was a significant improvement in attitude—some 78 per cent later confirmed approval of the communications with 70 per cent recording acceptance of company policy.

REINFORCING FACE-TO-FACE DISCUSSION

Select the technique that matches employee expectations

Gardner Merchant, the market leader contract caterer, then part of the Forte Group, was concerned about the expense and difficulty of keeping management up-to-date with countless changes—some large and some small—across the dozens of locations in which they operated. Managing director, Garry Hawkes, with his director of corporate affairs, Bob Cotton, called in communications consultants to look at this problem and recommend solutions.

An audit of existing communications and, particularly, the gaps in these channels in reaching management, showed a number of interesting points. Many managers did not read or take notice of newsletters as they felt they were too impersonal. Top management was well regarded as well as face-to-face meetings.

Despite his extensive travels round the group, it was impossible for Hawkes and his top team to visit all 6000 plus locations. The considerable distances that many participants would have to travel made centralized meetings prohibitively expensive on a regular basis. Some managers identified that they wanted 'personal' communications of the type they received at management meetings but without all the hassle. They were also very keen to have a channel for feedback so that their views could go back to top management for comment.

The results of this study, and a number of comments from managers, suggested that some form of closed circuit television conferencing might be appropriate.

However, the final recommendation was somewhat different. It proved to be much more effective than either closed circuit television briefings or distributed video news programmes. The proposal to reinforce personal visits by directors and annual conferences was an audio news magazine modelled on BBC radio feature programmes such as 'You and Yours' or 'Science Now'.

The tapes used a professional producer and interviewer who acted as a link man for the whole series. Interviews were carried out with key personnel and these were tested to determine the acceptance of the messages and to fine tune the presentation. This found, for example, that no more than one telephone interview per programme was acceptable or recipients began to feel that key people were not making themselves available and so not rating the communications as important as it truly was.

The programme was originally named 'Radio Reigate'—because of the location of the company headquarters, at that time, which had been synonymous within the company for 'management'. At the time of the management buy-out, the concept was continued but the programme was renamed 'Five Star Sound'.

Some 600 copies of the first edition were produced, initially to cover all senior and middle management at all main locations. The tape was issued with a questionnaire. The company also set up a phone line which recipients could telephone with their queries, comments, observations or questions. These were strictly followed up and answered in future programmes. When respondents on the phone line and other research indicated that a particular interview or story had not been well received, then this would be examined by talking to some of the commentators or going back to the original topic to check whether the right angles had been exposed.

Radio Reigate was an immediate success and won a public relations award. Much more important, it won the approval of employees of the company and became a part of management communications.

Research among recipients showed a more than 95 per cent usage rate with over three-quarters of all recipients listening to all 30 minutes of each tape. One reason for this was that an audio tape can be listened to in the car, in privacy and at any time the recipient decides—even in short pieces, as a story or news item at a time on each of several short journeys. Those managers who did not drive to work were playing it on home audio systems; some even used Walkmans to keep up-to-date on the train!

Interest in early issues was such that the production quantity had to be significantly increased. However, the cost of additional copies of the audio tapes could be counted in pennies with the biggest single item being the distribution cost. Management tried to introduce a return system for old tapes so that these could be recycled for use by an audio magazine for the blind. This had to be abandoned as so few wanted to part with the tapes.

Five Star Sound, as it is now known, may well have been the country's first audio news magazine by a commercial organization. Audio magazines are now accepted as a standard part of the communications repertoire of techniques.

Some observations, in summary

1 Employees should be considered the primary audience for they have the ability to make or break any communications plan.
2 The contribution they can make to enhancing the impact of public relations will be considerable, and often at no cost.
3 Treat your employees as your home team, part of the information network with a two-way function between the company and all its external publics.
4 Make sure that your public relations philosophy is professionally presented to employees, for discussion, before any external communications.
5 If you fail to win the support of your employees for what you are planning, then much of your external communications will be wasted.
6 One of the most important influences on employee attitudes to company public relations will be the attitudes your managers present ...
7 ... therefore, you will need to gain the commitment of all levels of management to the plan and their support of your aims and messages.
8 Try to test this acceptance by finding out what views are expressed outside formal company situations—in other words, when the boss is not there!
9 As part of your eyes and ears, use the many external contacts that employees have as a source of useful information on external perceptions.
10 In employee communications areas, the public relations and personnel disciplines—and respective bosses—must cooperate completely.
11 Human resources must rightly be responsible for all personnel policy but, equally, public relations must handle the communications.
12 Make communications part of your employees' responsibilities; appraise them, train them and provide them with the necessary assistance.
13 Expect all employees to contribute positively to both better internal and external communications, as well as suggesting improvements.
14 Consider the use of some *meetings plus core messages* information process internally, such as the cascade system or team briefings.
15 Use printed material for accuracy and 'transportability' to reinforce key verbal messages presented at such briefings.
16 When you cannot expand on a point (for example, stock exchange rules or the competitive position) explain why.
17 Above all, trust your employees for they are on the same team. People tend to respond very positively to being briefed in confidence.
18 However, make quite clear what is confidential and what is not—and what the 'official line' might be when talking to non-company third parties.

19 Build all internal communications procedures on personal briefings (face-to-face, whenever possible) ahead of any external announcement.

20 *Remember*: Briefed today and in the papers tomorrow—such joy. The other way round—such grief!

21 Differentiate clearly between when you are asking for views to help decide policy and when you are asking for support for decisions already taken.

22 Set up parallel systems to feed back up to management the concerns of employees and their views on communications problems/opportunities.

23 Check on the communications flow, both ways, to identify and help those who hold on to information to give them power over their staff.

24 People only talk when people listen, so start a listening philosophy from the top. Encourage your managers to welcome unwelcome views.

25 Listening does not compromise a good manager; it helps that person to be more decisive, for the views of those affected and their likely reactions will be known.

26 Analyse the information needs of employees appropriate to their roles in the company, but create opportunities for those who require more detail.

27 Harmonize communications across divisions and across countries so that while they may be different, to suit local needs, they will be consistent.

28 Do not wait until legislation or trends force new communications efforts but undertake these voluntarily and as early as possible.

29 Make sure that such developments, trends or company employee communications policy changes are relayed to all divisions.

30 Put your employee communications policy into writing, publish it widely and include it in new staff inductions to ensure maximum support.

8

Public affairs

Set the agenda for legislators and opinion leaders

Public affairs at the heart of public relations

Today, major organizations cannot operate to full effect without a proper understanding of the political climate at local, national and international levels. What is happening in the public arena will have a direct effect on what can and cannot be done, not simply in the legal or legislative sense but in terms of what is publicly acceptable. The basis of public relations is that organizations can only succeed through a public consensus that allows them to pursue their legitimate aims.

Decisions in the public sector are being shaped, influenced or implemented by civil servants, politicians, government researchers, local authority members and officers, lobby groups, national assemblies, and international assemblies, such as the European Parliament, the European Commission, NATO, OPEC and the United Nations.

Oddly, much of what we describe as 'public relations' is actually closer to private relations—communications between tightly defined groups of people, defined in the sense that the communications audiences are the 'publics' upon whose consent the organization depends for its success ... though these publics could be financial analysts, union leaders or civil servants. Often, public affairs can be one of the most important elements in a broad public relations programme; it is involved with the planned management of those political and public issues that decide the future of the nation and, therefore, affect the organization.

Business leaders need to be familiar with the programmes of the main parties, particularly those in power or likely to be in power. Not only can legislation be a factor, but changes in employment rules, social services, investment, planning and regional policies can also have a direct impact. Increasingly, local and national governments are becoming involved in public issues such as the environment, safety, food, health and hygiene, which means that the organization also needs close coordination between its issues management plans and its public affairs activities, as these are likely to overlap.

EMPLOYING A WORTHWHILE PUBLIC AFFAIRS ADVISER

Public affairs requires an understanding of how public opinion is shaped, whether by pressure groups, by specific opinion leaders, through planned, focused campaigns, by special interest bodies or the media. Our legislators (and those who advise our legislators) are all influenced by the same process. You also need to remember the importance of what is happening at local level in county and city halls ... and the interaction between all these and the statutory bodies that exist to manage sectors of our public life.

One of the most important and difficult tasks in public affairs is identifying what matters from the volumes of published and private information that may have *some* relevance. If a public affairs adviser is to provide an effective service to the management of the organization, then he or she must be able to sift, sort and précis just the information that is important, at exactly the right time.

To filter this material demands a full understanding of the organization's business and a clear brief on where the managers see it heading. Possible sources of information in the UK would include *Hansard*, official government business publications, trade media reports, surveys and studies by specialist associations, speeches by political leaders, party publications and summaries of the proceedings of the European Parliament and Commission.

Also, it will be essential for the management adviser to build a database of those individuals who are the key players in the movement of opinion on your topics of interest—for example, those MPs and MEPs on committees that will promote change, those public figures, academics and researchers whose views are respected. Commercial organizations run computer services that offer a rapid analysis of experts and interested individuals, but this can be no more than the starting point for an understanding of the influences at work.

Of equal importance as knowing the information is knowing the relevance of it. The chief executive needs to be confident that the public affairs adviser has the ability to interpret and analyse the basic information that will be presented. Such analysis needs to include, for example,

- at what stage is the thinking?
- how likely is it to result in change?
- what factors may affect its progress?

- how would this impact on the organization?
- does it involve the whole business sector?
- are there others who may be affected who will be interested in having some input into an initiative to modify, redirect or reverse the proposition?
- which public figures, experts and opinion leaders (who have already or are likely to air views) will carry weight?

Making a submission in the legislative process

Knowing what is happening and its possible impact are only parts of an effective lobby. It is what you do about it that matters. The preparation of the programme of activity can be crucial. Direct approaches may be relevant where a key politician or official needs to know your company's view. This must be presented factually and positively.

Remember also to cover the possible arguments *against* your case. If you want support from those who may influentially argue your cause, it is little less than courtesy to run through the contrary arguments you feel they should expect to face. You will never again win the support of someone you have inadequately briefed who, in good faith, then walks into a wall of opposition points of which he or she had no idea and no ability to refute.

Third parties who will be influential—such as officials of professional bodies, even competitors—may need briefing so that they will support your views. On some major public issues, it is appropriate to 'go public' and involve the more respected and influential media. This needs careful consideration. A carefully presented case may be convincing if put privately, and public or media pressure can sometimes jeopardize this and create antipathy. However, once entrenched positions are established and confrontation seems inevitable, it may be sensible to appeal to public opinion—accepting that any behind-the-scenes influence has usually been abandoned by then.

The construction of the political lobby requires special skills and may well involve the employment of specialists, many of whom are not in general public relations at all. However, whether the chief executive is running the lobby, employing a public affairs specialist or the parliamentary division of a consultancy, it is useful to appreciate a few broad principles:

1 Particular attention to identifying the right individuals is central to success.
2 An effective and carefully considered case, with evidence, must be developed.
3 The counter-arguments (and their strengths and weaknesses) need to be

understood and may need to be discussed when seeking support from people who will be asked to back your case. They cannot afford to look ill-informed and be humiliated.

4 Timing of the presentations is critical. Some attempts to persuade are made too late, when views have been developed beyond the point of influence.

5 The identification of those who are likely to be supportive should be carried out early as they can become ambassadors for your case.

6 Those who need persuading from different views can be tackled later, when the tide is beginning to flow in your direction.

7 Do not overlook those who have an interest or responsibility in the relevant sector, such as constituency MPs (and MEPs), as you should receive, at least, a friendly hearing for your perspective.

8 Check out those on the special interest all-party and party backbench committees, for example, as they may already be informed on the subject matter and be receptive.

9 Mount a parallel approach in Whitehall as well as Westminster; you will need Civil Service backing behind all political initiatives.

10 The parliamentary media can often put weight behind your case if it offers an interesting story for them, but use as much diplomacy and skill in briefing them as MPs, MEPs or civil servants. They are often easier to contact at Westminster than general press reporters.

11 As all legislation has to go through the Lords and many of them have special expertise, briefing the right peers can be invaluable; some have government posts and many of the more active have the ear of ministers. They also have an important power to delay legislation.

12 When generating support, take advantage of all offers of help and make specific suggestions of where help will be most valuable.

13 Brief everyone involved very thoroughly, particularly if changes are necessary in strategy or tactics, explaining the reasons.

14 Keep all briefings friendly and businesslike with no more than appropriate hospitality.

15 Sometimes short office meetings with one or two people will be more valuable than long discussions over the dinner table.

16 Make sure that you always advance a positive argument rather than only being critical of alternative proposals, for everyone likes reasons for action.

MAKE SURE YOU SAY WHAT YOU MEAN

The language for briefing must be simple and direct, avoiding jargon. The chief executive is unlikely to prepare the case for the organization—though there are worse things the person in that position could do, provided he or she does not get possessive about the copy. The chief executive must certainly be totally satisfied with all written documents, briefing material or presentations.

This is not the place for guidelines on good English but short sentences and active verbs are always best. Good communicators have enthusiasm and confidence. In his long career in Allied Lyons, before becoming chairman of Normand Motor Group, Struan Wiley presented many successful cases both inside and outside public affairs. No one ever misunderstands his message, yet he explains the simple origin of his direct style.

> My first boss checked thoroughly everything I wrote. This meant corrections had to be made. In the end, he said the best way round the problem is to keep the sentences short. Other than full stops, only use punctuation in exceptional circumstances. The result is shorter, more concise and clearer communication.

Wiley is right. In fact, the most important point in writing copy is to keep it simple and short. Make sure everything conforms to your personal style—particularly if anyone else is drafting material for you.

Do not get hung up about rules. Ending a sentence with a preposition is not something 'up with which I will not put'. You may also find split infinitives in this book, for this 'rule' is really tedious pedantry. And do not be embarrassed to start a sentence with 'and', if it works.

Any comments credited to the chief executive should be written—or finalized—by that person. There are, however, a number of reasons why it may not be wise for the chief executive to direct his or her own lobby. There will be other responsibilities and these may well take the chief executive away at exactly the time the lobby needs his or her full attention. Also, the chief executive's direct involvement does not allow the various levels of contact or provide the 'longstop' option. With a lobby run by an adviser, the chief executive can come in, wherever appropriate, as a heavyweight.

PRESENT YOUR CASE TO ALL INTERESTED PARTIES

There are likely to be other influential groups that will require special attention. These may include trade and professional bodies, educationalists, pressure groups and local government. To communicate effectively with such groups it is very important to identify their own aims and appreciate how these might relate to the organization's aims.

Any public relations programme aimed at opinion leaders will only be successful if it can create understanding between these special interest groups and the organization. Wherever possible, it should *also* be an aim to create goodwill and support. However, where the special interest group is directly opposed to the interests of the organization, this does *not* mean that no attempt should be made at communications ... or that it is impossible to achieve understanding.

It is important to understand the position of all important external groups—particularly those trying to exert pressure for change, such as a campaigning consumer body, a group of dissident shareholders or the animal welfare organization, exampled above. What is their case? Is it factually based? Who are they trying to influence? How are they attempting this? If there is validity in their claims then this may suggest appropriate policy changes within the organization. (For this reason, a key target for pressure groups should be the public relations advisers to the organizations they are attempting to influence!)

Political democracy is intended to work in the best interests of *most* people. Similarly, the information democracy should ensure that all the best arguments are presented and the opinion which emerges is in the best interests of most people.

DO NOT RELY ON TRADE ASSOCIATIONS ALONE
In much of Europe, the role of the public affairs adviser is still not fully accepted. The function is far better understood in the USA, where the concept of the political chief executive has been one of the key features in the development of communications over the last decade or two.

In contrast, many British (and many European) businesses do not seem to recognize the need for political monitoring and political action. Many businesspeople believe that an occasional social contact with politicians, topped up by information from the media, constitutes an adequate background against which to spring into action should the need arise.

In addition, a number of trade associations claim to have a competence in political monitoring, but in many cases this barely exists. British public affairs specialist, Douglas Smith of Westminster Advisers, quotes the disturbing experience of hearing the head of a major trade association seeking to calm fears over an impending bill, saying, 'Relax, we are still squaring it with civil servants.' This comment was made blandly in the House of Commons itself, with MPs present, on the day when the bill under discussion had its first reading and all concerned knew it would be law within months. Some companies may be leaving political monitoring and lobbying to trade associations that do not have the expertise to tackle this critical area.

Much of the lobbying undertaken by some trade associations, individual companies and organizations is somewhat basic; it may make them *feel* good, but will have very little influence on the shape of legislation. Too often, the case is being presented too late and without enough authority or substantiating evidence.

An intelligent public affairs campaign should not be required to deal only with contingency situations. The organization should be maintaining continuous parliamentary contact and monitoring developments. You need to be aware of possible trends and political feelings at an early stage—often at the stage when ideas are being shaped in the 'think tanks' (the Adam Smith Institute and such like). This will eliminate the need for emergency measures at a later stage in the legislative process.

In the public affairs area in the UK, the decision-making process has many levels, from junior to senior civil servants, from backbench MPs to cabinet ministers. The organization that wishes to influence the decision-making process will be working at all relevant levels. While the European level is of paramount importance, lobbying at national parliamentary level continues to be important.

Ministers can often be the most valuable source of contact. Their active involvement will help establish their own reputation for action, upon which their political future is based. In planning any presentation to a minister or a ministerial department, it is helpful to have an idea of the style of the minister and his or her department. This can usually be established by watching the public and television performances of the minister concerned, and reading all his or her policy statements and speeches. These will probably indicate the minister's areas of special interest; and it may also be sensible to seek the advice of your local MP.

ENSURE CONSTITUENCY MPs ARE FULLY BRIEFED

Probably the most important factor in developing the representation of a parliamentary case is to understand how the parliamentary processes work, the roles of the MPs, civil servants and ministers and an appreciation of the importance of timing. As with so many areas in the complex world of public relations, there can be no real substitute for employing the best professionals possible to handle specialized sectors. The director with a responsibility for parliamentary affairs does not necessarily need to know how to handle all issues. However, it is essential to have the skill to know when to call in expert advice. There remain basic aspects of good communications which have an influence in the parliamentary area. These need to be handled by the public relations specialist as part of a broader communications programme.

Every organization should ensure that it has a satisfactory relationship with all relevant constituency MPs. This must be regardless of what their parliamentary allegiances may be. These MPs should know the company and have an understanding of the style of its senior management and what it is trying to achieve. This understanding will ensure that there will be a number of informed views on the organization within the Houses of Parliament; the constituency MP may not just be the one associated with the organization's head office as there will be a constituency MP for every depot, regional warehouse or distribution point.

Each should be briefed and should meet the senior manager at each location: a Friday may be most convenient as many MPs are then in their constituencies. Having established the initial contact and given the MPs the opportunity of meeting senior management as well as staff, and of seeing the organization at work, it is sensible to keep the members updated on company developments and management views on any proposed legislation. A local press picture, or a radio or television slot, are usually popular with the visiting MP.

PRESENT THE CASE TO ALL KEY COMMITTEE MEMBERS

But a working relationship with a constituency MP does *not* constitute parliamentary relations. In an information democracy, it is reasonable that the best case will emerge through a process of argument and counter-argument. All sides in every case have the democratic right to present their arguments in the best way they can. Consequently, it is fair to say that an improvement in parliamentary liaison by companies would help create better understanding ... and, possibly, a more sympathetic climate of parliamentary opinion. In our information democracy, the principle is 'let the best case win'.

Opportunities to influence legislation exist not only for trade associations and commercial organizations but also for charities, professional groups, social bodies and societies. Perhaps the best starting point for parliamentary relations for these groups would be the party backbench committees and the all-party committees relevant to their areas of interest. Such committees welcome input from informed organizations on current issues; it is possible to find a committee in the British Houses of Parliament on virtually any area of professional and business interest.

If the campaign is likely to involve a high degree of sophistication or know-how then it might be advisable to retain a parliamentary consultancy. Consideration might be given to retaining an MP as an adviser. But it must be recognized that while the MP can provide information and guidance, very limited time will be available to help the organization. Equally important, as the MP has to retain independence, he or she is less likely to want to put forward the client's point of view than might an ordinary constituency MP. Public relations practitioners are advised to ensure that any special relationship is properly published. MPs should always declare any special interest where this is necessary, and always in parliamentary affairs.

Focus your efforts for an effective European buy

Britain, with its 11 partners (at the time of writing) in the European Union, previously the European Community, shares a unique position in world legislative practice—the 12 EU members are subject to both national and binding transnational legislation. And, clearly, the transnational legislation of the EU will continue to be of increasing importance.

The European process differs somewhat from the British, in that the European Commission—in effect, the civil service of the European Union—initiates legislation. This is first considered by the Council, then by the European Parliament and the Advisory & Economic Social Committee. Since the Maastricht Treaty came into force, the European Parliament has the power of co-decision on many matters. But even before that, in practice over three-quarters of its amendments found their way into legislation, even though its powers under the Single European Act of 1987 suggest, in theory, that it will merely be consulted.

It is possible for organizations to make direct representations to the Commission in Brussels; however, it is also possible to direct an input through UK parliamentary channels. Examples where this has been successfully undertaken include the debate over fishing limits, the retention of the mile and the pint as UK units of measure, the protection of door-step deliveries of milk and many others.

However, it is preferable, recommends Tony Pearce, managing director of the Access European network, to operate through a European grouping or trade association, whenever possible. The Commission and the Parliament prefer to hear the views of European groupings but will, of course, listen to any organization wishing to present a serious perspective.

The UK parliament (unlike the European one) does not have enough time to debate all impending European legislation. There are select committees on European legislation from both the House of Commons and the House of Lords and they are expected to identify all draft directives and regulations that should be discussed in the House. An organization wishing to present evidence to either of these committees should arrange to discuss this with the clerk to the committee.

KEEP YOUR EURO-MPs FULLY INFORMED AND UP TO DATE

There are 567 seats in the European Parliament and each MEP has more power and influence than in the early stages of the assembly. Political groupings are of some importance, but do not allow the complexity of relationships to deter you from keeping close to your constituency MEPs—not just for your headquarters' operations but for every location you operate. Germany has 99 seats, France, UK and Italy 87 each, Spain 64, Netherlands

31, Belgium, Greece and Portugal 25, Denmark 16, Ireland 15 and Luxembourg 6.

Every organization in the UK is within the constituency of one of these 87 British members of the European Parliament. Organizations should consider presenting their case to their constituency MEPs–they know how the system works, what is possible and what is not. Most will advise on the thinking of the Commission on particular issues, for this body has significant power and considerable influence.

UNDERSTAND THE POLITICAL STRUCTURE OF EUROPE

Perhaps British organizations have not been positive enough in presenting their case. Possibly this is a result of the limited understanding of the workings of the European parliamentary system. Useful sources of information for would-be campaigners include the House of Commons library (which lists all committees and party groups), the *Civil Service Year Book*, the *House Magazine* (the unofficial guide to parliamentary activities), the commercial parliamentary monitoring services, the European Commission and European Parliament Offices in London, which provide guides and information. The Public Relations Consultants Association has published a useful introduction to European lobbying, written by MEP Ben Patterson. The Department of Trade and Industry is also particularly helpful and will provide information and advice.

To appreciate how to influence the legislative process in the European Union, it is important to understand the structure of the inter-linked elements.

The United Kingdom became a member state of what was then the EC on 1 January 1973. There are three 'European Communities' to which the 12 member states all belong, which make up the EU to which we informally refer: the European Coal and Steel Community (ECSC) set up by the ECSC Treaty signed in Paris on 18 April 1951; the European Economic Community (EEC), set up by the EEC Treaty signed in Rome on 25 March 1957; the European Atomic Energy Community (EURATOM), set up by the EURATOM Treaty also signed in Rome on 25 March 1957.

However, of more current relevance are the four main community institutions, all of which play a role in shaping legislation: the Commission, the Council, the European Parliament and the Court of Justice.

The Commission

This proposes policy and legislation. The Council of Ministers and the European Parliament then discuss and, if appropriate, adopt or amend the proposals; the Commission also implements the decisions taken by the Council of Ministers and supervises the day-to-day running of European policies. The Commission is the 'guardian of the treaties' and can initiate action against member states that do not comply with EU rules. It has its own considerable powers in some areas, notably competition policy and the control of government subsidies.

The Council

This is the Union's main decision-making body. It adopts legislation on the basis of proposals from the Commission, taking into account the views of both the European Parliament and the Economic and Social Committee. The term 'Council' embraces not only ministerial meetings from the Council of Ministers but also council working groups of officials from the member states and the committee of permanent representatives of the member states in Brussels (COREPER) which prepares discussions in the Council of Ministers.

Specialist councils have evolved dealing with particular areas of policy. The main ones are: foreign affairs (including trade policy and general issues), agriculture, budget, finance, industry, the internal market and research.

Councils are attended by the relevant ministers from member states and by the Commission, which is present as of right and participates in discussions as an equal partner. The relevant UK minister is usually obvious from the title of the Council. For example, the UK is represented on the internal market and on the industry and research councils by a minister from the Department of Trade and Industry (DTI).

The European Parliament

This is a directly elected body with 87 members from the UK. Under the EU treaties, its formal opinion is required on most proposals before they can be adopted by the Council. Members are elected for a period of five years: 1999 will be the next election year. The secretariat of the Parliament is divided between Brussels and Luxembourg, although the Parliament's plenary meetings are mainly held in Strasbourg and its committee meetings in Brussels. A plenary session chamber has been built in Brussels and this hosts 'mini-plenary' meetings several times each year.

Most of the detailed work is done by its specialist committees, divided by subject area, which examine Commission proposals before they are put to the Parliament. When consulted on a proposal, the Parliament refers it to one of these committees. The committee appoints a 'rapporteur' for the proposal, that is, an MEP charged with preparing a report on it. The committee then discusses that report and may amend it. Each report includes a draft opinion on the Commission's proposal. This draft opinion is put to the Parliament as a whole by the specialist committee, and is adopted (sometimes with further amendments) as the Parliament's opinion.

The European Court of Justice

This rules on the interpretation and application of European laws. It has judges from each country in the Union. Judgments of the court are binding on each member state. (A *court of first instance* has been created to relieve it of some of its excessive workload.)

HOW DOES BRUSSELS WORK?
The EU is not just a set of procedures and institutions but is run through a complex matrix of individuals, all with their special responsibilities and perspectives. Remember also that in all the Union institutions there are 12 nationalities working together. This makes for cultural and linguistic diversity, and some quite marked differences of approach. However, all EU officials are committed to the same treaty objectives and there is therefore much common ground between them.

Virtually all EU officials speak several community languages. French and English, in that order, are the most widely spoken. Written texts for internal discussion are usually produced in either French or English. More formal documents, such as draft proposals from the Commission to the Council, are translated into all nine official EU languages.

In addition to the formal channels of communication, there are also informal ones. Officials working in different community institutions on the same subject are likely to be in close touch with each other. There are also close contacts between officials and other Brussels-based personnel, such as the member states' permanent representatives and the Brussels press corps. It is worth being aware of these cross-currents. For example, one EU contact may well be able to introduce you to other useful contacts in other institutions.

UNDERSTAND THE PROGRESS OF EU LEGISLATION
There are usually three stages in actually influencing decisions in Brussels:

- gathering information
- agreeing your action plan
- making the necessary contacts with whom you need to discuss your perspectives.

The DTI has prepared some helpful information and will always offer more topical advice than can be presented in this book. However, the following suggestions should be useful.

The first step in any campaign to influence decisions in Brussels is to obtain clear and up-to-date information on what is happening. One thing the

European legislative process produces in abundance is information. Additionally, many publishers and consultants offer newsletters and information services, drawing on the basic documents. So how do you set about establishing what you need and how to get it?

Trade associations and chambers of commerce can often help. The DTI publishes information covering the current EU legislative programme, while specialist industry publications, from trade associations or elsewhere, may help the public relations adviser to stay in touch with the community issues likely to affect that person's business. Consultants with expertise in EU matters can also help with gathering and interpreting data.

Whether the organization approaches the EU directly or indirectly, it is important to bear in mind that dialogue with Brussels is a two-way process. The public relations adviser will want information from the Commission and the other institutions about their plans, and will want to influence those plans. But they, in turn, will value the information the organization can offer about its particular sector.

The Commission relies upon information from various outside sources in order to draw up its forward proposals. For any piece of legislation, there will be a list of key contacts the executive responsible for the lobby will need to make and maintain. Make sure these contacts have a written note of the organization's concerns, but do consider face-to-face meetings too.

USE EUROPEAN LOBBY SPECIALISTS
The Brussels machinery is accessible and willing to listen to a well-prepared case. An efficient trade organization with a lobbying brief will concentrate on establishing effective contacts at all levels throughout both British Houses of Parliament and in the European legislative system. This cannot be undertaken on a part-time basis by a general public relations practitioner operating across a broad spectrum of company communications activities—or, even, operating within the consultancy world. As a consequence, the importance of the specialist public affairs consultant is increasing steadily. Some large companies (and larger consultancies) employ public affairs advisers to concentrate on this area.

The corporate influence on legislators at national and international level is an area where the chief executive will wish to be personally involved. There is considerable expertise available to help you to win in the corridors of power.

Some observations, in summary

1 Public affairs is all about issues in the public arena and, ultimately, what the public, through its legislative processes, finds acceptable.

2 Do not attempt to present views at the public affairs level unless they will have a consensus of support by specialists or public, once understood ...

3 ... in other words, do not waste time on lost causes or arguments you have been unable to win elsewhere. Everything you say will be checked.

4 Structure your public affairs activities to cover local, national and (where appropriate) international politicians, civil servants and their advisers.

5 This is a specialist arena not for the amateur, the inept or faint-hearted, so the cheapest approach is to use the best advice you can buy.

6 One of the essential (but, sometimes, tedious) activities is to monitor, sort and sift the volumes of information to identify the items that matter.

7 From the right information must come the analysis of the implications, trends and the current state of play to enable you to plan your strategy.

8 Perhaps your best investment will be in building a reliable, up-to-date and accurate database of all those of influence on your key issues.

9 When building your case, remember to develop the counter-arguments, as those briefed will want to know how to deal with any challenges.

10 Keep the language of briefing simple and direct, avoiding jargon.

11 Consider carefully when a private lobby is most effective and when it may be necessary to go public to apply pressure through popular support.

12 Use your professionals to lay the groundwork in public affairs so that the chief executive can come in at the close or as a longstop, if necessary.

13 Know the competition—those who will be putting counter-arguments to yours or trying to achieve the opposite to your desired effect.

14 Should your opponents be using misleading arguments, consider briefing them yourself to prevent them using inaccuracies in their case.

15 Make sure your trade association is aware of your plans and liaise closely but do not rely on them to present an industry brief effectively.

16 Ensure that everything is well planned and that all who are likely to be involved are briefed to minimize the need for 'firefighting', should your plans be threatened.

17 Your constituency MPs, of all political persuasions, expect to be briefed and can not only support the case but can offer helpful advice.

18 Party and all-party committee members should be briefed individually or in groups, and be certain to give everyone an equal opportunity to meet you.

19 In the UK, present the case both to civil servants and ministers. They like winners, which strengthens their track record of parliamentary success.

20 At the EU level, you may need to use different procedures as it can be more effective to operate through a trade grouping.

21 Key influences will include members of the European Parliament and officials in the relevant directorates-general (DGs) in the Commission.

22 Cover all MEPs who have a constituency involvement with your company or the issue, using both formal and informal presentations.
23 In London, Washington, Brussels or other legislative centres, use local and specialized professionals, not your general public relations team.
24 Exchange information across your operating markets, even briefing legislators on what is happening in other countries, where this may be helpful to them.

9

Corporate/investor relations

Build a corporate reputation that becomes the company

Coordinating financial and corporate relations

As with other chapters in this book, many of the recommendations here will cover very familiar territory for those directors with relevant specialist experience or responsibilities—in this case, those involved in financial and corporate sectors. However, many readers will have expertise in other disciplines and these notes will primarily be directed at them so they can take a full part in board discussions on this area of responsibility for ALL directors.

The company reputation is very significantly shaped by how it undertakes corporate communications. The bedrock of all public relations activity—community, employee, marketing or parliamentary, for example—should be the interrelationships between the company and its corporate audiences. Central to such corporate public relations—and part of it, in my opinion—must be financial/investor relations. Though this is a highly specialized branch of public relations, it is potentially so high profile and core to all company operations that it must be considered part of the broadest corporate communications efforts.

Of course, these suggestions primarily cover quoted companies; however, even private companies and non-profit organizations have some need for financial communications and many of the points in this chapter apply to such bodies.

Corporate public relations

How can corporate public relations contribute to the achievement of company commercial aims?

Consider an example of a company that moved from a production orientation in a domestic monopoly market to achieve a customer focus across highly competitive international sectors. One element of this planned development was a broad integrated programme of corporate communications. British Gas was one of the government privatizations that attracted more than its share of concern; at the time, some critics believed that a state monopoly was simply being changed to a commercial monopoly.

Chief executive, Cedric Brown, believes that major change can only be achieved successfully through the effective use of corporate public relations planned and run by professionals: 'Good communications is absolutely vital to be a world class success in today's environment. This starts at the top and reaches all levels. The board must deliver professional communications both inside and outside the organization.'

As a public utility, the company provided service to some 42 million domestic consumers. Management felt that this was provided with both a good level of service and value–though these messages were not fully communicated, and certainly not to opinion leaders.

Even after privatization, some of these areas were neglected and, as a result, the industry regulator and politicians made operations more difficult for the company. Margins were squeezed and the company was forced to allow competition not just into the market but into using existing gas facilities, on a shared basis. Today, over 39 per cent of the gas served to larger customers is provided by competitors through British Gas pipelines.

Action had to be taken to get some important messages over, explains Brown, so the company recruited a top communications professional. Since then, the corporate reputation has significantly improved and the company enjoys regular constructive dialogue with a whole range of decision makers. British Gas is using communications both as a tool to facilitate change as well as to initiate change, through developing two-way relationships across all corporate audiences.

Corporate public relations presents the company to the broadest audiences and many other aspects of company communications should be run in a consistent way under this umbrella. Some city financial advisers do not agree and feel that investor relations should be independent of all other activity.

Financial relations versus public relations

Indeed, should financial relations be operated separately from the broad public relations programme? Consider the following case:

According to an in-depth analysis by the *Financial Times* of the biggest scandal to hit the City in the decade, unacceptable communications practices were central to the loss sustained by countless institutional and private investors. Before this company—a top exporter and winner of several Queen's Awards to industry—collapsed so dramatically, it had made a series of acquisitions. These will somehow have to be unbundled following revelations that the chief executive published information that is now believed to be misleading. This information was used in good faith by analysts and respected City journalists in their reports; it not only held the share price artificially high but may have been a factor in winning some sensitive defence contracts. The City Takeover Panel has already censured the board and forced the resignation of the chairman, Lord Craskeman. All the directors could face a bar from holding future office if the criticism is sustained of their not being on top of what was being done in their names by the company public relations.

Central to the case being prepared by the Serious Fraud Squad is the fact that the company had no written public relations policy and communications had never been formally reviewed by the board. The earlier resignation as a director of barrister and ex-cabinet minister, Sir Paul Hilverson, has forced the prime minister to dramatically overhaul the rules on MPs' special interests; Sir Paul is believed to have played a pivotal role in recent confidential discussions on Libyan trade links.

No, thankfully, not an actual report but an imaginary drama that will hopefully never come to pass. Yet each of the elements has validity and has been seen in recent news stories.

UNAUTHORIZED CONTROL OF PUBLIC RELATIONS

If I were a director of a public limited company, such as the fictional case above, I would certainly want to know what the public relations policy was and what the communicators could or could not do in the company name— especially without the directors' knowledge. At the least, I might want to prevent any misinformation and make sure the company was not allowing any of those less-than-totally-ethical practices that might be undertaken by those exceeding their authority. This might prevent directors being unknowingly involved in the fictional activities that formed the report above. Remember Guinness, Polly Peck, Coloroll, Queens Moat Houses and many others? Did all the directors of these companies know and approve what was being done?

How can a director be certain of what is happening in the day-to-day public relations arena unless corporate communications is actively and positively directed from the board and from nowhere else?

On a more positive note, surely one of the best services a director can offer the company is to ensure that it operates to the best possible standards, is sensitive to the needs of all the stakeholders, and projects its case with pride and vigour. Is that not good corporate relations?

It is relevant that the report of the Committee on the Financial Aspects of Corporate Governance places much stress on communications, including the feedback role that might normally be part of a formal public relations programme to support investor relations.

> If long-term relationships are to be developed, it is important that companies should communicate their strategies to their major shareholders and that the shareholders should understand them. It is equally important that the shareholders should play their part in the communication process by informing companies if there are any aspects of the business which give them cause for concern. Both shareholders and directors have to contribute to the building of a sound working relationship between them.

Reputation and investor relations

Good corporate relations is part of running a good business. It builds pride and confidence and helps senior executives to sleep better at nights.

Recently the *captains of industry* survey, by MORI, asked senior directors of major companies in the UK which aspects of company business could be most affected by a strong or weak corporate image. The top factor was shareholder loyalty, according to these leaders. Interestingly, four out of five rated customer service by far the most important factor in maintaining or improving a corporate reputation. Favourable media coverage was the next most important. In other words, behaving well (looking after customers and getting positive news coverage for good management) creates a good reputation which, in turn, helps create sales.

According to a separate study, also by MORI, a good reputation can be a tangible business asset. Seven people in ten among the general public consider that 'a company that has a good reputation would not sell poor quality products'. Whether this is always true is less important than that it should be a widely held public belief.

This general view can be an important factor in shaping corporate policy in individual companies. Indeed, what the chairman says, how the factory managers treat their neighbours, the presentation of company lorries and the courtesy of drivers can all have an effect on the bottom line. Adopting a public relations perspective on management means more than avoiding damaging mistakes; it means taking advantage of every opportunity to ensure that all comments, decisions and actions reinforce the corporate reputation.

Research confirms that this reputation (which, after all, is built from these and many other direct and indirect factors) influences buying decisions. For example, shoppers are more likely to try something new from a trusted name; people would be 14 per cent more likely to buy a new frozen food product if it bore the name Heinz than if it were from a large but unspecified company. That 14 per cent advantage is likely to be a major factor—more than any product benefit and, certainly, far more than any price differential. Indeed, such an advantage may support premium prices.

MORI chairman, Bob Worcester, believes that familiarity breeds favour not contempt. Nine times out of ten, in most industrialized countries, there is a high correlation between how well people *know* a company and how well they *regard* it. If a company has a good reputation among those who know it, by increasing its visibility it can increase its public regard. And, he adds, at the same time the public's propensity to buy its products, invest in it, apply for a job, recommend its products, and so on, increases significantly.

Over half the British public believe that 'old established companies make the best products'. Unexpectedly, 40 per cent claim to 'never buy products made by companies of which they have not heard'. This is obviously not so, but it is clearly how a significant proportion of the public feels.

Management must back corporate messages

In any group, there will be a small core who will tend to lead opinion. They may be speakers or writers or may hold office in trade or professional groups—or may simply be those that attract the attention of others when they speak. Public opinion can often be moved by a handful of people, while some major decisions require only a few to tilt the balance one way or the other. It has been calculated that some recent takeovers have been won or lost as a result of the views of less than 100 people.

Yet, while thinking about those vital opinion leaders, do not forget the others within the company. In Chapter 7, on employee relations, the potential for everyone to be a member of the public relations team was discussed. Each has an influence, and although not all may be major opinion leaders, some will!

The top 40 or 50 managers in a large organization have an importance far in excess of their numbers or nominal authority, observes Taylor Woodrow's director of corporate communications, Mike Beard. He finds that they set the mood of the business and anyone feeling their pulse will know the health of the enterprise. From his experience, it is vital that they are melded into a team;

they must be at least as well informed as key external audiences such as the top 20 shareholders or analysts. As communications skills are variable in any group, he feels that serious gaps can be left through relying entirely on a cascade of information from the board.

To ensure that this key group is reinforcing corporate relations, the chief executive should supplement normal management processes with direct briefing on matters of corporate strategy. These might include briefing notes, repeats of City presentations and an annual management conference for this group. Their contacts will be widespread among corporate audiences such as business opinion formers, the financial community and the public sector. Properly briefed, they can be a formidable force, adding considerable weight and conviction to the messages from the centre among these groups.

Building the corporate programme

In many respects, the chairman, the chief executive and other senior directors should form the interface between the organization and the many publics with whom it must deal—backed, of course, by a senior and united management team.

A year or two before being asked to chair the Committee on Corporate Governance, Sir Adrian Cadbury wrote an excellent book outlining the roles of the chairman in representing the company. He says,

> The chairman is the link with the shareholders; he should also be responsible for company relations with other outside groups. It is for the chairman to put across the company's aims and policies to all those whose confidence in the business is important. (Sir Adrian's comments to the author, based on his views expressed on page 19, *The Company Chairman*, Director Books, 1990.)

Indeed, the chairman's responsibility for the public face of the company also means that that person is the guardian of its character and conduct. Sir Adrian adds:

> The standards in the company are set from the top. It is for the chairman to ensure that everyone in the business knows what the company stands for and what standards of conduct are expected from them. (Page 20.)

He also observes that it is essential that companies present their past record and future opportunities positively to the outside world. The outside world judges companies not just by the kind of business they are in but, above all, by the competence and flair of the people who are running them. The chairman has the responsibility for conveying to the public the ambitions of the company and the abilities of its management.

Building strong corporate relations

Just like an individual, a company needs a rounded personality. Different facets of this personality may well be more relevant to different audiences but each perspective should be part of the whole and not a completely different face. In other words, shareholders and potential investors, as well as investment advisers, will be primarily interested in the financial performance of the company; they will have an interest in the products and services, as these are the items that generate the profits.

In contrast, their interest in local community relations and environmental policies might only be to the level that it has an impact upon financial trading. However, it may be very difficult for the investment market to assess the potential impact of policy in these sectors unless this is explained by the directors. For example, a small change in EU environmental legislation, which may not be something of which investors would be aware, could have a big impact on operations and, therefore, position the company at an advantage or disadvantage in comparison with its competitors.

Similarly, a corporate audience, such as environmental regulators, might be particularly concerned about this legislation and the company's operating and environmental policies. These may be of greater importance than the financial position of the company, though they cannot be divorced. For example, if the company is trading profitably then it will be better able to make the changes necessary to meet the new directives. This is the situation with all corporate audiences—each will have its own particular focus but needs to have a view of the company 'in the round'.

It will be considerably to the advantage of the company if all the corporate audiences are clearly identified. A communications network needs to be set up to ensure that each of these audiences is getting a broad picture of the company, its policies and its operations. Specific focus on specific groups should be within this broader context.

Clearly, the financial and trading activities of any quoted company will remain one of central importance, simply because of the possible focus of media attention and the availability of published company information. For example, your company may be invited tomorrow to tender for an important piece of business for BT; or your son or nephew might be invited to attend an interview for a place on a graduate training scheme.

A glance at the financial columns or a quick check on one of the financial databases will bring you up-to-date with the company's recent activities that might have had an impact on its trading. Yet, other important aspects such as its procurement, contract, tendering and payment processes may never get that level of media coverage and so will be unknown. That is natural and proper; however, the key point to remember is that financial communications for those companies that are quoted will always remain a central element in corporate communications.

Creating investor relations

Sometimes there is confusion over corporate and financial relations. Shareholder relations, some feel, is corporate relations. But the corporation has many corporate audiences which are not primarily City/investment. Local and national government, professional and trade bodies, suppliers, employees and prospective employees, trading partners such as wholesalers or retailers and, above all, customers are as interested in the company as they are in its financial performance.

The company has a role in its local or national community that can be of considerable importance to many people. You do not need to be an investor in Grand Metropolitan or even a supplier or neighbour, let alone a customer, to have considerable interest in the company, its philosophies and its progress. We are all part of the corporate audience for Grand Metropolitan. The direction and effectiveness of its public relations demonstrates that the company recognizes the broad constituency that follows its activities with interest.

Many companies, charities, professional bodies and others will have stakeholders who may not be shareholders in the conventional sense and who may not be the focus of normal investor relations.

As we saw, looking at research under the setting of objectives, companies that are well known will create better customer attitudes and potential loyalties. Of course, corporate relations and financial relations cannot be artificially separated—and it may make practical sense to run these together. Certainly shareholder/investor relations will have a direct impact on the corporate reputation.

CONSIDER THE BROADEST CORPORATE CONSTITUENCY

The financial operations of a commercial organization really cannot be separated from its trading activities. It must make sense to project the financial credibility of the company and the skills of its management, just as strongly as promoting the products and services that it offers.

The relevance and importance of financial public relations has grown in recent years. The specialists in this sector now have access to the chief executive and have become important boardroom advisers. With the interlocking aspects of the financial, corporate, parliamentary and marketing relations, there is a strong case for the overall adviser being a public relations professional. But, if the adviser is to be credible to board colleagues, then very special expertise, courage and skill are required.

The focus of public attention on the *trading* performance of public companies and the growing understanding of the role of marketing are creating a much healthier business environment. The City is not the introspective group of financial institutions sometimes portrayed in television drama!

Investment advisers in the modern world not only want to know more about an organization's production capabilities, retail outlets or the services it offers, but are also looking at the market, competition and international development.

Projecting the management capabilities

More companies are recognizing the synergy between various aspects of corporate communications. The public relations adviser who combines the responsibilities of marketing communications, corporate *and* financial relations is fortunate indeed, as these are the three most important areas of an integrated company communications programme.

Many senior practitioners consider employee communications to be the fourth area for truly integrated public relations. Warren Newman, head of UK corporate relations for Général des Eaux Group, observes that many companies still regard employee communications as the responsibility of the personnel people. Although finance, marketing and human resources directors are all responsible for their own areas of activity, the corporate relations director should be responsible for ensuring that all audiences get the same message at the same time and by appropriate means.

It is not enough for a public company to be efficient and profitable. It is essential that the policies it follows, and the products and services it offers, are known and understood by the publics with whom it works. It is equally important that all financial institutions on whom the company depends are fully informed about the organization, understand the policies and respect the management capabilities.

The company cannot spend too much time on communications, comments Sir Edwin Nixon, deputy chairman of National Westminster Bank, but it should never attempt to present a picture publicly which is not backed up by the facts. It is essential that messages are presented in simple terms to the audience identified, but these must project the reality.

The commercial and trading activities of the company are closely linked to its financial performance, as reported to the City. Financial advisers prefer to work with companies they know and respect; no matter how specialized the operating sector, it is important that they understand the significance of the business, the quality of its management and the potential for commercial development.

It was once a criticism of the City that it always seemed to be one crucial step removed from the business activities of the companies concerned. This is certainly less true today; in recent years a number of factors have changed both the financial realities and public perceptions. These factors include the growth in public interest in financial matters (remember when the City pages were the City *column*?), the increasing internationalization of the financial world, developments in private investors and the opening of new opportunities for smaller companies to raise finance.

The financial sectors (including banking, merchant banking, broking and the major stock exchanges) are now internationally competitive, not just as a result of European harmonization, but through the development of 24-hour global trading and the geographic positions of London, New York and Tokyo, as the financial centres of the world. These are located in the three main international economic centres, Europe, the Americas and the Asia/Pacific region; by coincidence they are also spaced across the global time zones, so that trading activities are spread, almost, throughout the 24 hours.

Major companies are able to decide where to float, where to raise capital and which multinational advisers to select to help them across, say, the dozen or more financial communities that may be of significance to them. Despite some dramatic ups and downs in stock markets and confidence across the world, there has been steady progress towards more freedom, opportunity, scope and professionalism in the financial community. The financial public relations industry has also matured alongside this development.

Most general practice public relations consultancies of any size now offer specialist financial relations advice—and those companies that concentrate solely on this area have grown in both number and size. At the same time, the public relations adviser in major corporations has found that financial relations has become an increasingly important part of his or her work, as well as one of the services in which management colleagues expect the greatest expertise and judgement. The central element in financial public relations is to create the environment within which the management of the company is best able to achieve commercial aims.

Those making investment judgements about the organization are highly professional and are working in one of the toughest business environments imaginable. Therefore, companies trying to establish effective communications with them will need to be equally as professional. This will usually involve building effective relations with four main groups:

1 The major institutional investors, such as insurance companies, international groups, pension funds and investment trusts.
2 The professionals who advise and represent the major shareholders, such

as the stockbrokers, merchant banks, the corporate lawyers and accountants.
3 Private investors and shareholders (no longer always small players and, collectively, often of some importance).
4 The financial media, trade publications and commercial research and investment services that inform and influence these groupings.

Public relations practitioners in the financial area need to be very close to the corporate policy makers they are representing. Their activities are regulated by the law and some rather strict regulations–tightened since the concerns over insider dealing in New York, London and Tokyo. In the UK, these include the various Companies Acts, the Stock Exchange regulations and the takeover and corporate governance codes. The company will be judged by its performance ... and much of the appraisal of this performance will result from the accuracy, candour, timeliness, integrity and overall quality of the information being issued.

Appointing a public relations adviser

When making a public relations appointment to handle these areas the board will have to structure the adviser's role so that he or she can be on the inside, involved in policy and properly briefed, ahead of the game.

This puts a substantial responsibility on the adviser's shoulders, and explains why timid people do not survive in what can sometimes suddenly become a fierce world where much depends on the effectiveness of both the advice and the implementation. In a takeover battle, as in any battle, there are no prizes for coming second!

Of course, companies that have their shares listed on stock exchanges have legal obligations covering the information about their performance that they must issue to shareholders. This includes the announcement of results– usually preliminary, interim and year-end. The publication of the annual report and the AGM (at which shareholders and their advisers are briefed on and can ask questions about the performance of their company) can also be significant in the financial calendar.

Notice of the announcement of results is usually issued in advance. The timing and control of the information is particularly important and the public relations executive will normally be handling the advance notice to the appropriate stock exchange, preparation of news releases, briefing relevant journalists, planning meetings with analysts, and attending any press conferences or individual interviews that might be judged appropriate.

There are also regulations relating to the issuing of information that could have an effect on the share price, such as new issues, board changes, disclosures, changes in holdings, acquisitions, significant investments or disinvestments, major product or corporate developments, mergers and other takeover activities.

A market in securities which works efficiently is necessary for the confidence of both the investors and the companies whose shares are being traded.

The responsibility of a stock exchange is not just to regulate the buying and selling of shares but to ensure that the prices of transactions are based upon reliable information and that shares are made available at the same time to everyone involved. Clearly, the information issued by the companies is an essential part of this communications process.

Project consistent messages

Other communications relevant to the commercial performance of the organization must present consistent and effective messages. For example, information and literature that might be particularly important would include the annual report, trading summaries, background briefing documents on markets and products, bid defence documents, major speeches by senior executives, parliamentary evidence and summaries for special audiences such as employees, customers, suppliers and so on.

Corporate advertising can be an effective public relations tool and a powerful method of putting controlled messages in front of broad audiences quickly and efficiently. However, it can be costly and does not involve the two-way communications element of, say, discussions and presentations; nor does it have the third party credibility of media comments. But, with the size of audience involved today in some financial communications situations, it can be effective to back up other activities.

In recent years, television joined the press as a medium and a broader range of advertisers are involved, including flotation candidates, banks, insurance companies, building societies and other financial service groups. Some of this advertising is not presenting financial information but is corporate in nature, projecting the strength of the organization; equally, some of this advertising appears to be selling financial services but is really designed to do a corporate job on behalf of the advertiser—all financial advisers are also personal buyers of financial services. However, advertising has often been used as a technique to inform shareholders about developments in, say, takeover battles, though its effectiveness needs to be carefully considered in these circumstances—any hint of 'panic communications' (interpreted by investors as a belated effort to cover a perceived previous lack of communications) could well be counter-productive.

Plan for all contingencies

Planning for financial crises, such as an unwanted takeover bid, should be considered alongside other crisis planning activities, even if different communications specialists would be involved. The whole of the company issue planning strategy should be coordinated: a manufacturing disaster, for example, could affect employees, investors and customers.

In some companies, financial public relations may be linked to parliamentary relations. As an illustration, there could be a parliamentary dimension to such eventualities as a bid which may need to be referred to the Monopolies Commission, significant redundancies, the exposure of international trading barriers, the opening of new international markets and developments in relationships with those government departments that may be customers of major corporations.

Professional investment specialists are still influenced by attitudes; effective communications will not counter any evidence that they judge professionally, but *can* add an extra element. This might enable a company's shares to stand out from the thousands of others currently quoted on the UK's stock exchanges.

Build loyalty: you may need it

Until the 1980s, some public companies only recognized the importance of the loyalty of their shareholders when they were threatened by a takeover. In the past, it was not unusual to find that the public company did not even have a complete record of its shareholders and so was unable to communicate with them directly and promptly.

No share register will ever be fully up to date, though modern technology brings this possibility closer. The publicly quoted company will also have a complete current list of all advisers who might influence investment. Occasions may arise during the year when the company will wish to issue information directly to them. This must be done with discrimination. Investment professionals tend to view with suspicion any apparent extravagance, such as glossy brochures and unnecessary reports on company progress. The simplest guideline is to issue only information that is helpful to their professional decision-making; for example, if there were a significant change in the company's market, the organization might have undertaken research indicating why they should be making a particular investment. This analysis may well be of some interest; but a corporate brochure on a new expensive house style may not.

Financial advisers have to be very concerned about the loyalty that needs to be shown to the shareholders—who are able to withdraw their money at a moment's notice. As a general rule, it is safer to assume that there is *no* automatic shareholder loyalty and that investors invest only for the return they receive. Therefore, if a company wants to be able to carry its shareholders through difficulties, then it needs to communicate consistently with them over a period of time. It is of limited value taking emergency whole-page advertisements to try to establish some rapport with the shareholders. Of course, if the speed of developments requires a very prompt response, then such a technique can be used to convey information, but it must be no substitute for regular communications: certainly such actions do not always generate goodwill. Some research even suggests that such actions undermine existing confidence and support.

MAKE PERSONAL MEETINGS YOUR FIRST CHOICE
City support is essential at all times but particularly, for example, when a rights issue is planned or a new acquisition or market development is being negotiated.

There can be no substitute for face-to-face meetings to help strengthen the credibility of the company. Many companies with strong relations in the City ensure that their chairman, chief executive and finance director hold occasional but regular meetings with advisers in City circles. Care needs to be taken to ensure that selective information is not being given in advance to some shareholders. The wisest course is to hold such meetings to explain the background to published information, available to all shareholders—taking care not to introduce new information. Directors needing to be clearer on these points should read the report on corporate governance.

The City columns of the national and provincial press and key trade publications provide an important source of information for people making investment decisions. In dealing with the media, it is essential that the person publicizing your public relations develops a reputation for accuracy, speed and honesty in all press statements. Any blurring of the truth, evasion, exaggeration or inaccuracy will damage the practitioner's reputation.

News stories need to be sharp and short. It is essential that, in addition to the name of the public relations executive responsible for the story, the company director to whom the media can talk is also included. Preferably this should be the chief executive.

ESTABLISH RELATIONS WITH COMMENTATORS
Individual meetings with City journalists (not necessarily editors) and the chief executive are not normally as necessary as some chairmen feel. These are really only productive when there is a major story that can be discussed at the meeting. This might provide an exclusive article relating to the growth of the

company. Alternatively, an informal press lunch might provide an equally valuable opportunity to brief an individual editor on the background to an expansion into a new market.

Very few City journalists are likely to look in much depth at most listed companies, except at the times of the announcement of the interim and final results, acquisition activity and possibly the publishing of the annual report.

The AGM is usually of limited media interest unless the chairman is making an updated statement on performance or some extraordinary activity is expected from shareholders. Briefings for investment advisers can include some background on the company, its development, its attitude towards the market, future potential, investment policies and expansion plans. It would be normal for these to be presented by the chairman or managing director. For convenience, many of these are held over lunch, but a good lunch should never be a substitute for a good presentation.

Briefing meetings can be particularly important for companies with provincial headquarters, who might not have quite such regular access to City advisers.

The annual report
Obviously, one of the most important influences on the attitudes of both the investing community and wider corporate audiences towards the company will be the annual report. The figures are always the most important part. The emphasis should be on the clarity in presentation of the information.

The chairman's report should be crisp and factual and should not contain over-optimistic language or industry jargon. Pictures of the directors should be treated with care to avoid the suspicion that the annual report is being used as an ego vehicle! Of course, investors want to see what the custodians of their money look like, but there are both imaginative and dull ways to show them. In one sample of annual reports, GEC just used a picture of one director (chairman, Lord Prior); Whitbread used small action shots of the senior people plus a quote relevant to their direct responsibilities (with, interestingly, all employees at all levels identified by name in the captions to pictures); and Grant Thornton used informal action pictures of the directors at work.

More and more companies who are considered leaders in this field are improving the quality of presentation of the annual report and accounts. However, it is no coincidence that these companies also concentrate as much attention on the depth and clarity of the factual information. They do not make the mistake of substituting an attractive overview of the company for a concise analysis of the company's performance; such an analysis can be helpful as it will generally go beyond the statutory information requirements.

Corporate messages must be credible

Some specific activities may be undertaken to project the corporate personality of the organization. These will be important for quoted companies as they can have an influence upon the investor market and, therefore, its financial performance.

Such corporate activities may be of even greater importance to non-quoted companies who do not have the analysts, City commentators and financial media to discuss and project their trading record and financial performance.

There are two aspects of a corporate relations programme for the non-quoted company. First, all activities and visible aspects of the company must be planned to ensure that they project the corporate messages. As a simple example, whatever Roadline's corporate policy may be it has to remember that a very large number of opinion leaders travelling the roads of the country will be influenced (positively or negatively) by their fleet of vehicles. Should someone propose that an attractive trading tag-line might be 'Your Friendly Freighter', then, equally, someone had better be sure that the drivers support this concept and that the company is employing neither policies to force drivers to cut corners to meet schedules nor employment procedures that produce an exemplary collection of roadhogs.

The second key factor is to consider whether specific 'umbrella' activities might be considered to project corporate messages across the broadest range of audiences possible. Should this be the case, then sponsorships, community relations programmes, corporate advertising, business in the community style initiatives, educational support and/or other activities might be considered. Any such scheme that is proposed should be tested against the corporate objectives. Ideally, activities can be planned that have a corporate support role yet also back up marketing and employee relations at the same time.

In practice, effective corporate relations can have a measurable effect on reputation. People relate to people and the links between corporate and community affairs can be particularly valuable in projecting the human face of the organization. Major construction company, John Laing plc, believes its own policies in this area have made a significant contribution to enhancing the company's reputation. As John Farrow, group director with specific responsibilities for community affairs, advises: 'Actions speak louder than words in the field of public relations. In developing a lively community affairs policy, we are able to demonstrate that we care about people and the environments in which they live and work.'

SETTING CRITERIA FOR SPONSORSHIP

Agreeing a policy to link sponsorship, community and charitable involvement within the corporate framework

Some method of evaluating such activity against a corporate communications strategy is helpful. The following—which was prepared by the company's public relations manager, with the advice of an outside consultant, to a brief from the company's marketing director—is an example of a first draft strategy document created for board discussion by a major international insurance broker, in advance of undertaking a number of successful sponsorship activities; it ties community and charitable support into one coherent whole. As this is a confidential strategy approach, the directors have asked the company not to be identified, so for the purposes of this case study we shall call them InsurCo.

The development of a corporate sponsorship policy for InsurCo, with recommendations on community involvement and charitable donations

Background

InsurCo is a new kind of insurance broker with the aim of solving the most demanding risk management issues of specific businesses and industries across the globe. To achieve this, it needs to create an environment of understanding and support across a broad range of audiences critical to its success. A range of communications and marketing techniques are likely to be used in an integrated and seamless matrix. The aim? To create among those publics with whom InsurCo is in partnership—clients, industry bodies, professional advisers, legislators, neighbours, employees—the feeling that 'I know InsurCo, I have heard of the company, I understand what it does, it has a good reputation and seems to be the kind of company worth dealing with/working for/recommending/buying from/talking to', and so on.

Quite a challenge. Sponsorship has been part of the communications mix in the past. Has it worked? Does it have a role for the future? What could we learn from our experiences? What could we build on from the successes? These are among the questions that need to be addressed.

Investigation

Central elements in the investigation were a series of interviews with senior members of the management team to identify their views, not so much on what has been done but on the role that sponsorship might play in the future.

Individual views are not being reflected in this document, for a consensus largely evolved. Where this was not the case, these notes make this clear.

Other sources of information included records of activity, reports on previous company participations and experience from other companies.

The need for policies

Sponsorship can be expensive. It can create positive or negative perceptions. Many companies undertake activities that reduce their commercial effectiveness. Some do not exercise tight control and so expend an immeasurable amount of money and effort that is directed through divisional resources and budgets.

It would help everyone in InsurCo making policy decisions to have some central policy and guidelines. This would keep expenditure and the direction of activities under control.

It would allow some process for the evaluation of proposals and of activity undertaken, as well as measuring effectiveness and, therefore, decisions for the future.

The principles

Sponsorship should never be undertaken because it is a good thing to do; because of the competition; or because of a particular interest in the activity. It must be undertaken to a defined strategy and this document sets the first approach towards such policies.

Elements

There are a number of elements to consider:

- the potential to create awareness
- the opportunities for exposure of the name or identity
- the 'associations' that surround the event or activity
- the relevance to the target audiences
- the entertainment provisions (at different levels)
- the logistics involved in organization
- the history or track record of the activity

- the solus or cooperative sponsorship proposal
- the calibre and capabilities of partners or organizers
- the media interest and publicity opportunities
- the direct costs of the sponsorship
- the exploitation costs of the activity
- the incidental costs, including executive time
- the cost-effectiveness comparison across opportunities.

Each of these is discussed in outline and the consensus view of executives noted, where appropriate. These are shown after each of the following brief comments *in italics*. Such comments will lead us towards our strategy. Note that none of these is a literal quote but all are amalgams of views expressed.

Awareness

Often a central consideration in a sponsorship opportunity will be the likely awareness that can be created for the name or identity of the sponsor. This is not the same as the publicity. Awareness should be related to the audiences of importance to the sponsor. An event may create the maximum awareness among six key people with no publicity.

Also, awareness may not be enough alone. When Gillette originally sponsored cricket, awareness was very high; however, a significant proportion of the public surveyed thought that Gillette was some long-forgotten cricketer like W.G. Grace! Therefore, the branding of a sponsorship is an important factor, as Gillette demonstrated when they increased their profile and improved guidelines on using the logo in association with this sponsorship.

The general view among InsurCo directors was that a good level of awareness needed to be a factor when considering a candidate activity. This needs to be aimed at industry and specifier levels but not at public levels.

Name exposure

A consideration will be how effectively the name can be exposed. A 2-inch logo on a racing car or a badge on the driver's overalls may equate to no exposure. In contrast, the Round the World Race seems incomplete without Whitbread in the title. Or, from the same stable, the Stella Artois Tennis Tournament or, from another sector, the Booker Prize for Literature. But what about the Milk Cup or the GM Vauxhall Conference? Do we need Everest to complete the title the Horse of the Year Show?

Any event that we support must be clearly seen as an InsurCo activity, that belongs to us and cannot be referred to properly without our name.

Activity associations

The activity itself sends out messages and can be surrounded by an environment that may be positive, negative or neutral. Speedway and dog racing are downmarket. Horse racing can be down- or upmarket, depending on the event, course and level at which it is supported. Betting shops are down and Ascot is up though, to some, over the top. Wimbledon is classy but classless, though Henley is establishment.

A county clay pigeon championship can be very upmarket, but discreet at the same time. Banger racing would be cheap and nasty. Or would it? Suppose it were a community effort supported by government to get energetic car-mad young people off the streets? ... and so on.

We only want to be associated with activities that reflect that InsurCo is professional, well-organized, responsible and a leader in a sector that makes a major contribution to economic and business prosperity.

Relevance to audience

A hypothetical illustration: why support three-day horse trials if you are selling double glazing to people in terraced houses and research confirms that they see the sport as being for the privileged with too much time and money? What *we* enjoy is not the test. Who are we trying to reach and what is of interest to *them*?

We are targeting decision makers at middle and senior levels, plus opinion formers such as key editors.

Candidate activities are broad, including golf, major spectator sports events, theatre, the visual arts, or business education/training with a relevance to the insurance and financial services sector.

Entertainment

Some activities (sporting events, for example) may give exposure and entertainment opportunities. The Whitbread race gives some limited entertainment opportunities (the start and the stopover points, plus an awards dinner) but this is clearly secondary. Grand prix racing, Wimbledon and Henley can give good entertainment opportunities without any need for sponsorship.

Opportunities for focused, limited scale entertainment in groups of 12 to

20, possibly as part of a major event. During work hours without partners but with business angle or social with partners on evenings or weekends.

Organizational logistics

There are plus and minus factors in being responsible for organizing an event. The pluses are control, quality, exploitation, 'ownership' and strong company association. The minuses are cost, diversion of management, need for special expertise. Hanging the name on an existing event is the alternative, with the opposite plus and minus factors.

No strong views were expressed on this, other than InsurCo is an insurance broker not an event organizer so non-InsurCo personnel with the right expertise will be needed to handle logistics if it is to be a newly created activity.

Track record of event

Sometimes a new event or activity can create considerable news interest. Equally, a well-established event may have had all the wrinkles smoothed out. Certainly, it is easier to assess the likely response and results from an event that has a track record and has had to deliver in the past.

If we decide to be associated with an existing event it can only be one that has an impeccable record, with organizers prepared to consider our own views and input. We expect to see a defined return from participating.

Solus sponsorship

The supporting company can take the sole sponsorship role or the primary role. For example, Players may sponsor the Lotus Formula One team but involve many secondary sponsors all of whom want action and response in return for their contribution. This can cause conflict but does reduce the cost to the primary sponsor.

InsurCo should be the sole sponsor of an event designed to generate better awareness and to influence business contacts and prospects. This need not be the case for entertainment opportunities.

Capabilities of partners

The professional capability of the organizers of the event or activity can have a major influence on the results. Their efficiency might need to be balanced against possible resistance to new ideas: 'We've been doing it this way for X years', etc.

We would only want to work with a credible organization which would not involve us in logistical problems and would deliver the performance promised.

No strong views on this other than those above.

Media potential

The news interest in activities can be because they are in the calendar and generate stories (Wimbledon, say) or because they are unusual (The National Chess Championship). The former type of event has stronger staying power and stability. The latter may be relevant if an area exists that could be of public interest with the right promotion (basketball, say).

News coverage of the event would be useful, but is not the central criteria; media entertainment opportunities might be valuable. No one wants to be associated with an event that may be newsy but is not worth while.

Potential cost

- The sponsorship price and package
- Exploitation costs
- Incidental costs

The true cost of any sponsorship will include the up-front asking price, plus the costs of generating the maximum benefit plus the indirect costs that arise from local budgets, company personnel costs, travel, executive expenses and time. All of these should be included in the calculation of the real cost. Similarly, in the calculation of the potential budget, the corporate and divisional monies that are currently being (or have recently been) spent should be totalled.

Views on group expenditure of the right activity ranged from £1 million per annum to zero. All were agreed that discretionary divisional spending was more significant than might appear and this needed some control.

Cost-effectiveness

No sponsorship should be undertaken simply because it is the 'thing to do' or makes us feel good—though both may be valuable side-benefits. The activity should be undertaken to support corporate strategy, to specific objectives—ideally measurable—to an agreed budget. The success in putting those messages in front of that agreed audience should also be measured at the end to appraise the cost-effectiveness.

Some recent activities may have generated a significant audience and positive media coverage, but are not so appropriate today to reach the key decision makers. Criteria for effectiveness need to be established.

CHARITABLE DONATIONS

Observations

It is clear from discussions and our limited investigations (supported by all senior executives interviewed) that the company is involved in contributing to many charitable organizations and 'good causes'. This represents both enthusiasm and a keenness to support activities that are viewed as being appropriate by the individual managers. However, it will be difficult to be precise about how much the company is donating in total and it seems likely that the goodwill is being dissipated through spreading support thinly and/or not getting recognition for this effort.

To help to develop a policy, it might be helpful to look at some of the observations that arose in discussion.

The reasons for charitable donations

It must be recognized that not all donations are to official charities. It is likely that some are not only to good causes that are not organized as charities but may not even be strictly organized as official bodies. This does not mean that such donations are wrong but it is worth recognizing this point.

Let us consider some of the reasons why a company might make small-scale charitable donations.

1. *It is the 'right thing to do'*
Does a company have a moral responsibility to distribute largesse? It could be argued, almost in some biblical sense, that the company has, and 'sections' of the community have not and the wealth should be redistributed. However, the biblical comparison is not helpful. An individual may give in a saintly way until he or she has nothing. A company cannot do that because it would cease operating, throwing countless people, directly and indirectly employed, out of work. Equally, if the company is not making profits, is it excused from donating some of this 'negative' surplus? Should an organization be filling gaps left by the government, society and the voluntary sector?

On balance, most people would agree that the company has a commercial, operational and ethical responsibility towards its customers, employees and shareholders and trading partners—though some argue about the order in which these groups should be. If it behaves properly with respect for its neighbours and the community within which it operates, and pays its taxes, then it can be argued that the contribution that it is making to the economic well-being of the community through its activities is the end of its moral responsibility.

2. *Goodwill can be generated towards the company through supporting the right causes*
In a recent survey, some 70 per cent of business and financial journalists agreed that they felt better disposed towards an organization that has an active role within the communities in which it works. Such an active role is open to many definitions. However, charitable and good cause donations could be part of a corporate community involvement.

However, it is difficult to measure the goodwill that is generated by such activities. Indeed, in some cases—often unknown to the company—minimal goodwill may be generated and, on occasion, this may even become ill-will. For example, a local cause feels it needs £200 to achieve something and is offered £100. This can look very petty from a multi-billion pound operation. Equally, some causes may not gain support of management and, therefore, achieve no support. Others may win some support but are viewed as being less deserving in the eyes of the community. Clearly, this is a minefield and some policy needs to be agreed.

3. *Employees will feel better disposed towards the company*
It is possible that some employees who are successful in their appeals will achieve an enhanced status in the eyes of their colleagues within the good cause they are supporting. For the reasons discussed above, this is not guaranteed. They may go back to a committee meeting which has expected them to raise £200 and say they only managed to raise £100. However, this supposed benefit needs to be looked at carefully. All employees will have their own social or community interests for which they might be most encouraged if the company were to donate, say, £1000. Should the company donate £1000 per employee to the good cause of each employee's choice? Clearly not, but it would be a policy. However, more seriously, it does give us some guidance towards agreeing a policy.

Some possible guidelines

To develop a policy that can be agreed at a senior level within InsurCo, it might be useful to feed back some of the broad observations made by the executives that we interviewed.

If the company were to be involved in formal charitable/good cause donations, then these might be orientated towards organizations that have:

- a formal, established structure;
- either local branches of registered charities or organized groups;
- educational and training bodies, particularly those focused on the less-advantaged;
- some direct relationship to the communities within which InsurCo works;
- some direct connection with active and enthusiastic employees within InsurCo.

From this can be drawn the basis of a policy that would include all donations through the approved group.

COMMUNITY INVOLVEMENT

Coordination

Elements of community involvement are of a charitable nature and should therefore be closely coordinated, possibly by an umbrella policy which links charitable contributions and community activities.

Definition of the community

All seem united that the only community that would be of real relevance would be that within which InsurCo works. There is no support for the concept that a major company has to fill a gap that is left in community welfare by the government.

There was mixed response to the suggestion that companies have community responsibilities. On balance, there was little strong opposition to some modest level of support and there was some marginal positive feeling towards community activities that directly have a relevance to InsurCo and could be seen to be of goodwill benefit.

Even within this framework, what constituted the InsurCo community was not universally agreed. The four areas that were accepted were:

- the financial services industry;
- the City (and particularly the insurance sector);
- communities within which employees live;
- communities within which InsurCo has significant operations, notably London.

The financial services sector is probably better covered through the company's normal public relations activities, particularly media relations.

The insurance community within the City clearly has some relevance but this might also be better covered through proposed sponsorship activities.

It was generally agreed that the communities in which employees lived were too diverse and any activity orientated to those areas would be spread very thinly and would generate minimal benefit.

The community within which InsurCo operates was considered relevant, although there were mixed feelings over the benefits of a commercial, entrepreneurial group financially supporting a local mixed community largely run by those with left-wing sympathies. At worst, such contributions may be greeted with hostility and generate ill-will and, at best, some thought, support might be seen to be cynical or patronizing. Any backing for community involvement must be handled with great sensitivity.

Candidate activities

Those activities that involved personal and human response were largely felt to be the most sincere and beneficial. Some of these require management time but no cost. Examples that might be supported included:

- *Facility visits*—Schools and colleges that wish to see how a large company worked might be allowed to make suitable visits.
- *Careers' talks*—Community groups that ask for an executive of InsurCo to talk to them can be assisted. Speakers could be provided on a wide range of topics but those targeted at young people/school leavers would probably be most appropriate, particularly careers guidance.
- *Reciprocal support*—In contrast, should InsurCo ever be looking for volunteers or special assistance, then consideration would be given to local community groups. This might include buying paintings for offices from the local art college, allowing charity collectors, local artists to use the foyer under strictly controlled conditions.

Above all, those activities targeted at young people and with a focus on careers, particularly in insurance, would always take priority.

SOME PROVISIONAL CRITERIA

Community support

1. Local communities where major facilities are sited would be preferred.
2. Activities which focus on young people and their careers will be a priority.
3. Financial contributions alone will not be supported where there might be an alternative source.
4. Specific activities preferred, not those where the InsurCo contribution is but part of 'something in the hat'.
5. Activities where there is a personnel link with the company would be top priority.
6. Support 'in kind' would be considered, subject to the above criteria. No effort to be considered in isolation but all eligible for support to be related to charitable donations and sponsorship to ensure the selection of the most appropriate.

Charitable contributions

1. Criteria broadly as with community involvement.
2. Clearance of all projects through a suitable committee.
3. One major goodwill cause to be supported each year—possibly by a ballot of employees.
4. Additional budget for smaller discretionary contributions, also to be approved by the committee. Such small donations not to exceed a nominal figure to be agreed, say, £250.
5. Budget for major activity and discretionary grants to be decided by management committee.
6. Annual report on activity to be prepared by chairman of the review committee for discussion by management board.

Some observations, in summary

1 The company reputation, according to research and common observation, is significantly shaped by corporate communications.
2 Good products and reliable customer service have proved to be factors in building a good reputation ...
3 ... while a good reputation is an important element in shareholder loyalty, as people like to invest in companies of which they can be proud.
4 However important investor relations may be, it should always be considered as part—often a significant central part—of corporate relations.

5 In fact, consider the corporate public relations as the umbrella for all company communications, working to harmonious objectives.

6 The chairman and board carry the ultimate responsibility for company performance, delivering the excellence of communications to project this.

7 The directors must spell out and control what is said in the company name, and policy must be checked and approved at board level.

8 Make sure that the communications process is sensitive to the needs of each of the stakeholder groups and monitors their approval of corporate actions.

9 Corporate governance demands an intelligent two-way communications process, understood and supported by each director.

10 The recent guidelines also make clear the importance of feedback so that shareholders can advise the board of areas of concern.

11 It is also clear that corporate responsibilities mean that the chairman is the guardian of the character and conduct of the company.

12 Be sure to include the identified opinion leaders from each sector in the audiences addressed by corporate communications.

13 A particularly influential group will be your own top managers who need and deserve special treatment to weld them into a powerful team.

14 Issue all briefing materials to this group and consider a regular presentation on the corporate position by the chief executive.

15 Each different corporate audience needs special information but make sure this is against the backdrop of the overall company position.

16 Do not allow financial communications to overshadow the many other important areas of communication with other company audiences.

17 In all activities make sure that the capabilities of your management—preferably a team of managers—are being forcefully presented.

18 Build shareholder interest and loyalty through consistent and relevant communications rather than panic efforts when you need their support.

19 Focus investor briefings around face-to-face presentations, using members of the board and top management, to demonstrate team strengths.

20 Make the annual report the keystone document that identifies, in the style you can control, everything that you believe the company represents.

10

Issues and crises

Plan issues management to be your reputation insurance

Plan to protect your reputation

The corporate reputation is an asset that should be treated like any other. Indeed, much of this book is focused on matters of expanding and developing the reputation. However, it is important to consider methods of protecting the reputation when things go wrong–a form of reputation insurance.

Many companies (but by no means all) have crisis plans which are intended to protect their reputation should an emergency arise. Unfortunately, this is an area of public relations that is still developing and there are too many lightweight concepts whose proponents are over-claiming for the benefits that will derive from their particular philosophies.

The argument is roughly as follows: You can pollute half of Berkshire, poison most of the residents of Guildford, turn the hair green of those who use your product and kill half your workforce without much damage to your reputation, as long as you follow the advice in this reassuringly expensive 3-ring crisis plan binder. This tells you that someone senior must turn up at the scene of the incident, look sympathetic and good on camera, and make the right soothing, apologetic noises.

The reality is that companies should be planning not to have 'incidents'. To that extent, this matter is much bigger than public relations.

LOOK AT ISSUES BEFORE PLANNING FOR CRISES
As argued elsewhere in this book, management should take one step back

from contingency planning or crisis management. The board should have a clear view of all likely and unlikely issues that could be facing the company and its markets over, say, the next five years.

Some argue that if public relations disciplines are being properly implemented it may well be one of the more effective methods for getting all levels of management to take these responsibilities seriously. If your public relations professional is monitoring all issues, he or she will also be presenting an analysis of the risks that can result. Line managers who would rather cross their fingers and think that the unthinkable may not happen, may be galvanized into preventive action!

All members of the senior management team should participate in this issues audit which can be undertaken by in-house or external personnel. There are very sound arguments why this should be run by the public relations discipline. Members of this team have no specific line responsibility or concern; they should be tuned into the marketplace; they will have a clear view of the broad range of perceptions of the key audiences upon which the organization depends for its success; and, above all, they should have independence of all vested interests.

My own experience with issues audits is that most of the issues that demand attention are well known within the company. It only requires candid, confidential interviews with key line managers and directors to identify all of those that need to be considered. It can be helpful to talk to external bodies such as trade and professional groups, associations, government departments and so on, to get their perspectives; clearly, most companies know their own business so these bodies rarely identify practices that are not well known within some department or division of the company.

CIRCULATE THE ISSUES INDEX FOR COMMENT

A document circulated among top managers which identifies all these issues and the possible impacts upon the company is an effective starting point at which to begin managing activities within this environment of issues.

Clearly, the company has to have a stance towards each of these issues, some of which it will be able to control and some of which will be external. As a simple example, a company manufacturing small domestic appliances may see public concern about packaging and be encouraged to shift from plastics to recyclable paper or card-based alternatives. The company may decide to go with this trend or to evaluate alternatives that are currently not recyclable. Many plastics are environmentally more friendly than their supposed recyclable paper and cardboard alternatives.

One US electrical equipment manufacturer has taken to packing all products shipped to store in non-food-grade popcorn. It is a superb alternative to polystyrene beads, is cheaper when produced in quantity and has at least as good an ability to absorb shocks as the plastic material that it replaces. After use, this 'packaging' can be fed to chickens, pigs or even pets. Alternatively, it can simply be composted.

In this example, the company clearly has a high level of control over the stance it wishes to take towards these issues and the routes that it might consider following.

However, it may have little or no influence over moves towards legislation suggesting bubble insulation for small domestic appliances and the elimination of the earth cord. Other safety standards, service back-up, replacement and guaranteed policies may also be affected by legislation.

Appraising the issues for potential opportunities

An intelligent issues-appraisal procedure in operation at Heatrae-Sadia enabled the company to identify a trend likely to evolve towards longer guarantees on electrical appliances. The company scored a marketing first and scooped a major share of the market for its electric showers and heaters by being first with a two-year guarantee instead of the traditional one-year period.

External legislation may be a factor over which the company has little control. However, by auditing issues alternative approaches to each can be developed and, from this, might spring a crisis management plan to deal with contingencies or emergencies that might arise. Clearly, such procedures should be run in parallel by management efforts to minimize the possibility of such contingencies.

An effective public relations operation can play a key role in keeping line managers on their toes and, to some extent, acting as devil's advocate. To take an example, consider Townsend Thoresen and the disaster that struck it when one of its ferries put to sea with bow doors opened and nearly 300 people were drowned in the ensuing sinking of the vessel. The crisis management was appalling, but even if it had been brilliant it would not have brought back any of those victims. However, if an issues management system had been in operation, perhaps the hazards associated with a procedure that allowed (indeed, encouraged) ships to sail with bow doors open might have been treated more seriously.

How could a non-technical public relations person prevent a marine tragedy that could not be prevented by the marine specialist? Quite simply. Marine specialists knew the hazards but had failed to get the board to override the commercial pressure to turn the ships round quickly. Commercial needs took precedence over safety and, indeed, the decent values by which a company should be run. The public relations adviser has no line loyalties, no concern about seniority, no axe to grind.

The adviser should be responsible to the chief executive (or equivalent) and this means advising him or her of any company practice that could be damaging to the company's reputation. If the adviser had been running an issues management programme, then all the senior directors and managers would have been interviewed regularly to identify anything on the horizon that might have an impact upon the company and any practices, trading activities, competitive influences that could similarly affect the corporate position.

It was clear from the inquest and the inquiry on the Townsend Thoresen disaster that many senior managers within the company were extremely concerned about the conflicting pressures on turning ships round quickly in harbour and maintaining the highest safety standards. It is not unreasonable to believe that a strong public relations professional with the backing of management to take responsibility for issues management would have become aware of this. The chief executive would have been asked to give this important area immediate attention.

The process that is sometimes called a 'reputation risk management' is close in many ways to the idea of issues management. Reputation risk management is sometimes defined as the discipline designed to protect the reputation against threats. In other words, packaging trends and public concerns may be issues over which the manufacturer could have a good degree of influence. Industry legislation and competitive activity may be issues where it has not.

To take one of these as an example, the traditional metal electric kettle market was wiped out almost overnight by the introduction of a new product design—the plastic jug-type kettle. Manufacturers even with dominant positions in secure markets need to be constantly looking at everything that could endanger their position.

Preparing for possible crises

A sensitive monitoring system is absolutely essential for an effective crisis management programme. The media information network is likely to be at least as effective as the company's and quite likely to be last to react. Remember, too, that some threats to the reputation may begin quite modestly.

South West Water first became aware of a major incident when they began receiving complaints from their water customers. At first, it did not seem too serious. Eventually, and after a long lapse of time, they were aware that a chemical supplies company had delivered a load of aluminium sulphate used in water processing; the unaccompanied driver had dumped this in the wrong tank, and it went straight into the water supply with potentially disastrous results.

There was a lead time of several days between the incident occurring, the company acknowledging responsibility and identifying precisely what had happened. For at least part of that time, it seems likely that members of the team dealing with the incident were aware that it was far more serious than they were admitting. This was an extremely dangerous period as such misleading information is certain to be identified at a later stage in any inquiry.

APOLOGIZE PROMPTLY, WHEN APPROPRIATE

One difficulty in such situations is that it can take time to establish the facts ... and when the media spotlight may be glaring on an organization time is not in plentiful supply.

Understandably, there is a strong instinct to play for safety. Indeed, some legal and insurance advisers would prefer the company to say nothing. Any comment, they argue, can have an effect on any future legal claims or court actions should negligence or misdemeanours be suspected. Yet, to offer no comment can destroy a company's reputation by making management look indifferent to the hazard or actual harm that might be created by an incident.

If the company reputation is to be protected, early and sensitive comments are essential. Remember the concept of the corporate personality. Would an individual retain much respect if no comment was offered on a tragedy that he or she was involved in and may have been responsible for?

From his own experience, Sir Jeremy Morse, banker and past chairman of the Institute of Bankers, contends that apologies are an important part of public relations for large organizations.

He recommends prompt apologies for particular errors and omissions. However, the company needs a policy issue on what to do when things go wrong in a bigger way—accidents, catastrophes, and major management failures. Such cases are complex and there is a natural temptation to hide behind the complexities while sorting out the problem. But, in fact, he maintains, it almost always pays to issue an early apology: something major has gone wrong; we don't know all that is involved; we shall sort it out as quickly as we can; meanwhile, we apologize to those affected, etc.

This may lead to the organization being blamed for matters that turn out to have been someone else's fault.

Nevertheless, there are two central reasons why this is usually the right course. First, externally, the public respect an apology freely given rather than one that comes after a considerable period of stonewalling. Second, internally, an early apology frees managers to sort out the problems far more effectively than if they are still maintaining an outward front that nothing is wrong.

An effective procedure planned in advance is essential to minimize damage. It can even pay dividends. Black & Decker produced a substandard product, yet the company's prompt and open handling of complaints actually saw sales increase for the replacement model.

Similarly, Heatrae-Sadia, mentioned earlier, recalled a potentially lethal electric shower with such efficiency, candour and speed that not a single negative news report appeared. Indeed, public recognition of the company's caring stance saw sales rise to cover what might have been the crippling cost of the no-quibble recall and rectification process that had been set up within 24 hours.

Establishing a crisis management team

The company needs to form a crisis management team. Ideally, this will be composed of a number of individuals, all of whom will have been trained and know how to work together. The company will need more personnel allocated to this team than are actually necessary. Some are certain to be away, ill or on holiday.

Equally, there needs to be more than one leader of this team to cover such an eventuality. The crisis management team should encompass a range of skills other than communications. These might include senior executives from within sales, marketing, customer care, operations, personnel or industrial relations. Ideally, these should be personnel at the most senior level. The advantage of having such a mixed team is that they bring a range of expertise and improve the chances of various aspects of any crisis being well covered. Each member of the team needs an understudy.

ESTABLISHING INCIDENT ROOMS AT EACH LOCATION

An incident room should be established at every company location. Quite often this will double as some other function room, such as a reception, canteen, briefing or interview room. However, it is helpful if it is equipped to deal with the emergency—for example, a locked cupboard containing all essential items.

Note that each location may need more than one incident room as these can be closed off or inaccessible when the incident is, for example, a fire or an explosion.

ESTABLISHING A TRAINING AND POLICY MANUAL

The issues management team will develop a crisis manual. This is a practical document full of essential information, not only to help the team in handling the incident but in providing background material that can be issued to deal with enquiries. Copies of this manual need to be available at every incident location and it is particularly useful if this can be in electronic form on computer so that high-speed print-outs of background to various products, situation, safety records and other items can be available instantly.

The 3-ring crisis handling plan—which details exactly what should be done in each incident and is often prepared by specialists with minimal company input—is extremely unlikely to be used and will sit on the shelf gathering dust. A document that has helpful and immediate information is much more useful.

Copies must be kept by all members of the crisis team both in their offices and at their homes. Members of this flying squad are also advised to hold in constant readiness a packed bag with any emergency items that may be necessary, such as a change of clothing, portable telephone, spare batteries, the crisis manual, a company telephone list, a key media list, direct telephone lines, television and video recorder with blank tapes, computer terminals with modems, action check lists and so on.

In dealing with a major incident, your company spokespeople will need to be able to handle the media effectively. In many cases, the media will be aware of the incident before the company. The most credible company spokesperson will always be the most senior. There are some basic guidelines that should be considered when dealing with journalists in an incident situation.

- Ensure that spokespeople are fully trained.
- Give the media the fullest information possible. Even if you do not have full details of the incident, useful background on the company, its record and trading activities will be helpful to journalists.
- Establish a media relations strategy as early as possible and ensure that all are fully briefed on it.
- Make sure that everybody is as helpful as they can possibly be with the media, dealing with all questions they can cover and logging those they are unable to answer so that they can be called back.
- Get on top of the situation early and maintain control. Decide the agenda and manage the media information to that.
- Use pre-prepared information. With television journalists it is extremely useful to have available maps, plans and aerial photographs of all locations so that they can be used with a spokesperson to discuss the incident, where it has happened.
- Honour all commitments to the media. If information will not be available for half an hour, then make sure that it is and that it is disseminated to those who have asked for it.

- Get the information out as quickly as you can, even if this means supplying it part by part.
- Ensure that you are disseminating information through other channels of communication—telephone and fax should not be forgotten—so that other audiences such as employees are not totally reliant on the media for their understanding of what is happening.

Making personnel aware of their responsibilities

As noted earlier, Townsend Thoresen suffered a tragedy that should have been anticipated. The public fury over the hopelessly inadequate response ensured that its name could never be used again. The press office was not manned at the time of the tragedy and it took the company precious time to respond. The news was instant. It was on our radio and televisions while company officials tried to gather a response team. When they did, it was not impressive.

Television showed us press officers handling distraught public enquiries, writing phone numbers in the margins of newspapers. The chairman eventually arrived at the scene, back from holiday. In one of those horrific examples of misjudgement, he was interviewed wearing a shockingly inappropriate straw summer hat.

The death of the passengers through maritime malpractice was a shock. The way the management seemed to have prepared for the possibility of an accident was unforgivable. And they were not forgiven.

Could they expect anything better from a real tragedy? The company responsibility is clearly to minimize risk, hopefully to the point of eliminating it. But any company running ships, coaches, buses, trains or planes would be considered recklessly casual if it were revealed that it had no adequate plans to handle a major incident. Even if it were not the company's fault, lives could be threatened through terrorism, sabotage or suicide.

Yet when a British Midland plane crashed on a motorway killing many passengers, the speed and sensitivity with which the company reacted brought out the maximum public sympathy at that awful time. The chairman was on the scene in less than an hour, personally directing a well-drilled contingency team. As well as assisting the emergency services, he talked openly to the media so that anxious members of the public could be as fully informed as possible. The support operations behind the scenes were equally as efficient. British Midland was able to recover and is, today, one of the leading and most respected independent airlines of Europe.

The emergency role of senior personnel

When the *Exxon Valdez* split open in Alaska, spilling millions of gallons of oil, senior executives were slow to visit the scene until forced by public pressure. Some 30 000 customers sent back their company charge cards in disgust. The reputation damage to the company was enormous; the financial damage incalculable.

Perhaps the best-known crisis management programme that recovered a frightening situation was the one that Johnson & Johnson undertook following the malicious poisoning of their Tylenol product. This had been the best-selling analgesic, contaminated by someone with an irrational grudge; at the time of the crisis, a survey confirmed that 94 per cent of consumers were aware that Tylenol was associated with the cyanide poisonings.

The details of this horrific incident have been well reported elsewhere, but it is useful to note that the strategy Johnson & Johnson adopted involved a total recall and a new product relaunch. This recaptured its market share and, eventually, additional sales because of the goodwill generated towards the company. It was a clear example of turning a potential disaster into an opportunity. Clearly, in this case, the company was not negligent or at fault in causing the original problem, which was the work of a deranged blackmailer.

This illustrates the more important point that the public do not automatically approach every company problem with a negative perception. Their opinions and attitudes are very much shaped by the response of the company. Johnson & Johnson wasted little time in recalling millions of bottles of its Tylenol capsules, and spent half a million dollars warning physicians, hospitals and distributors of the possible dangers. As the *Wall Street Journal* said at the time, 'The company chose to take a large loss rather than expose anyone to further risk.'

The company adopted a worst-case approach to the problem and insisted on a total recall even though the original problem was only in the Chicago area; the testing of all recalled products actually confirmed that only 75 of some 8 million tablets were contaminated, and these were all found in one batch.

Perhaps one of the keys to the prompt and responsible approach adopted by Johnson & Johnson was that the company had a well-published credo, which identified its primary responsibility as being towards its customers. A company may safeguard its reputation by writing a policy that will help employees make decisions.

One visible action that the public can note and respond to is the seniority of the managers allocated to deal with crisis. A criticism of the Exxon company was that top executives did not immediately respond and it was some considerable time before anyone in authority actually arrived at the scene of the *Valdez* disaster in Alaska.

In contrast, Warren Anderson, chairman of Union Carbide, immediately flew to Bhopal when his Indian subsidiary suffered an unimaginable manufacturing accident. This produced a poisonous gas cloud which, in one night, had killed 1200 people—and the death toll was rising hour by hour. He knew he risked almost certain arrest and an obviously hostile reception but believed that it was his responsibility.

He defied the advice of some legal colleagues to accept responsibility and expressed both regret and concern. This established Union Carbide, equally, as the victim of this tragic disaster. It also positioned the company as the leader in establishing what went wrong and what needed to be done to rectify the tragedy that had been created.

Union Carbide may have mismanaged some aspects of the tragedy, but they did have the sense to respond promptly, calling a press conference at their head office on the very first day. This contrasted with, say, the Firestone Tyre & Rubber Company officials who claimed that nothing was wrong when Firestone 500 tyres first began disintegrating.

The speed of the media

It is important to remember the speed of response of the media. Journalists can often be the first to be aware of many incidents—sometimes even ahead of management. The news about the Flixborough chemical factory explosion was around the world in minutes because a radio journalist happened to be cycling near the plant.

When the Gulf tanker, *Betelguese*, unloading at Bantree Bay, caught fire and exploded at 1.00 a.m. on a January night some years ago, a senior journalist from the *Irish Times* was actually watching the shipping in the bay through his binoculars from his holiday cottage. The ship literally blew up before his eyes. News of the disaster was being flashed around the world on the wire services within ten minutes of its occurrence. It was over an hour before the public relations people were advised.

What starts as a small story can also become a very big story, even if no direct single tragedy, accident or incident is involved.

Subjective comment can cause irreparable damage

Lever Brothers had enjoyed a high-profile multi-media launch of its advanced detergent, New System Persil automatic washing powder. A report by the National Eczema Society throwing doubts on the product, quoted in *The Guardian*, was the start of a major problem. This was picked up by the *Sunday Mirror*, later the *Daily Mirror* and virtually all the national UK publications. Market share collapsed.

It is important that the management should remember that many new products will have potentially critical audiences. Some journalists are also interested in manufacturers' problem stories.

In the case of the Persil powder, research eventually undertaken suggested that only 1 in 10 000 people might have had a dermatological reaction related to its use. However, that was too late and the damage had been done. Better warnings on the packet and more detailed explanation over its enzyme base might have prevented the problem in the first instance. This proved to be a case where an issue audit before the launch might have identified the risk—it would certainly have prepared the company to deal more promptly with a problem before it could cause such damage.

The original and potentially world-beating sweetener to replace sugar (but with none of the disadvantages of saccharine) was cyclamate. Its credibility was severely undermined by an extremely negative report from a small US research institute which linked the product with claimed carcinogenic properties found in tests it had undertaken.

This led to massive media exposure of the supposed risks. These reports took the company by surprise and it was very slow in response, but the damage was so severe that the product was withdrawn. Eventually, some serious reservations about the research were recorded but, by then, it was too late.

The makers of aspartame—perhaps most famously known under the Searle brand name NeutraSweet—were much more careful in the preparation of the market. The information they produced for journalists and other commentators minimized the possibility of any such damaging and possibly irresponsible reports. It has swept on to become a billion-dollar seller with minimal negative comment.

Check procedures with realistic tests

An emergency exercise is an excellent way to test the procedures. A simulated emergency will be agreed among a very small group of people—the smaller the better. To make this an effective test, other members of the emergency and crisis teams must be able to react in exactly the way they would with the real thing.

The testing will be a good way of evaluating how effective training has been. No set of procedures can work perfectly and any test will identify a number of areas that, hopefully, will only need slight adjustment but, occasionally, may need major reorganization.

Head of Public Relations for British Airways, Peter Jones, has had considerable experience of developing and running crisis management systems. On a number of occasions—sometimes the real thing and sometimes tests—he has been able to check out practice against theory. One critical factor, he believes, is that you must contain and separate the incident. The rest of the business has to continue or you will have no business.

From his experience, you might only use 50 per cent of whatever the crisis manual says, but you will never be able to tell in advance what that 50 per cent may be. However, the one constant factor is that the speed of modern media gives you an absolute maximum of 60 minutes to get the incident communications under control. Broadcasters can be on air in seconds and on many occasions they may be the first on the scene. The tone of those early broadcasts can set the tone for the whole incident.

While the natural focus is on external communications, it is critical not to forget to keep your own personnel and your business partners fully informed. For example, if a plane is involved in an incident and your counter staff are not briefed, then they cannot adequately deal with the naturally concerned enquiries of other passengers. 'Believe me,' adds Jones. '*I don't know equals I don't care.*'

COMMUNICATE SIMULTANEOUSLY TO ALL AUDIENCES

Managers need the ability to see the crisis from the public perspective. For Rhone-Poulenc's biggest facility in the UK, we helped run an exercise to test emergency procedures. The aim was to check communications alongside essential rescue and containment operations. The company had simulated an explosion on site in which a number of people had been severely 'injured' and perhaps some may even have 'died'. The test allowed company personnel to identify any weaknesses, sharpen their skills and check coordination with emergency services. It ran well and identified some areas where improvements could be made to minimize problems should, heaven forbid, the real thing happen.

The senior site manager was an example of command and authority as the unnerving 'incident' unfolded. Just one factor caught him by surprise. He had dealt very effectively with a 'local radio reporter'—in actuality a member of my staff—who had grilled him on the incident. He had forgotten that such comments could be broadcast locally within minutes—indeed, factory neighbours might have heard or seen a real explosion. He was very disturbed when the next telephone call was from a tearful and very worried local neighbour, convinced that her husband, who was working on that shift, had been killed.

The management, in dealing with the accident and emergency services, had remembered their responsibilities to the media but had forgotten that telephone lines would be instantly jammed with calls from anxious friends and relatives. Emergency procedures were adjusted in this and other areas as a result of this experience. Although the woman calling was only a member of the consultancy team, the adrenalin had been running so high that the plant manager was genuinely shocked by the thought that in reality this could be the widow of someone on his staff who had been killed.

On another occasion, during a similar test, the consultant posed as an aggressive television reporter and grilled a hapless employee of a leading distributor of hazardous materials at its Thameside plant. He challenged the executive over the hazards of the butane stored at one of their facilities. He bullied the man into admitting that he lived 20 miles away and that he was glad that 'I'm not a factory neighbour, because my family would never feel safe.'

An executive from the nuclear-waste reprocessing plant in Sellafield, Cumbria, casually commented after a leak of radioactive vapour: 'This sort of thing happens every day in industry.'

An official in the steel industry protested about what he felt to be unfair reporting of a fatal accident with the comment: 'Our industry is improving standards all the time. We have only killed four people this year.' No doubt comforting news for the widows but not very impressive to those who are not thinking in statistics but in human terms.

The moral is to think about what you are proposing to say. Run through it. Review your plans and, above all, test any procedure—for every incident has the potential to create new problems and from these come the lessons that bring constant improvement.

TESTING THE EMERGENCY MEDIA PROCEDURES

Make sure all are briefed and supportive to ensure positive results

Whitbread, the major UK food, drinks and leisure group, has an effective and well-tested crisis plan. It has helped the company through a number of situations that could have been damaging to its reputation. Usually everything runs smoothly, but not always—and it is the odd hiccup that comes from running the procedure that helps keep everyone on their toes and sort out such wrinkles.

Marketing director, Stephen Philpott, recounts a crisis well-handled with only positive media coverage, but it could have been otherwise.

The company markets Heineken beers in the UK. During one normal business day, he received a call from the company in Amsterdam. This advised him that around 240 000 bottles of Heineken Export that Whitbread had sold in the UK might contain tiny glass particles. They had to run an instant product recall.

The crisis came in the middle of a holiday period, as might be expected, when news was quiet; the recall attracted more news interest than it might have done at a busy time. The company was pressed from all quarters for interviews. The public relations professionals of Heineken and Whitbread agreed that Philpott should calm concerns by undertaking a series of interviews. Most ran as planned, including the main BBC news at 9 o'clock, News at Ten, and most of the nationals.

GMTV were keen for a special piece to run in their national morning news programme and a late-night situation was planned. Philpott and his public relations adviser would meet the television crew and interviewer at around 11.30 p.m. to carry out an interview at one of the Thresher wine merchant shops in central London. All arrangements were made with the manager, but when they arrived the shop was closed and no one was to be seen!

After a couple of telephone calls, they found that the manager had received counter-instructions from his area manager who had instructed him not to get involved. The Whitbread team were unable to find anyone at that time of night with the authority to persuade the shop manager to go against his boss's instructions.

By now the interviewer was getting impatient, the crew tired and irritable. The potential for disaster was considerable; the interviewer could have commented that he and his crew were denied access to the shop to film the potentially hazardous product. Philpott could have been filmed regardless in circumstances that were far from ideal.

Happily, while the options were being discussed, an enterprising colleague negotiated the use of a nearby office. Due to the openness of the Whitbread team, the interviewer was level-headed and accepted the situation in good humour. The result was a fine and fair interview.

Stephen Philpott's advice after the experience is to check and double check every detail. Anticipate everything that could go wrong and have an alternative available. As Philpott ruefully adds, one other lesson from this incident is that all personnel attending any such crisis situation or interview now carry with them all necessary personnel and emergency telephone numbers.

Some observations, in summary

1 If it helps to persuade colleagues to make the commitment, consider your crisis plan as part of your reputation insurance.

2 Be cautious in appraising the potential contribution of recommendations as there is considerable over-claiming for some simple solutions.

3 The best crisis plan when running any organization is to run it in such a way that you do not have damaging incidents.

4 Before planning any crisis or contingency plan, sit back and analyse all the issues that could affect the organization's reputation or trading.

5 Brief your public relations personnel to prepare the issues audit or, if necessary, acquire experts to help them.

6 The senior executive allocated to pilot this project through the company must have direct and easy access to the chief executive or chairman.

7 The first step in any issues audit is to start with interviews internally, as most potential issues will be known to specialists within the company.

8 Next, look at external audiences—an independent view is one good reason why public relations people may be best suited to manage this project.

9 Before making judgements on issues, produce an index of these for circulation and comment within the company.

10 Following such comments, develop a corporate stance on each issue, involving input from your specialists but endorsed from the top.

11 Remember that competitors may review issues which are to your advantage (positive), to your disadvantage (negative), or neutral.

12 An intelligent issues audit will not only solve potential problems, it will identify many new business and market opportunities.

13 Your crisis plan should spring out of the issues audit, reflecting the mission statement or the corporate objectives relating to its key audiences.

14 This plan will cover more than communications—it will need to involve safety, marketing, human resources, personnel and other disciplines.

15 The final plan will have to be signed off by the chief executive or chairman after discussion, amendment and a formal presentation to the board.

16 Concentrate on the principles and not the terminology—for example, this issues/crisis planning is sometimes called reputation risk management.

17 The central element in the plan, if it is to be of practical use, will be the early warning system that monitors issues and identifies potential crises.

18 Agree with your legal and insurance specialists the stance that you will adopt should a crisis arise. Never play down your position for legal safety.

19 Apologies and expressions of regret can generate understanding, and can ease the pressure on executives trying to find out exactly what happened.

20 Intelligently phrased, such apologies do not need to be an admission of liability.

21 Parallel with the development of the plan, establish teams to handle such crises and ensure that they have the essential range of skills.

22 Create an appropriate incident room at each location, plus a spare one on a different part of the site in case an incident should make the first room inaccessible.

23 Ensure that these rooms have the necessary facilities that, at a moment's notice, can be brought into operation for the team dealing with the crisis.

24 Train your flying squad; make sure there are back-up personnel for each member; and that all are equipped and prepared to depart at a moment's notice, with bags packed, passports ready and so on.

25 Ensure that the crisis plan tightly integrates the communications, human resources, marketing and safety disciplines.

26 All personnel on the crisis team need appropriate media training, plus familiarity with the basic company information for use in interviews.

27 All line management (to a level to be agreed) need training in crisis handling so that an incident is not vested in the hands of a few specialists.

28 Remember that many personnel such as security guards, lorry drivers, secretaries, and telephonists may be involved and need briefing.

29 All personnel need to know how to behave, the extent of their authority, the lines of communication and their responsibilities.

30 Prepare standard company information on such areas as products, manufacturing processes, safety records, shipping, distribution procedures and so on.

31 Ensure that this information is available in hard copy and, above all, electronic form at each of the incident rooms.

32 Any PCs or word processors used must have the appropriate modems so that they can be electronically connected across the company network.

33 Do not rely on public communications but ensure that the team is equipped with portable telephones, shortwave radios, transmitters, portable satellite dishes, as may be appropriate.

34 Ensure that all communications is targeted at all audiences and not just at the media, with appropriate contact lines or enquiry personnel.

35 Above all, run regular tests, checking safety response and media handling; consider using your public relations people as hostile journalists.

36 Set up debriefing meetings with all members of the team to improve procedures; invite the emergency services to attend and comment.

11

Personal skills

Develop your own expertise to communicate effectively

Establish honest media relations

The chairman, chief executive and other senior directors use professionals to help plan and run communications programmes; but they will need personal skills if they wish to lead from the front. In this chapter we are looking at business communications skills rather than interpersonal capabilities, though they do share some elements in common.

Just as the chief executive is really the chief financial officer, he or she is also the chief public relations officer for the organization. The chief executive may delegate the day-to-day management to a professional or may ask for professional advice, but he or she must ultimately take personal responsibility for the effectiveness of communications and, therefore, the management of the company's reputation.

When researching this book, I asked Margaret Thatcher's media chief, Sir Bernard Ingham, for his views on the basics that are essential if communications is to work effectively. His suggestions are directed mainly at the public relations adviser but they apply equally to the director who wants to understand the key factors in managing the company spokesperson or for those occasions when the role must be taken personally.

From his many years in the hot seat in Number 10 (and more recently as a consultant), Ingham confirms there are six essential criteria for establishing good media and public relations. The executive responsible for public relations must:

1 secure top management's endorsement and support for a positive communications policy;
2 know the facts and their implications, the organization's policy and the mind of its boss, and have the status to contribute to the formulation of policy, taking necessary initiatives;
3 have a positive, active approach to communications rather than a reactive one; public relations is intended to be building bridges not defensive barriers;
4 be able to communicate complex material in simple relevant and everyday terms, with the authority to translate jargon;
5 be continuously available both in good times and bad; running to earth when the press pack is in full cry does not help the hunted or end the chase;
6 never lie or deliberately mislead, as bridges to the media and public collapse under the weight of deception.

Hopefully, not too many readers will be running to earth with the press pack in full cry on their heels, but, as Ingham adds, this positive proactive approach is the only sound basis for successfully managing an organization's reputation.

Conveying the key message

The spokesperson needs these personal characteristics to represent the organization properly, but *information* is also needed to convey the message: company plans and aims, the state of the market, competition, audience perceptions and public expectations, for example. And, as Sir Bernard rightly insists, the message will become confused unless it can be communicated in simple terms.

One central point in preparing much material for business communications is the need to eliminate anything peripheral and to get briskly to the message. For example, at a seminar or a staff briefing, the message has to be in the first sentence. If it is not, the audience will listen impatiently and hypothesize on what the key message will be. Fairly soon, they will get bored or irritated and you will have lost them.

Some research suggests that a speaker has as few as six seconds to capture an audience. Even being generous, you will have no more than half a minute to get them interested before irritation sets in.

A press interviewer may accept just a little of the preliminaries, but a radio or television interview cannot waste a second. You need to develop the skill of condensing complex arguments into simple points that retain the essential truth, without distortion.

Always tell the truth

Indeed, there is a very considerable skill involved in living by the truth. While it is true that fabrications require much greater powers of memory, it is also true that the truth imposes its own burden.

In business there are constant pressures to bend, fudge or obscure reality. The lawyers may tell you that too much candour might strengthen legal claims against the company. The insurers might urge you away from anything specific to avoid compromising the policy. The marketeers sometimes insist that too much information will erode the competitive edge. The financiers can detail the City regulations and conventions that inhibit openness. Even those lovers of truth and transparency, the public relations advisers, may occasionally press upon you the wisdom of the truth, nothing but the truth, but not necessarily the whole truth.

But all this advice creates considerable problems. The director who says nothing may not be lying, but could later be accused of negligence for not having said what needed to be said—being economical with the truth, as they say.

Yet again, the truth, the whole truth and nothing but the truth could leave the company without any customers, investors or employees. How do you strike a balance?

The answer is not to view this as a moral problem but simply as a practical one. There can be no arguments over the morality. It has to be truth, nothing but the truth and (as close as humanly possible to) the whole truth, as may be appropriate at the time. Where secrecy or confidentiality dictate, it is often the best policy to make it quite clear that there are elements that cannot be disclosed, and explain the reasons.

ALWAYS QUESTION AND TEST ADVICE

There is another matter that complicates these decisions. Sometimes, advisers advise as if the organization were working in a vacuum and it has total control over all decisions that it makes. For example, your marketing professionals may ask you not to announce the major export order that the company has just won; there might be a second one in the pipeline and they don't want to alert the competition to this opportunity. It sounds logical and sensible but, in reality, it is a totally flawed argument. The organization placing the order with you may be quite pleased about it and may have its own reasons for wanting to talk—officially or unofficially.

Other business people involved may see aspects of the deal and may talk about it within your industry, which might include shippers, handling agents, secretaries, telex and fax operators, insurers, bankers and countless others. They may also discuss it with friends in the media.

There is another weakness in this argument: it makes the assumption that you only obtained this order because your competitors were not aware of the opportunity.

It is very probable that any intelligent buyer placing a major order will be as aware of the competitive position as you are. After all, it is in his or her interest to obtain quotes from as many competitive sources as possible. Therefore, there is a strong possibility that the competition are already aware of this potential business. Even if they were not, the winning and delivery of such a major order is bound to come to their attention sooner or later if they are the sort of competition you ought to fear. And if they are not the sort of competition you ought to fear, why all the secrecy?

EARLY COMMENTS CAN WIN MAXIMUM ATTENTION
The truth is that when you make the announcement you win bonus news points in the media, with your employees, with government, with suppliers and business partners, with your shareholders and with everyone else who is interested in your success. On the other hand, hold the news until it has become common knowledge and you not only lose these opportunities, but you run the risk of irritating people who wonder why they were not properly informed.

Try ringing a trade journalist about an order you should have mentioned three months previously and you might receive a very chilly 'I heard about that ages ago from your competition; it is a pity that you didn't tell us at the time you signed the deal because we could have given you the front page plus a 24-page supplement on that!'

TACKLE BAD NEWS AS VIGOROUSLY AS GOOD
As good news is best divulged early and honestly, this is even more important with bad news.

Your legal advisers may ask you to say nothing about the accident in which a number of workers were injured. Any apology might be interpreted as an admission of guilt and this could be used in the action they could take for damages against the company.

What heartless, pathetic nonsense. If you are not sorry for injuring someone you employ, then you should not be employing people. Whether the accident was due to some fault on the part of the company, some negligence, or simply the inattention or carelessness of the person concerned, the company still carries some responsibility. If the company is proved to be at fault, you want to make recompense voluntarily, speedily and vigorously and not rely on the pressures that might be produced through the legal system—with all the negative associations that that will create of a company that neglects its responsibilities and has to be forced to behave decently.

You will want the legal advisers to check over the statement, but never allow them to prevent you from making any comment.

Listen before speaking

If you have been successful in your career, you have had to be decisive. Perhaps, on occasions, you have had to make a decision before you were fully comfortable and certain that you had all the facts. The risks from delay had probably reached the point where they would soon exceed the risks from some small element of misinformation.

But are you sure you are always told what you need to know? The decisive leader is often not the one that colleagues want to risk challenging with a contrary view. In all areas of business, listening is important but in communications it is vital.

I was once asked to organize some key media interviews for Howard Schultz, a distinguished US management adviser who has been interviewed around the world countless times. I would rather upset my client than have him make a fool of himself through not being properly briefed. (I was not always so bold and made many painful mistakes through temerity, as reported elsewhere in this book.)

On this occasion, I decided I would explain the whole principle of media interviews, on the basis that UK media may be somewhat different from those in the USA. (Of course they are not in any significant way that would affect the advice.)

After a polite start, I was a little surprised to see him begin to take notes. 'Fascinating,' he said later. 'Very helpful.' It turned out that he had never had the opportunity to discuss the basics and some of the points were new to him. All the other advisers with whom he had worked must have made the same mistake that I nearly did.

The point of the story is not to make assumptions. At the very least, test them. You need to know the other person's point of view. After all, you learn nothing when you are talking, only when you are listening.

Test your conversational investigative skills

Try the club test. Next time you are in relaxed circumstances with a few friends raise an interesting topic. If possible, select something you do not normally discuss, say, the influence of television upon social behaviour.

The opening stages of the conversation will probably fall into a pattern of which there are only the two main versions: you will start with a statement or with a question. Either way, the intention will be very similar. Usually, you want to gain some idea of the other people's points of view on the topic. This could be either because you have no views or because you have strong views.

If you have no views, it may be that you want to know if they have ideas that might be of interest. Or you may feel not very well informed about the subject and wish to test whether they have better knowledge.

If you have strong views, then you may want to test if they agree with your views or not. If they agree, then you can discuss the various points of the issue. If they disagree, then you can have a lively debate challenging each other's views, gathering up evidence and clarifying your thinking.

If their arguments are not as good as yours, you may try to persuade them and enjoy that satisfaction. If their arguments are better than yours, you may be persuaded or, at least, may modify your own perspective.

Try it. You may find that you do something instinctively in social conversation that we sometimes completely omit in similar situations in our businesses. That is the fundamental fact-finding phase that should always come before the development of a point of view or case. There are few conversational debates that do not feature one of these approaches at the key start point.

You say, 'I think that violence on television is having a terrible effect on the behaviour of young people,' and you pause to see whether your friends will agree or disagree with this assertive statement. You will then adjust your comments accordingly.

Alternatively, you may say, 'Do you think there is any link between violence on television and the behaviour of young people?' You will wait to see whether they agree with the implication within the question, or not, and adjust the rest of the conversation accordingly.

Whether you want to know what the others think because it will affect how you think, or whether you want to know what they think so that you can adjust the argument to have the most influence over their thinking, you are undertaking fundamental research.

Practise and extend your media skills

This book cannot cover the detail of how to prepare, write and issue news: there are many excellent publications on that subject. But these can be useful skills for any director, not only as insurance for the occasion when he or she might be thrust into the limelight but also as a positive attribute that can help to project the company and its values.

The simplest guidance for dealing with the media is to treat all journalists as you would like to be treated. To do this, you need to imagine yourself as a journalist. If you believe that journalism is an interesting, worthwhile and professional function, then you will have no problems. If, on the other hand, you would have rather been born Stalin than a journalist, then think about this.

Many people derive great satisfaction from criticizing the media. This is particularly true when the media attack our own organization or something that we hold dear. But remember that, in a democratic society, journalists are often the only independent group employed to expose lies, fraud, deceit and dishonesty. They may all get it wrong sometimes—or some of them may get it wrong sometimes—but on balance they do a very effective job in helping to protect freedom, truth and integrity within our society.

It might be superficially attractive to wish, say, *The Sun* to disappear, but who is to decide which media should be allowed to survive and what they should be allowed to cover? Censorship is still censorship even if it is intended to be benign, and history tells us that an imposed will (such as some form of benign censorship) soon ceases to be benign if it is unaccountable. In other words if you want a free media then you have to accept the simplification of issues by the *Daily Mirror*, the excesses of *The Star* and the lunacies of *The Sport*.

If you favour some form of control over what the media might publish, perhaps through some independent body, then which side might they have backed when Distillers resolutely, consistently and vigorously resisted media claims that there might be harmful side-effects to Thalidomide?

The role of the journalist is clear. *A journalist has to produce news that is of interest to readers, listeners and viewers.* If industry gets bad media, then perhaps it's because industry is not particularly effective at putting over its case.

UNDERSTANDING THE JOB OF THE JOURNALIST

If you want the best possible and fairest reporting of your company then it is essential you treat journalists as if you understand the job they have to do—and not only understand it, but support it and try to assist.

Obviously, you are aiming to build a good reputation among the public but you must start by building a good reputation among the media. You need to be respected for the speed and efficiency of your approach, the integrity of your information, the candour of your answers to questions, the access that you allow to facilities and personnel and, above all, the equal vigour with which you tackle bad news and good news.

Every company has its disappointments as well as its successes and nothing impresses a journalist more than a chief executive who is candid about the problems. It is simple psychology. If the chief executive can be open and honest about bad news, then perhaps the journalist can have a little more trust in the good news he or she is given at other times. With journalists, respect is like love: give a little and you get a lot in return. Certainly, it is very short-sighted to irritate a journalist.

I knew a managing director of a leisure company who hated the media. After the inevitable row he would have with each journalist that his benighted press officer lined up for him, he used to triumph, 'Sorted him out. Won that argument.'

But, as the equally inevitable ensuing coverage demonstrated, he lost every row—at least in the eyes of the readers, who were the only ones who counted.

As entrepreneurial film-maker David Puttnam comments, remembering his own occasional combats with journalists, 'I have always shared Oscar Wilde's view that a man cannot be too careful in the choice of his enemies.'

Look for programme opportunities for your organization

The ability of radio and television to reach an audience can be appreciated from the cost of the advertising! Advertisers spend this sort of money because of the audience it delivers, the attention it achieves and, most important, the results it produces. Yet both radio and television are available media for good editorial ideas: too few of these come through business channels. 'Any Questions' and 'Question Time' both have difficulty in finding enough business people with views and the ability to express them directly.

The effective public relations adviser working on behalf of the company will be creating broadcast news opportunities, and it is necessary to know how to handle a radio or television journalist when approached to provide information or facilities. As you may be the object of the story or the subject of the interview, it is wise to understand the fundamentals.

- Determine the programme that is to contain this item.
- Will it be live or taped?
- Will the contribution be edited?
- Who else will be appearing?
- Who will conduct the interview or discussion?
- What topics or questions will be covered?
- Will there be an opportunity to see/hear the final programme before transmission?
- Will there be a live debate to counter any misunderstandings or damaging assertions from other participants?

A contribution that is to be edited will give the person being interviewed a little more time, even an opportunity to correct any blunders. Also, the interview can often be arranged at a more convenient time—even in your own office—thus avoiding an inconvenient journey to the studio.

However, it must be remembered that you do not control the editing. Maybe the answer when you got it wrong, or the embarrassing mistake, will make better television. Have you never seen an interview and wondered why on earth such an experienced person said such a thing? Maybe the interview was run for 20 or 30 minutes to get the key 30 seconds they really wanted.

Can you be confident that they might not leave out the response where you explained the errors in all their 'facts'? Also, will your comfortable office be an ideal setting when the interviewer starts asking about your third world markets or possible redundancies?

It may not happen to you, but why take the chance? Live appearances are nearly always preferable to recordings, believes Sir Anthony Cleaver, chairman of IBM UK. While apparently more demanding, you have an equal chance with the interviewer. He also adds the practical recommendation that you should always have in mind the three key points you wish to convey. Make sure you express them regardless of the questions asked.

Sir Anthony remembers being interviewed on a number of occasions on an agreed topic, when the discussion suddenly moved into an unexpected area. In a pre-recorded interview, this shift can be edited out making the interviewee sound hesitant and lacking confidence. However, in the live interview, the viewer or listener can appreciate the sudden change. With experience, you can deal with these firmly and take them in your stride, winning the support of the audience.

'Always go for the live opportunity' is sound advice that I would totally endorse. I would also add that you should start with the point you wish to leave with the listener or viewer. It will give the interview punch and guarantees that whatever else may happen, you have at least stated your most important point.

Sam Whitbread, director of Whitbread and past chairman, adds two simple rules, well worth following, that he has followed from his earliest days in business. He remembers being given instructions he did not understand because his boss had forgotten the young man's inexperience. *Hear what you say through your listeners' ears. See what you write through your readers' eyes.*

Consider the journalist's point of view

Journalists are people. They are moved and motivated by the same things that move and motivate all of us. They respond well to being treated properly; they like being treated with consideration; and they do not expect to be fawned over.

You do not need to be a personal friend of a journalist before he or she will write a fair story. Even if you are a personal friend, he or she would be a fairly useless journalist if you did not get a bad press when you deserved it.

There is no great need to wine and dine a journalist—though many people make this a hobby. On the other hand, it helps if you are on passable terms and, if the way to discuss business in a busy day is over lunch or dinner, then so be it. However, never organize a lunch just to get to know a journalist; if you waste that person's time, he or she may never want to know you. It is perfectly acceptable to set up such a meeting if you have one or, better still, two or three good stories to discuss.

Good stories are not what your public relations department or consultancy issued as a news release the previous week. Good stories are items that the journalist may not be able to obtain from other sources—early warnings or items in more detail, those that may have a personal slant or give some background of which the journalist will be unaware.

Keep any off-the-record comments to an absolute minimum. Once a year may be excessive! Remember that 'who gossips with you, will gossip about you'. If you can avoid keeping something 'off the record' it will be a great advantage, as the chances of being misunderstood will be minimized. In other words, assume that everything you say is intended to be used by the journalist. This means that you must be particularly careful with those things that you might say after a few glasses of wine.

Never use phrases such as: 'You can quote me on this.' They are pretentious, corny and the sure sign of an amateur. Leave the journalist to decide what is to be quoted, as he or she is expecting to be able to quote you on everything. Most things said after such a phrase are usually utterly uninteresting, such as, 'We are the fourteenth largest manufacturer of widgets in Western Europe.'

Michael Grade, chief executive of Channel Four, is one of those rare media entrepreneurs who is also as adept when he is the subject of the news—as he has often been in his career. He has summarized a few rules of his own that he has learned over the years:

- Never complain to journalists who criticize you. Never thank them if they are complimentary—just be accessible and friendly at all times.
- Never, never lie to a journalist, any journalist. Always remember that journalists have a job to do—try to help them to do it.
- Always correct factual errors, either by seeking a right to reply or by letter for publication, or with a personal note direct to the journalist concerned.
- Much public relations is about perception. If the perception of your company, or you, is just plain wrong, you have to take a long-term view

about correcting it. It could take years to turn attitudes around—you have to keep plugging away with your own message, over and over again.

- Oh, and remember, journalists are no different from you and me—they can't keep secrets either.

DEVELOP ANGLES RELEVANT TO THE JOURNALIST

Is your news something you would want to and expect to read in the publication you are briefing? *Plastics and Rubber Weekly* may be more interested in your widgets than 'Panorama'. If your topic is neither newsworthy nor directly relevant to the readers (or listeners or viewers) then why are you briefing the journalist? Is it hopelessly inappropriate or can it be developed to be appropriate?

Your plant extension being opened by your local paper may not even be of interest to the local newspaper. However, a thousand new jobs may be of relevance to a far wider range of media. Ten new jobs in a new sector or against a background of redundancy may be news. An opening by the 100-year-old retired pensioner may be of genuine human interest. An opening by the world's most famous talking parrot may be mildly amusing, but may be seen as a gimmick and may not generate a positive reaction.

Many companies get themselves into a mess by trying to focus on creating positive media coverage for those things that they consider to be interesting. They lose sight of—or do not even consider—what may be interesting to the journalist. What interests the journalist? What interests the public for whom the journalist is writing? The journalist is a hero if the 'scoop' proves to be correct; but out of a job if it's wrong!

When it comes to comparing what the organization feels and what the journalist feels, then it is a million to one that the journalist is likely to have a better idea of what is of news interest than the organization's chief executive. The key question a business manager should ask is: If I were a journalist, would I consider this of news interest to my readers/viewers/listeners?

It must be a weak approach to attempt to create good news when it suits the interests of the organization. The wiser position is to make public relations a permanent, continuous, strategic part of business management. In other words, your organization should make serious efforts to build relations with key audiences (including the intermediaries, such as the media and analysts) that encourages them to talk with knowledge about your operations, and to see your organization as a source of useful, authoritative information.

If you do this, you will not only gain much respect but any bad news will seem a lot better when you are obviously trying to help rather than conceal.

The managing director of Laurence Scott (at that time the UK's largest manufacturer of electric motors) once asked his public relations adviser to minimize the possible negative local media coverage following a most horrific accident. A crane operator had swivelled his unit, touched overhead power lines and had been electrocuted. The inquest established that to do this he had removed an important safety lock but, none the less, he had been a company employee, and was now dead, with a widow and young children. The company remained technically guilty of the offence.

The chief asked his young public relations adviser to talk to the editor of the local newspaper about the report that was due to be published on the accident and to get the story into perspective; as he explained, the company had a good safety record with very few serious accidents.

Nervously (and regrettably), the public relations officer duly spoke to the newspaper; the editor had missed the fact that an inquest had taken place and thanked him for that information. The editor then ran a major story, highly critical of the company, drawing attention to many other accidents the company had sustained across various plants. (That foolish public relations person was, in fact, myself!)

What I should have done (but experience and courage failed me) was to have convinced the managing director that, together, we should draft our own news story. This would have spelled out all the facts, our apologies and the actions that we had put in hand to prevent the occurrence of any similar accidents—as well as steps we had taken to ameliorate the tragic circumstances of the widow and the children.

It would still have been a big story but at least it would have been more sensitively handled. The company would not have seemed so callous, or manipulative, trying to use its public relations people to suppress the publication of a story that was genuinely in the best public interest.

The moral of the story is: think twice before trying to do deals with the media. Is it worth it? Why bother? Be tested by standards you can support.

I learned from that experience a lesson that public relations people only need to learn once. If you know something is not right, then you can be certain it is not in the best interests of your company or client, and your only duty is to say so.

Learn some practical media skills

Commercial media exist to provide news that is of interest to their readers, viewers or listeners. This simple statement of fact should be obvious, but it means that any company spokesperson must be ruthless in the application of critical standards to the preparation and issue of news material.

Some journalists seem to believe that a news sense is a very rare quality. In truth it is largely common sense. Bad news is not the only news; however, it is the exceptional that is the definition of news. If one taxi driver sets fire to his or her vehicle, then that is news; the fact that several thousand others do not, is of no consequence. The first naked football fan running onto the pitch may be news, but the 500th will not. There are two main reasons why bad news gets better coverage: first, it is more exceptional (murder, hijack and fraud are not yet the norm); second, people experience morbid curiosity in disaster and tragedy, perhaps because of the relief that they are not the victims.

Companies can use this 'new is news' factor to their own advantage. The first woman to chair a public company may be news. The first major contract for the sale of an unlikely consumer product (such as electric kettles) to Tibet is news. A survey showing that the average man has three (or 30!) pairs of underpants is news. A 63-year-old cleaner being invited to open a new high-technology laboratory is news. The winner of a travel scholarship who has never been abroad is news. The invention of a safety device by an apprentice is news. The invitation of all company pensioners to the launch of a new product is news.

It only takes observation of how the media work to recognize that central to any effective media relations campaign must be a hard core of news. And it is perfectly legitimate to create news. If it is new, has never been done before, is interesting and relevant ... it could be news.

Obviously, what is news in an engineering publication may not be news in the parish magazine. What is news for a local radio station may not be suitable for national television news. Let us look at some practical guidelines. You may not use them as often as your public relations advisers but, even so, it helps to understand the principles.

NEWS RELEASES

You should only issue news to those journals that will have a direct interest, unless you want to damage your media reputation. Do not scatter stories to all. Always provide a contact name and telephone number. Be certain that the telephone is properly manned, 24 hours a day, 365 days a year.

It takes many years of training and experience to be able to present information in the concise and direct style necessary for news releases to be used by editors. A basic writing ability is essential. But, with care and practice, an average writer can be developed into a good news writer. There are some guidelines that may be helpful:

1 Develop your writing skill. Draft, redraft, edit, polish and perfect the copy. Read publications and understand what makes news and how it is put together. Analyse the writing skills of good journalists. Understand the good; criticize the bad.

2 Always ask who, what, why, where and when and be sure that these questions are answered in every news story. Train yourself to eliminate as ruthlessly as you add. If material does not answer one of these questions, what is it doing in your story?

3 Write stories to suit the style of the publication. If, for practical reasons, your story has to go to a wider range of media, always draft it in the style to suit the most popular of these. Better still, produce different stories for different types of news outlet.

4 Always keep the copy tight, concise and factual. Never fudge an issue or create a misleading impression. Substantiate any claims. Separate fact from belief by putting the latter into quotes. (Research chief John Brown confirmed the vehicle exceeded 200 mph. 'We believe it's the fastest in the world,' said ..., etc.)

5 Write the story from the point of view of the journalist. Although it is a statement from your organization, it should be presented so that it can be used directly in the publication with the minimum of editing. Comment, observation or speculation can only be included in a story in quotes or footnotes.

6 Get the main news point into the first paragraph and preferably the first sentence. Organize the paragraphs so that the most newsworthy are at the top. This will allow the journalist to edit from the bottom. The paragraphs you can most easily afford to lose should therefore be those towards the end of the story.

7 Keep sentences short; use positive and not negative; use active verbs; avoid subordinate and inverted clauses; and omit any subjective material or superlatives. Keep separate points in separate sentences, and break each collection of points into separate paragraphs.

8 Put the copy into modern journalistic style. Eliminate any old-fashioned phrases, formal or pompous language, jargon peculiar to the industry, clichés or colloquialisms that are not accepted as standard current English (or appropriate language).

9 When you have written your story, check through and make sure that it meets these criteria. In particular, be certain that the news is at the beginning. Draft news releases can often afford to have the first two paragraphs deleted!

10 Go through your copy, tighten, edit, improve, check all spelling and punctuation. Get someone else to read it before it goes for release. Ask them to criticize and query. Avoid becoming sensitive about your own copy. Learn to be self-critical. Push yourself to the highest standard possible.

LETTERS

Publications like to receive authoritative letters on topics of interest to their readership. Be sure your company writes where relevant. Agree a corporate policy.

INTERVIEWS

Make sure your public relations executive has prepared briefing notes, arranged a convenient time and place for the interview, provided travel arrangements, lunch or other facilities that would be hospitable but no more. Train yourself in media techniques. Trust journalists and get them to trust you. Say as little off-the-record as possible; however, never lie or hide the truth. If the timing of a question or discussion is not convenient, then explain to them why you cannot help: offer to give them a story as soon as possible.

EDITOR MEETINGS

Make sure that you regularly meet the key editors for your industry. They should know you well enough to be able to talk to you at any time they wish. Make sure that your meetings with them cover some items of substance and are not merely social occasions. Therefore, pick up a strong news story for each editor meeting: then follow it up every 6 or 12 months, as may be necessary.

ARTICLES

Many publications carry authoritative articles. Make sure your executive is monitoring all publications relevant to your industry. If you see a news story which is contrary to your company's views, suggest an article as a follow-up. If you see a trend in the industry that others may not be aware of, suggest an article.

PLANNING

At all stages the executive responsible for planning the public relations activity needs to relate the communications objectives to the sources of information available to these audiences. Across the world, the news scene changes rapidly: new publications, radio, television, and other media opportunities are constantly arising. The result has been a major increase in outlets for broad distribution of news. At the same time many audiences are bombarded with information and are becoming more selective.

The effective media relations executive should be able to balance the need for broad news distribution and target communications at narrower identified audiences and opinion leaders.

Radio and television techniques

Company executives sometimes put too much weight on the influence of print media—mainly because their copy can be held in the hand, copied and passed on. Yet recent research suggests up to 90 per cent of news information may be received by most people via broadcast media. These are powerful channels and should be used. One television news slot can reach more people than all the popular national press combined.

PROGRAMME OPPORTUNITIES

Local stations are desperate for local news. In the UK, national radio programmes such as 'You and Yours', 'Science Now' and 'The Food Programme' regularly use commercial news items. Television programmes such as 'Panorama', 'That's Life' and 'Tomorrow's World' also use commercial news items, presented in the right way.

Local and national radio and TV can reach millions. Programme makers are all in the ideas business. The sheer volume of radio and television currently being broadcast in the UK means that there is a massive demand for good material.

In the UK, the annual, *Who's Who in Broadcasting*, will help identify the people who put programmes together. A news release may be an acceptable method of putting a factual news story in front of the news editor, though the personal approach is nearly always best.

Radio and television are immediate media. Stories will not last, timing is critical, and news stories need to be presented quickly to editors. Facilities for interview, location recording, studio guests and so on must be provided immediately they are required. Deadlines are tight and, with electronic news gathering, are becoming tighter. Live material from remote locations can now be directly slotted into news bulletins.

Timing is, however, important in another sense. The presentation has to be crisp, immaculate and professional. The radio or television audiences have the ability to switch off or change channels almost immediately. As a result of this, broadcasters are constantly working to keep a high level of immediate interest in their output.

The chief executive and the public relations adviser should know how to handle a radio or television journalist when approached to provide information or facilities. The public relations adviser has also to decide who will represent the company. Should it be the top executive? If it is important or strategic, perhaps yes. Or should it be a specialist director relevant to the issue under debate? And does that director have the necessary skills? Never assume that an articulate senior executive has what it takes, unless he or she has been tested ... or, better, trained.

Senior executives will have varying degrees of natural aptitude for handling broadcast interviews, observes Peter Middleton, chief executive of Lloyds of London. Very few books on management pay attention to the fact that managers have talent and what they achieve cannot be learned from studying techniques. However, to handle a key radio or television interview on instinct alone without some professional training would be foolhardy. It could put the whole corporate reputation at risk, he adds. 'I went to my first TV training session unconvinced of the value of spending this time—but within three minutes of the day's first interview, I had changed my mind.' Middleton was managing director of Thomas Cook at the time and the travel industry had suffered a number of accidents affecting holidaymakers. He simply had not anticipated the questions and when asked if he was content to let his customers die, he recalls that he 'dug a hole so deep it could have accommodated all London's refuse for a year!'

TRAINING

There are many excellent training courses available to help you or your colleagues present your organization's case in the best possible way. Make sure that all senior executives who may be required to broadcast are trained in the techniques. Decide whether you are going to speak on behalf of the organization.

RADIO INTERVIEWS

These tend to be less aggressive than television, but this does not necessarily make them easier. The listener will tend to be concentrating on other things— driving the car or digging the garden. The power of the spokesperson's personality has to come over positively. Gestures (or a fine face) will not help. The speaker has to make his or her words and voice sound interesting. This is a skill that can be developed.

Ironically, although the speaker cannot be seen on radio, the studio situation can be surprisingly confusing. Often there is only a short informal build-up to radio interviews. The interview subject can be seated and, in seconds, be broadcasting live over the airwaves.

Always take advantage of any rehearsal opportunity. Run through the points, checking tricky questions, but remember that the interviewer reserves the right to ask you anything. This might include subjects that have not been discussed in the briefing session. If the interview is taped, the interviewee can refuse to answer; the silence will have to be edited out.

TELEVISION STUDIO INTERVIEWS

On television, the concentration of the attention is onto the small studio area where the guest and the interviewer will be sitting. Therefore, it is easier to concentrate on the subject in hand. However, the surge of adrenalin can help some people sharpen their performance but stuns others into mumbling incoherence.

There is no substitute for experience. Watch television and see how it works. See how people deal with questions. Tape as many interviews as possible and rehearse your own answers to questions. Learn to identify the effective techniques and the irritating habits.

NEWS AND FEATURE PROGRAMMES

Learn the differences between the types of programme presented. News items are highly condensed, feature items might be slightly longer, while full-length investigative-type programmes can often be hostile.

You need to be very clear and, if necessary, firm with the programme makers to avoid unhappy situations. Every seasoned public relations professional will recount personal horror stories. Most arise from a simple misunderstanding over the objectives of the programme makers; they want to make interesting, relevant programmes, not promote your vested interests. Most will play this straight but some may be devious; all will put their viewers' interests ahead of yours—as you probably would in their place.

SPECIAL INTEREST PROGRAMMES

Both radio and television present special interest programmes. These tend to be less aggressive because the broadcasters are working in the same industry week after week. These feature programmes are dependent on the degree of cooperation received from people who work in the special interest sectors, such as gardening, antiques, motoring or leisure. This does not stop the broadcasters from hitting hard, but it does ensure that they are reasonably accurate and fair in any criticism.

Be sure you know what the broadcaster is aiming at before you, or one of your executives, agree to cooperate. Ask for a list of those appearing. Sometimes the name of the programme will indicate the angle quite clearly. The researcher may tell you the evidence to be used in other interviews.

LOCATION INTERVIEWS

There are a number of ways in which interviews can be organized. With major news events, a participant may be stopped and confronted by a camera or microphone. Be sure you are not caught out by such situations. Think beforehand about what to say. If this is limited by the situation—for example, a takeover negotiation—construct something that will still give the broadcasters a piece of useful television or tape. However, remember that you are in charge.

It is quite acceptable to make a polite excuse and break away when you have said all you wish.

TELEPHONE INTERVIEWS
On occasions, your organization will be asked to give a telephone interview: this should be resisted if possible. The quality will be bad and you have no control over the editing or usage of the material. The viewer or listener may even get the impression that it was not important enough for your company representative to go to the studio.

If your executive is in a studio interview, he or she may well have a down-the-line interview—in fact, talking to a studio monitor. Your executive must appear to be taking part in a real-life conversation with the interviewer. The best advice is to ignore the electronics and talk to just one real person. The same principle applies on down-the-line radio interviews, where that 'real' person may be a microphone in front of the studio guest.

PANEL DISCUSSIONS
Advanced preparation, as always, is helpful. Consider the points you would like your executive to convey. It is not always a good idea to be the first person to reply in a discussion. Equally, the executive should not let the discussion go too far before he or she starts to make points.

Make sure you express your organization's views effectively. You should be quite prepared to put normal politeness quietly to one side. Do not be brow-beaten by the chairman; the interviewee must answer the question in the way he or she would prefer.

SYNDICATED RADIO INTERVIEWS
In the UK, there are several organizations that will produce an interview on tape, syndicated to local stations. The basic principles still apply. However, as your organization is paying for the service, you will receive more help in the preparation. Remember that the final radio tape has to meet broadcast standards or it will not be used. The syndicating companies will not allow the interview to become soft. They, and you, want good usable material.

STUDIO INTERVIEWS
Face-to-face interviews are invaluable because your speaker is not competing for attention, though he or she is competing for the time. If the interview is live, then the duration of the interview will be known, and for that reason there is likely to have been more discussion beforehand about the areas to be covered. If the interview is filmed and edited, its length may depend on the

amount of interest the speaker is able to generate. Never allow a 5-minute interview that will be cut to 30 seconds on screen.

Consider carefully the points you want to make. You may need to identify the questions that are to be asked in order to weave these into your answers. Always treat the interviewer as a professional trying to do a professional job, but remember that he or she is extremely unlikely to know much about the sector you are discussing.

Plan your interview

Never bluff. Handle naive questions politely. If the interviewer is asking a simple question it is because the viewers or listeners would like to ask the same simple question. There are many ways of presenting the truth but avoid misrepresentations. Listen carefully to the stance that the interviewer is taking. If you need to challenge an assumption ('Many people believe ...'), do it firmly but politely, using evidence where possible: 'I can understand you believe that, but our research shows that 80 per cent of the public ...'

You must put adequate preparation into what you or your spokesperson is to say. Do not rely on being a spontaneous speaker. Concentrate on the good news and avoid temptations to justify yourself. Do not allow the interviewer to get on top of the situation. Keep cool and concentrate on essentials. Do not be diverted. Learn to convert technicalities into simple lay language. Do not say anything on-air or off-air that you might regret later. Prepare for yourself or for your executive a brief of the main points you wish to cover.

Do not drink (in any circumstances) before the interview. Wear clothes appropriate to the situation. Avoid annoying mannerisms. Concentrate on what you want to say, not on what they want to say. Think of interesting ways of illustrating your points. Keep it enthusiastic. Avoid jargon. Talk through the interviewer to the audience. Do not allow yourself to be interrupted. Correct any inaccuracies in the questions.

Look honest, sound honest and be honest—then you and your organization might be believed.

More businesses are organizing themselves to handle media investigations in a professional way. For many years journalists had free rein and could inflict considerable damage. The fault lay in the lack of awareness by many organizations of a need to prepare for such situations.

Investigative television reporting will continue to become better and fairer as organizations become better equipped to cope with the special requirements of the medium. These media will continue to increase in importance in projecting the organization's messages.

MAKING THE COMPANY BEHAVE PROPERLY

Demonstrating the damage to reputation of negative news reports

Let me quote an illustration of how to tackle a difficult situation positively. A leading manufacturing company for which I worked had a safety record that was the envy of the industry. However, one of its facilities in the UK seemed to be having a number of industrial accidents and, as public relations manager, this worried me considerably.

As I was also the editor of the in-house company newspaper, I had seen the safety reports, which seemed to suggest that something was wrong and, sooner or later, one of the accidents might not be so small.

After discussion with the safety director, we felt we needed to take further action. He had explained that as this was an older plant, it needed updating and a lot more spent on safety procedures. The safety record would have been even worse if it were not for the quality of management— but the potential for a rise in incidents was worrying. I wrote a report for the chairman on the damage to the company reputation that could be created by a poor safety record.

Arguments about doing the right thing because it is right, or treating people the way you would like to be treated, do carry some weight. These arguments have added significance if a bottom line impact can be demonstrated. Damage to reputation is bad for sales and bad for the share price. As all good public relations practitioners know, you can never rely on bad news keeping itself discreetly quiet.

The most powerful argument to the chairman was that there were countless sources by which the poor reputation of the company could become public knowledge. One of those might be through a crusading national television programme.

As these arguments were not winning the day, I decided to put it to the test. I commissioned a friend of mine, who was a freelance regularly working for the more sensational national dailies, to write a story—on two conditions. The first was that this was strictly confidential and would not be published anywhere. The second was that she would only use her normal sources and normal reporting methods to create her story. She would get no help from me, other than the initial point in the right direction.

The brief was deliberately minimal. Imagine, I told her (as might well be the case), that an employee or trade union official phones you off-the-record to tip you off.

With her assurance that she would not use this inside information to create her own news story, I asked her to check out the safety record at the plant in question. If anything of interest was found, she was to let me have the sort of story that she would write for, say, the *Daily Express*.

The story arrived on my desk two days later, making me feel I had been over-generous in the fee that I had allowed her in our negotiation!

However, she had earned every penny. It was sensational. It was terrifying. A pencilled note on the top of her copy advised me that if she had submitted this as a normal news story she believed that it would have been very big indeed—possibly even a page-one lead.

The headlines, as I recall, read:

How many more to die?
Lifetime worker killed by fiver economy measure

The story then went on to describe how maintenance standards had been compromised as a result of a company directive to minimize maintenance costs, as the profit forecast that year was looking depressing.

During construction, unknown to the company and in a period when the plant did not belong to the group, a subcontractor had installed a safety valve of inferior design. This was below the capacity required. It had been installed in a key piece of plant with a result that a maintenance worker had been killed by exploding machinery when the valve failed.

I read the story with horror. After a few moments to compose myself I went upstairs, just a couple of flights to the office of the chairman.

He had an open-door policy and we had already established a direct and constructive relationship. He looked up as I approached his desk. I kept a straight face.

'Please read this. It appears in the *Express* tomorrow morning.'

He was one of the most enlightened and positive bosses I had ever had. Yet, as I sat for those few seconds watching him read the story, I felt that maybe I had gone too far .... .

'Hell, Roger. We have to do something about this. It's not fair. It's gross.'

'Hold on. I think I can stop this,' I responded.

'How? Do you know her well? Can we talk to her and put this into perspective?'

'I am sure we can,' I hesitated. 'But, to tell you the truth, this story is not appearing in the *Express* tomorrow.'

'You've stopped it already?'

'No, sorry. Even my public relations skills cannot stretch that far. The reality is that this is not a genuine story. I asked a freelance friend of mine to write it. It is what could appear in the *Express* tomorrow.'

'How dare you,' he exploded. Then, after a moment of tension, he laughed. 'Point made. If we behave this way, this is the kind of story we could expect. Why not use the simple route? Why not tell me?'

'I tried,' I murmured. He had walked round the desk and slapped me on the shoulders.

'Well, you won't have to worry about things like this any more because you're fired!'

I gasped.

'Just kidding,' he grinned. Next morning a new safety procedure was installed across the company though I never understood how it arrived so coincidentally out of the blue.

Useful organizations

AA
      Advertising Association
Aberford House
15 Wilton Road
London SW1V 1NJ
Tel: 071-828 2771

ABCC
      Association of British Chambers of Commerce
9 Tufton Street
London SW1P 3QB
Tel: 071-222 1555

ACC
      Association of County Councils
Eaton House
66a Eaton Square
London SW1W 9BH
Tel: 071-235 1200

ASA
      Advertising Standards Authority
Brook House
2–16 Torrington Place
London WC1E 7HN
Tel: 071-580 5555

BAIE
      British Association of Industrial Editors
3 Locks Yard
High Street
Sevenoaks
Kent TN13 1LT
Tel: 0732 459331

CAM

Communications, Advertising and Marketing Education
Foundation (CAM)
Aberford House
15 Wilton Road
London SW1V 8PH
Tel: 071-828 7506

CBI

Confederation of British Industry
Centre Point
103 New Oxford Street
London WC1A 1DU
Tel: 071-638 8215

CERP

Confédération Européen des Relations Publiques
Rue des Petits Carmes 9
B-1000 Brussels
Belgium
Tel: 010-32 25112680

CIM

Chartered Institute of Marketing
Moor Hall
Cookham
Maidenhead
Berks SL6 9QH
Tel: 0628 524922

COI

Central Office of Information
Hercules Road
London SE1 7DU
Tel: 071-928 2345

CSO

Central Statistical Office
Government Offices
Great George Street
London SW1P 3AQ
Tel: 071-270 3000

EPO

The European Parliament Office
2 Queen Anne's Gate
London SW1H 9AA
Tel: 071-222 0411

IABC   International Association of Business Communicators
                        One Hallidie Plaza
                        Suite 600
                        San Francisco
                        California 94102
                        USA
                        Tel: 0101-415 433 3400

ICO   International Committee of Public Relations Consultants
                        Association
                        Willow House
                        Willow Place
                        London SW1P 1JH
                        Tel: 071-233 6026

IM   Institute of Management
                        Management House
                        Cottingham Road
                        Corby
                        Northants NN17 1TT
                        Tel: 0536 204222

IOD   Institute of Directors
                        116 Pall Mall
                        London SW1Y 5ED
                        Tel: 071-839 1233

IOE   Institute of Export
                        Export House
                        64 Clifton Street
                        London EC2A 4HB
                        Tel: 071-247 9812

IPA   Institute of Practitioners in Advertising
                        44 Belgrave Square
                        London SW1X 8QS
                        Tel: 071-235 7020

IPR

Institute of Public Relations
The Old Trading House
4th Floor
15 Northburgh Street
London EC1V OPR
Tel: 071-253 5151

IPRA

International Public Relations Association
PO Box 2100
1211 Geneva 2
Switzerland
010-4122 791 0550

IS

Industrial Society
48 Bryanstone Square
London W1H 7LN
Tel: 071-262 2401

ISB

Incorporated Society of British Advertisers
44 Hertford Street
London W1Y 8AE
Tel: 071-499 7502

ISP

Institute of Sales Promotion
Arena House
66–68 Pentonville Road
Islington
London N1 9HS
Tel: 071-837 5340

MS

Marketing Society
St George's House
3–5 Pepys Road
London SW20 8NJ
Tel: 081-879 3464

MRS

Market Research Society
15 Northburgh Street
London EC1V OAH
Tel: 071-490 4911

NPA

Newspapers Publishers Association
34 Southwark Bridge Road
London SE1 9EU
Tel: 071-928 6928

NS

Newspaper Society
Bloomsbury House
Bloomsbury Square
74–77 Great Russell Street
London WC1B 3DA
Tel: 071-636 7014

PC

Press Complaints Commission
1 Salisbury Square
London EC4Y 8AE
Tel: 071-353 1248

PPA

Periodical Publishers Association
Imperial House
15–19 Kingsway
London WC2B 6UN
Tel: 071-379 6268

PRCA

Public Relations Consultants Association
Willow House
Willow Place
London SW1P 1JH
Tel: 071-233 6026

PRSA

Public Relations Society of America
33 Irving Place
New York NY 10003
USA
Tel: 0101-212 995 2230

SE

Stock Exchange
Old Broad Street
London EC2N 1HP
Tel: 071-588 2355

UKECO   The UK European Commission Office
             Jean Monnet House
             8 Storey's Gate
             London SW1P 3AT
             Tel: 071-973 1992

Index